TRAVELS WITH PEGASUS

Also by Christina Dodwell

TRAVELS WITH FORTUNE
IN PAPUA NEW GUINEA
AN EXPLORER'S HANDBOOK
(winner of the New York Academy of Sciences award)
A TRAVELLER IN CHINA
A TRAVELLER ON HORSEBACK

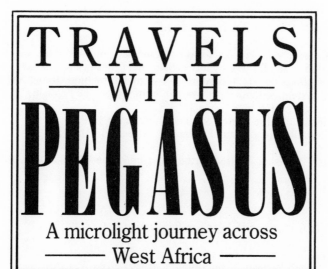

TRAVELS
—WITH—
PEGASUS

A microlight journey across
— West Africa —

CHRISTINA DODWELL

Walker and Company
New York

First published in the United States of America in 1990
by Walker Publishing Company, Inc.

Previously published in Great Britain by Hodden and Stoughton, Ltd.

Library of Congress Cataloging-in-Publication Data

Dodwell, Christina
    Travels with Pagasus : a microlight journey across West Africa /
by Christina Dodwell.
        p.   cm.
    "Previously published in Great Britain by Hodden and Stoughton
Ltd.—T.p. verso.
    ISBN 0-8027-1125-1
    1. Africa, West—Description and travel—1981-   2. Dodwell,
Christina, 1951-   —Journeys—Africa, West.   3. Ultralight
aircraft—Piloting.   4. Air travel—Africa, West.   I. Title.
DT472.D63   1990
916.604'328—dc20   90-12548
                                                            CIP

Printed in the United States of America

2   4   6   8   10   9   7   5   3   1

Contents

Acknowledgments

My first thanks go to David Young of Pegasus Flight Training for all his hard work, and for his superb photographic contribution to the book, also for teaching me to fly.

Of those who sponsored our flight, huge thanks to: Solar Wings Ltd for providing the aircraft and ancillary support; to Jacques Bonnard and Mobil Oil for efficiently providing fuel stashes and much help; and to David Hampshire and the staff of Guinness Cameroun for great support in Cameroun. Also, David and I thank Kodak for film, Ozee for flying suits courtesy of Mike Osborne, and Icom UK (VHF radio).

For co-operation and efforts beyond the call of duty, we are grateful to: Rex Hammond of the Department of Transport; Barry Cole of the Department of Trade and Industry; Barry Davidson of AIS (flight information); Michel Lagneau and Toby Dodwell of PEI; Humphrey Muna of Camair; Annie Brandt of SCAC; AOG in Paris; Jeremy Swift for route planning, and all who kindly gave us advice.

In Cameroun our special thanks go to: Alain and Noelle Lyonnet; Mr Brun and Avia Service; British Consul Anthony Walter, Vice Consul David Seddon, and Bob Arrowsmith; Tony Hickin and Wem Mwambo of CDC; Jean Guet, Christian Le Heron, and J. Tchuente of Mobil in Douala; Roger Eymin from Foumbot; Jacques and Monique Duchene (SCTA) Ngaoundere; Tibati Catholic Mission; Patrick Fonge in Maroua, and Adamu M. Mohammadou at Maroua Airport.

In Nigeria: to Colin Bunch and Chris Gray of British Caledonian; Chris Chimezie in Maiduguri, and Okere Canice in Potiskum.

In Niger: the Commandant of Zinder Airport; Alain and Muller Freres in Tanout; Peter Tunley of WWF in Iferouane; Amadou Sidibe, chef de poste at In Gall; M. Chaibou and the boys of Tchin Tabaraden; the Commandant of Tahoua Airport; Aladdin and Regina in Dosso; Daniel and Marlene Trevidic, and Wirguiss of Mobil in Niamey.

In Mali: Fiona Patrick, Save the Children, Douentze; Commandant Diallo at Sevare Airport; Hassan Bathily and Moctar Thiam of Mobil in Bamako; Richard Moorehead and all his WWF team in Youvarou; Michele Stigliano and Tom Wijderveld in Tombouctou; Samba Apho

Truaore in Goumou; Dr Fousseni Sidibe in Goundam; dear Ibrahim in Bandiagara; Robert and Nel van Bommelo, Ineko and Gerrit in Sokolo.

In Mauritania: Prefet Sarr Demba of Nema; Prefet Djime Sow of Oualata; Sheikh Ould Abdel, Mohammed Talib, and the Agricultural Dept of Ayoun; Ibrahim Wane and his family, and Felix, in Nouakchott.

In Sénégal: St. Louis Aero Club; Philippe Neau, Chris Hudson, and Michel Begtine of CSS in Richard-Toll; Mbaye Fall and Seyni Diop of Mobil in Dakar; Dakar Aero Club; Jean Claude Mosser and his family in Dakar; and British Consul Barry Williams. There are many others whose names are missing, people who it was a pleasure to meet and whose kindness to us gave us the strength to continue.

CD

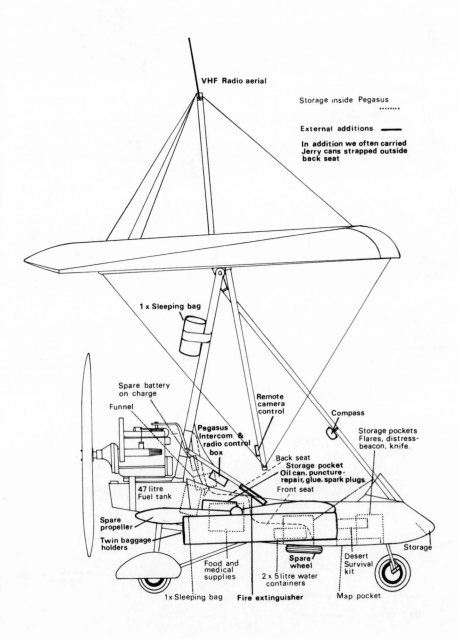

VHF Radio aerial

Storage inside Pegasus
. . . .

External additions ━━━

**In addition we often carried
Jerry cans strapped outside
back seat**

1 x Sleeping bag

Spare battery
on charge

Funnel

Remote
camera
control

Compass

**Pegasus
Intercom &
radio control
box**

Storage pockets
Flares, distress-
beacon, knife.

Back seat
Storage pocket
Oil can, puncture-
repair, glue, spark plugs

Front seat

47 litre
Fuel tank

**Spare
propeller**

**Twin baggage
holders**

Food and
medical
supplies

**Spare
wheel**

Desert
Survival
kit

Storage

2 x 5 litre water
containers

1 x Sleeping bag

Fire extinguisher

Map pocket

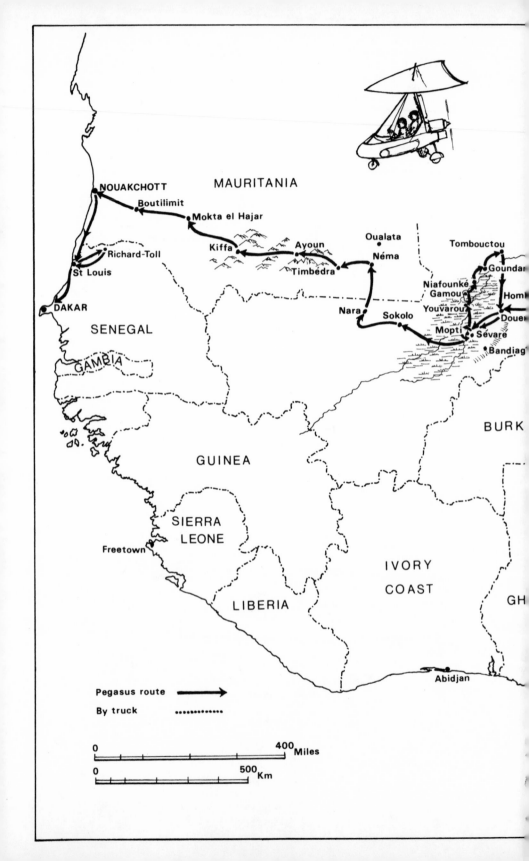

MAURITANIA

NOUAKCHOTT
Boutilimit
Mokta el Hajar
Kiffa
Ayoun
Timbédra
Oualata
Néma
Tombouctou
Goundar
Niafounké
Gamou
Hom
Youvarou
Doue
Mopti
Sévaré
Bandiag
Nara
Sokolo

Richard-Toll
St Louis
DAKAR

SENEGAL

GAMBIA

GUINEA

SIERRA
LEONE

Freetown

LIBERIA

IVORY

COAST

BURK

GH

Abidjan

Pegasus route ➤
By truck ••••••••••••

0   400 Miles

0   500 Km

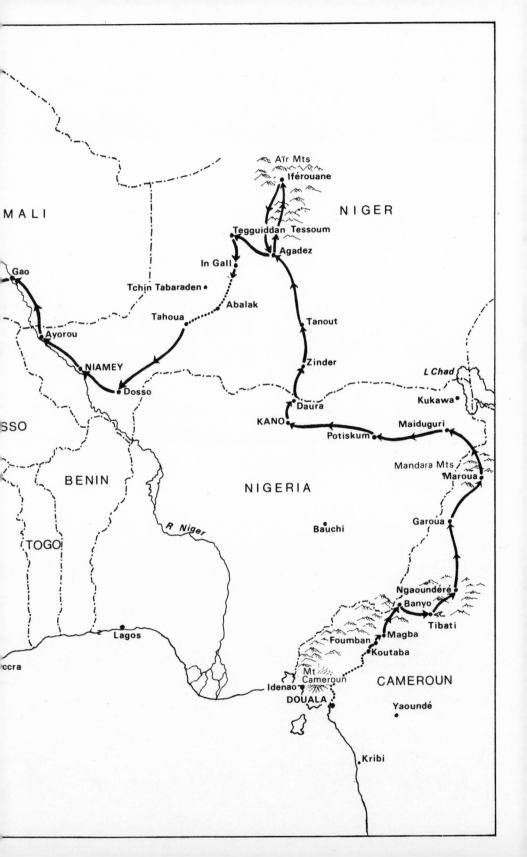

ONE

Pygmies and Palm Wine

It felt like sitting on a chair 1,000 feet above Wiltshire, with nothing between me and the M4 but some wires and cunningly jointed lengths of aluminium, and a red, white and blue sailcloth wing. The propeller behind me pushed us along at 45 mph with sudden slumps like a lift when we encountered wind turbulence. A marvellous view stretched over rolling green farmland with villages tucked in valleys, and I spotted three separate sites where men had hewn the shape of a great white horse on the chalky hillsides. And what could be more appropriate, for I was having my first experience of flying in a Pegasus XL microlight.

Exposure to the elements added to the wide open feeling. I was protected only by a helmet and flying suit, with a seat-belt holding me in place, as I pondered the shoulders of the pilot sitting on a lower seat in front of me using an A-frame bar to steer and make us climb. He pulled the bar in towards his chest and took his foot off the throttle, and we swooped in a dive. The tiny instrument panel held only a couple of gauges, one an altimeter showing us to be dropping at 300 feet a minute. A shallow glide, the engine idled and the propeller's buzz grew quieter.

The pilot's voice came through the helmet intercom telling me to reach past his shoulders and take hold of the control bar, and try flying. It was exciting but I wondered when I would begin to like it.

Having travelled on land and water, flight was the one medium I hadn't yet tried: by horse I'd crossed thousands of miles in Africa and in the Middle East, and by canoe I'd paddled solo down the largest river in Papua New Guinea, the Sepik, down Africa's Congo, and China's Yellow River. Just when you know how to do something is the time to move on and start

13

learning again. The danger is complacency. But hitherto the thought of a light aircraft, apart from being too expensive, had also been too restrictive. I didn't fancy being cooped up behind windows and tied to official airstrips. I should not have been able to land as often and as flexibly as I needed in my sort of travels. I'm far too inquisitive, and if there's something interesting below, I would want to go down and have a closer look.

Microlighting could have been made for my method of travelling. Serendipical! You're not enclosed, you can fly low and slowly, going into regions inaccessible to ground transport, and can land on a mere seventy-five yards; you can even detach the wing and fold the whole thing up into two parcels when you get tired of it.

But I am not an enthusiastic mechanic, and I would not want to be tied to the machine for a whole journey. So, despite my usual preference for solo travel, I could see lots of good reasons for acquiring a Pegasus two-seater tandem and I would take along a professional pilot who could look after the machine's health and welfare en route. But this didn't mean I'd be chickening out of learning to fly myself. I'm not good at taking a back seat; and since the pilot would be there all the time, why not learn on the trip and put in my twenty-five hours' flying practice as we travelled?

Where to do all this? Flying a microlight is a chilly business at the best of times, so I wanted to go somewhere warm. I felt a hankering to return to Africa and the part of Nigeria I'd been born in and left finally at the age of sixteen. Though I'd come to England for six years in the middle and done all my schooling here, my childhood in the bush had left memories of vast plains shimmering with heat, palm forests, and great fat chieftains who bounced me on their knees. Some were still cannibals in those days, but it was no threat, just a custom. I'd returned again to Nigeria, aged twenty-four, and begun my first horseback journey from there. That African journey, a three-year marathon, had led across the Sahara, down into the equatorial forest belt, across southern Africa and up through East Africa, ending in Ethiopia with the arrest of myself and horse and pack-camel by the Revolutionary Army because the country was in the grip of civil war.

For this air journey various pilots recommended I flew down the eastern side of Africa: it would be safe and enjoyable. In contrast, West Africa was considered to be the pits. No micro-light had attempted its crossing and no one knew what sort of difficulties might be expected. I'd always rather go for the unknown.

What appealed to me was a 7,000-mile route starting from the equatorial rain-forests of Cameroun, going north to Lake Chad, then through northern Nigeria, across sahel and desert, into Agadez in Niger and the remote desert mountains of mid-Sahara. From Niger to Gao and Tombouctou in Mali, then Mauritania and down along the Atlantic beaches to Dakar in Sénégal. Perhaps it was a bit ambitious but there was only one way to find out.

As for the pilot-cum-flying instructor-cum-mechanic, I had been so impressed by the ability and common sense of David Young, the pilot in my introductory flight, that I asked him if he wanted the job. I proposed a four-month trip, his work being to keep the microlight airworthy, and to pilot and teach me to fly. He agreed with enthusiasm, an intrepid man, game for an adventure. And he thought it would be easy to teach me to fly.

The forward planning and obtaining of special flight permits, needed in military-ruled countries, was part of my work. Long-distance microlight flights have always involved a ground sup-port vehicle, but I didn't see why we couldn't manage without such tedious encumbrances. Anyway, the journey would not be an attempt to set up any record, nor was it going to be a race. We could strap our baggage on to the aircraft's frame and be self-contained, with an extra large fuel tank to give us a range of about 200 miles. The engine, a reliable Rotax 447 cc, used a two-stroke combination of oil and super petrol.

Suspecting these would not be available at the back end of West Africa, I asked advice from the international office of Mobil Oil, who said it would be a nightmare and they suggested I applied for their sponsorship. So I put in an application offering to stick that glorious flying horse emblem on my wings. In return, Mobil agreed to stash fuel in jerrycans for us through-out our complete 7,000-mile route. In remote spots the jerrycans would be left at military outposts or with chiefs of villages, and the cans would be sealed so we would know if someone had tampered with the fuel. This was a likely problem where petrol was scarce, and anything could be used to top up the can. Bad fuel is one thing in a car but different when you're high above the ground. Being realistic, I thought the idea of stashing jerrycans hadn't a hope of working out, but it was certainly worth the chance.

Our departure would be mid-November. Lift-off minus five days was marked by rapid exchanges of telex with a freight company in Douala, Cameroun, who said my microlight hadn't arrived. The London office assured me it definitely had been sent. The Douala office confirmed they had not received it.

Lift-off minus four. They found Pegasus but didn't have any paperwork. New papers would be sent on the next flight. I was refused visas for Nigeria because I had no flight authority number or military clearance, for which I'd applied three months previously and had continually pestered the authorities to send me in writing. West Africa is a nightmare of bureaucracy. Temporarily failing there, I put in applications for Cameroun visas.

Lift-off minus three was Friday 13th, my last working day in London. The Cameroun visas were given special clearance but the signing officer was out indefinitely and had locked away our passports. Meanwhile the Nigerian High Commission agreed to grant our visas, though without the passports I could do little. They kindly authorised the visas to be issued in Douala.

Our departure itself, aiming for a seven a.m. flight to Douala, was thrown into disorder when David said he'd left his vaccination certificate in a drawer a hundred miles away. The airport official at Gatwick said it was compulsory. A helpful lady in a clinic wrote out a duplicate for us and we reached the security checks with only minutes to spare.

Our hand luggage was seen to contain bulky metal objects. Everything had to be turned out on the desk. They put aside all our distress flares and smoke signals, but agreed to send them with the flight purser and we ran to board the plane.

It was nearly empty. So I stretched out and fell asleep with nervous exhaustion. When I awoke we were above the Sahara Desert. Hours later, still above the desert, we began to appreciate its enormity. The Boeing pilot invited us into the cockpit to see his range of instruments. The most useful thing I learned was that their radio always monitors the emergency channel which we would use for distress calls.

In Douala we stayed with my brother's friends, Alain and Noelle Lyonnet, who had lived there for twenty years. Alain was learning to fly light aircraft, so was able to arrange space in a hangar, where David could assemble our microlight. While we waited for final permits I couldn't resist the opportunity to start my flying lessons in a Cessna. Where I wanted to fly was really a detour from our main journey. I was eager to go south down the coast and into the rain-forest, terrain David had categorically declared off limits for a microlighting novice. Hence the Cessna. We had to take a gendarme with us for my flying lesson. That was the law relating to light aircraft. When it came to Pegasus I wondered where the poor man was going to sit, and hoped the authorities wouldn't be expecting us to carry our regulation bobby hanging on underneath. But no, it was confirmed we should be an exception to the rule. I had got special permission for our journey by microlight, or ULM (Ultra Léger Motorisé) as they are known in French-speaking countries.

Meanwhile David, the local instructor, our gendarme and I all piled into the Cessna, were duly warned against overflying military areas and allowed to take off – *décoller*, unstick, in this francophone part of West Africa.

We flew south along beaches of white sands strewn with washed-up tree trunks, heavy forest timber, breakaways from big rafts of logs brought downriver to sawmills. David looked at them in terms of the hazards a microlight would have to face in an emergency landing. 'That's part of the difference between us and other light aircraft,' he said. 'They have dual ignition systems, twin magnetoes, we only have one of anything.'

Meanwhile I concentrated on the plane in hand, steering left, banking and using the foot-controlled rudder. Pegasus didn't have a rudder, nor a tailplane. Now beneath us was the forest, its canopy thick and colourful with splashes of maroon young leaves and palest green new growth on top. Above the canopy projected stately red-leaved biminga trees, an expensive wood used in furniture. Here they hadn't been felled, because being beside the ocean was not the richest timber area. The forest looked unmolested, primeval, and was a treat to fly over. I went up to 8,000 feet to get a panorama of the coast, then down to look at a wrecked ship on the beach. The plane was responsive to handle, and I felt quite relaxed because if necessary the instructor could have taken charge in a flash. We cruised at about 140 mph, though speed seemed to depend less on the power setting than on whether the nose was pointed up or down.

Our destination was Kribi, a small town seventy miles down the coast, where David and I hopped out and let the instructor fly back to Douala. Flying might be fun and I was looking forward to even better views from Pegasus, but I didn't want to miss out on what was going on at ground level. I had made it clear to David from the start that microlighting was for me a means not an end to travel. I can't resist rivers. Now I wanted to spend a few days travelling by canoe into pygmy country. I was encouraged by noticing several of the shy Ngoumba pygmies in Kribi market while I bought food, and fifteen miles out of town on the Lobe River we hired a battered, leaky, but basically strong wooden dugout. Its patches were cut from truck tyres and nailed on, and it came with two boatmen.

I was impatient to get deep into the forest and the motor pushed us along at a decent pace. The trees were already dense and some leaned out over the river, with veils of creeper hanging from their branches. Much of the forest was in flower, with tulip tree blossoms and poinsettias above tangles of mauve convolvulus and fluffy white-tipped pompoms like fibre-optic lamps. The river meandered and felt good.

Rounding one corner we faced a half-submerged tree with a flock of white egrets perched on it. When they saw us they kinked their necks and flew away slowly upriver to the next fallen tree where they alighted once more and sat like white candles. Each time we approached they took flight, a lovely manoeuvre, and they led us along. A couple of hornbills flapped across our route, black with grotesque casques and ungraceful flight, and above them flew a grey broadwinged bird of prey.

Our canoe was as tippy as most dugouts; some that came downriver past us were very narrow, their occupants sitting on the end, legs dangling each side, or balanced inside on the rim. Clement, the elder of our two boatmen, pointed to a village and said it was inhabited by pygmies, friendly ones but rather commercially minded to catch any tourists who might come up here. We didn't stop.

Night fell and the moon rose. We kept a lookout for dead trees in our path. The boatmen wanted to keep going until we reached a footpath leading to another pygmy village beyond the beaten track. A sudden noise of rushing water indicated we were about to hit a submerged tree; we dodged and slid beside it. The current grew stronger.

At the path we tethered the canoe and walked into the

forest. Fireflies darted about in the grasses underfoot while from nearby came a throaty rising warbling song. I asked Clement what made it and he said it was a luangala, a three-toed animal with a dog's head and short legs, which lived in trees, had a lot of fur, and came down at night to feed. Clement spoke reasonable French, having been to a mission elementary school. He was a sensible man who rented out his canoe when he wasn't fishing.

The village was dark and silent. The hut doors, made from interlaced strips of bark, were closed. From one door hung the yellow and black banded tail of a forest wildcat, which Clement told me marked the witch-doctor's hut and was *gri-gri*, or magic, to protect the village. If a thief came here to steal, he would fall ill, and only the witch-doctor would be able to cure him. From the deserted village the boatmen deduced that the pygmies were away on a hunting trip which could last for weeks. We slung our mosquito nets from the poles of an open shelter and lay down to sleep.

The next morning we made an early start and were quickly riverborne, heading on up into the interior. By eight a.m. the sun was growing hot. The river looked dark and muddy. Gradually its course grew narrower and the banks were overhung with trees putting multi-rooted tentacles down into the river. Strangler roots clasped their host trees, some of which had died and rotted away leaving the stranglers standing empty, making lacy cut-out patterns of knotted silvery roots. Cobweb enshrouded some low-branched trees, antelope horn ferns grew out of others. From the branches of 150-feet giants dangled corkscrew lianas, one with a cluster of ferns hanging like a decorative basket on the end of a hundred-foot vine.

A violent splash beside the canoe soaked me and I was just in time to see the large tail of a crocodile flapping over, batting the water as it dived. We must have caught it dozing on the surface. Clement guessed it would be an adult about six feet long. Then the motor suddenly cut out. We drifted and paddled to a sandy inlet so the boatmen could investigate the problem.

I got out. There were some wide five-toed footprints on the beach which the men said probably belonged to a gorilla. I thought they were teasing until I looked at the larger than human size of the prints. They led through a corridor in the forest, though no easy path, thorny and tangled. One big tree had root buttresses twice my height, and between these fins

19

jutted out large half-mushroom-shaped ant colonies. The bottom edge of each mushroom was frilly with scalloped curves and points, off which the rain could run easily, sheltering the nest. Beneath each were tiers of smaller mushroom shapes, and from them led out ant trails, enclosed tunnels of sand cemented on to the tree's bark running straight and high up the trunk, while other tunnels went around each fin to link up with the next ant colony.

Clement and his mate had fixed the motor and we chugged on. The men chattered, their language melodious with many long syllables. Some words had repeated sounds, the longest had a six-times repeat. I guessed it added emphasis. The river was now narrowing to less than fifty yards and sometimes the trees met overhead. We had to thread through a fallen one that just left us space to pass between and under its branches.

Ahead I could hear the roar of rapids. The boatmen said it would be rough for about a hundred yards but there should only be one bad patch. We entered the waves, which grew larger as we approached a bottleneck where the river was squeezed between rocks. Going up into a fierce stretch the motor began to cough and wouldn't produce full power. It didn't look good for us in the rapid, and Clement quickly swung the canoe towards an eddy which helped us to the shore. We decided to unload the baggage and carry it to a cove above the bottleneck, then try with motor and paddles. Again we were forced back by the raging current, so we retreated to the shore and pulled the canoe on a tow rope. With four of us hauling the rope, lining it beside the rocks, we reached the top of that rapid.

Late morning we saw a spiral of smoke coming from a pygmies' hunting camp and, stopping there, we found an untidy shelter of thatched leaves. Outside it sat three children and a woman busy breaking open the boiled shell of a water tortoise. She would add its meat to the pot of soup simmering on the fire. The eldest child was crushing a pile of wrinkled fruit; inside each were two black-skinned seeds that the woman said were also used in soup and she gave me some to try. They tasted like groundnuts. Then she passed us a honeycomb that her husband had captured the previous day by climbing a tree and smoking out the hive. The honey was delicious, though rather full of dead bees that had drowned in it, and before biting into a chunk we broke open the cells to let any live bees escape.

Upriver from the hunting camp we came to a broad rapid. The canoe was in mid-river and once more lacked the power to motor up, so the paddles came out again and with all four of us going at full force we inched forward against the current and finally gained the top. At the next rapid Clement suggested trying a side course between rocks but in no time we hit a rock. Clement and his mate jumped out on to an underwater ledge and attempted to pull us off, then haul us through a gap. Their efforts failed when they fell off the ledge and were dunked underwater, but fortunately they held on to the canoe to avoid being swept away. Urgently they pushed again, but the canoe was still too heavy. David got out and found a rock thigh-deep below him; he added his muscles and suddenly the canoe swung free, leaving him standing stranded in the river.

'Stay put,' Clement yelled above the rushing water. Rescue would not be easy: the channel was too deep and fast to swim, and it was too far to throw a rope. In desperation we let the canoe slip back and paddled furiously to make the stern swing out in David's direction. He clambered aboard looking shaken. Such happenings were not in the normal run of microlighting instructor's duties, but he was soon shaking the water out of his ears and laughing at the incident.

We struggled on up the rapid and into the calm pool above it. Here we found a fishing camp where we paused for a break. This was not a pygmy camp; pygmies are not fishermen and they usually avoid the river since it is the domain of another tribe. The fishing camp was deserted except for one woman, skinning manioc, a root that needs to soak for four days in water before it can be skinned and crushed for flour. She would use the offcuts for baiting her prawn traps. The smoke rack above her fire held an assortment of small scaleless catfish. The boatmen bought some and we picnicked as we continued upriver.

I had not intended to go up as far as this but I didn't want to turn back, allowing temptation to keep luring me forward. Clement tried to discourage me, saying the forest upriver was empty, outsiders never went up there. This, of course, made it all the more alluring. But when we passed the trail to another semi-deserted hunting camp and discovered from a local hunter that the pygmies had returned to the village where we'd slept the night before, I agreed we could turn round and head downriver.

We descended without using the motor; it was more peaceful to paddle, listening to the birds' songs and watching their flight patterns. Since we would soon begin flying in earnest, David started teaching me the principles of flight. 'Flight is possible because a wing generates lift in two ways: by the angle it meets the airflow, called the angle of attack, and by the aerofoil shape of its wing. The air gets split as it passes over the bulge of the wing. Look at that cormorant's wing. See, it's fatter on top.' He pointed to a bird drying its outstretched wings in the sun. 'This means the underwing is shorter from front to back, so the molecules of air are forced to go faster over the top which creates a pressure differential. Less pressure above, more below the wing; that creates lift. The faster the airspeed, the more lift gets generated. It's really simple.' Then he started trying to explain the effects of drag in induced and parasitic forms, thrust versus weight, equal and opposite forces, and my mind began to reel.

Without the motor we heard the roar of the biggest rapid from afar. Clement said it was just as bad from this direction, so David offered to go on foot carrying the things we couldn't afford to lose, while I shot the rapid with the boatmen. It was immense fun but they wouldn't let me paddle, insisting I sat down and held on tightly with both hands. Further downstream we hit a rock and three submerged trees, but without causing any serious damage.

Just before sunset we reached the path to the village. I was puzzled because no canoes were moored there but Clement said pygmies never used canoes, they walked in the forest. At the village we met fifteen men, half the population, who had come in advance of the main hunting body and had brought a live crocodile, tied by its nose and hind legs. They had also caught a porcupine and a wild pig, which would arrive later.

To catch the porcupine and some succulent forest rats, they had used hunting dogs, but not for the wild pig. For this the method was nets, into which they drove the pig by making a lot of noise. They showed me the spears they used, two yards long, lining the haft at sight and stalking their prey before lancing the spear at close range. They were not accurate at long range. Several men carried bows and arrows. They said they also hunted antelope and elephants; not gorillas, although there were some locally, but they were afraid of men and stayed hidden.

I became friendly with the one-eyed proxy son of the chief who could speak some French; someone had poked out one of his eyes in jealousy because he went to a mission school. The boy had no thought of revenge, he said he wasn't as big as the bully and, since his father was dead, no one sided with him. It was the chief here who had seen the boy's meekness and good manners and brought him to live as his son.

The chief was also the witch-doctor, and I noticed the *gri-gri* had been taken off his door. As they sat around the lamp eating supper I watched the silhouettes of the chief and two big men, a bat-eared dog, and a scrawny cat, all sitting in a circle. The men ate manioc wrapped in banana leaves with viper soup. The animals were given the bones to crunch.

I was asked to contribute some money for village provisions, which I did happily to repay hospitality. The 'provisions' which had top priority turned out to be a crate of beer. With beer, One-eye said, they would dance night and day. They needed to celebrate the spirit of a child that had died recently. The dance would ease their grief and perhaps the child's soul would pity them and send them a new baby. Without more ado I despatched Clement and his mate to fetch the necessary supplies from a village trade store six miles away.

One-eye's real name was Quoi but it took me some time to work this out because every time I asked his name he said *Quoi*? (French for 'What?') and I thought he hadn't understood the question.

The night was a restless one because the pygmies were sounding drums, impatiently waiting for the boatmen to come back. From time to time the tapping would become a riff of drumming. One youth was stroking a six-string guitar, its strings held by curved sticks at different angles. He tuned it by pushing the twigs apart.

Soon after dawn the drumming began in earnest. I walked half a mile along a dew-drenched path to wash in a sweetwater stream. It was a lovely walk under arched bamboo whose glades were cathedral-sized hollows in dappled leafy half-light. When I returned dancing had already begun under a thatched shelter which wasn't tall enough for me to stand in. The chief's deputy taught me how to use a spear. He was little over four feet tall. Then I sat among people and watched the dancing; men in the centre sometimes lunging towards the seated ones, picking out individuals, then rejoining the middle, turning and stomping; while women danced with uplifted arms and flicking hips; clapping and chanting, low voices overlaid by higher ones picking up the chant behind the leader.

The chief lifted up a naked baby to dance in his arms. She wore only a talisman of three stones threaded around her waist on bark string. Behind the shelter the early mist was rising off the forest. Feeling slightly an intruder in this poignant family scene, and knowing my crew had a fair distance to cover that day, I chose my moment to interrupt the dance, which indeed looked likely to continue for hours, and said our goodbyes, wishing them much fertility.

When we left the village we paddled downriver as our motor had conked out, pausing to check the fish nets our boatmen had set on their way to buy the beer. Slowly the river grew wider between banks of raffia palms, and was dotted with encampments we hadn't seen in the dark on the way up. There were parked groups of canoes filled with prawn baskets. On the bank I noticed a large reptile, a yard long, clambering over some prawn pots and it flicked out a long forked tongue. Crocodiles don't have tongues. This had to be a monitor lizard.

The breeze coming upriver grew saltier. The sun was hot, and the younger boatman was wearing the cover of the outboard motor over his head as a sunhat. That's called improvisation. I asked him if canoes could go out of the river-mouth into the sea, but he said they'd be smashed up since the whole river goes over a waterfall, landing on the beach.

We stopped at Clement's home and, leaving our gear at a local café, David and I set off to the beach to see these falls. A man we met on the way offered to lend us his small sea-going canoe in which we could paddle to the bottom of the waterfall. Actually it was a one-person canoe, so we took turns. I surfed the canoe in on ocean waves towards the great white thirty-foot cascade. Some rocks showed under the waves but I only hit one which tipped me over into the sea, though it was easy to clamber back aboard. The waterfall was a three-pronged chute and I played around in the fierce current at the base of each cascade before allowing my canoe to be swept back out of the river-mouth into the sea.

That night we camped on the beach, and dined on a dish of prawns. I woke in the night, listened to the pounding surf, and went into the waves for a swim. Then ran down the beach to get warm, and take a look at the falls by moonlight.

In the morning the fire revived quickly with coconut husk kindling and splinters of wood from half-hewn canoes lying above the tide line. We breakfasted then moved north up the beach; a day of surf with thundering waves to play in: I couldn't want anything more.

The first flight of Pegasus in Africa was for journalists in Douala, and the second was inland at Yaoundé for Cameroun national television. This was the best way of allaying official suspicions, letting people know about our flight, and of thanking our sponsors. I took a back seat for the flying, not wanting to admit I didn't know how. I still wasn't keen on the sensation: being up there sitting in the sky, held in place only by a seat-belt. It made me think that people weren't meant to fly, they were supposed to keep their feet on the ground. 'What am I doing up here?' I wondered continually.

The microlight puttered along steadily at 45 mph, bouncing in slight air turbulence. The wing flexed and its tensions changed as David dipped us in a medium-bank turn, calculated by keeping the middle of the wing on the horizon. The microlight's safe flight relies on its design and a lot of people gave their lives to make them airworthy, in Britain and in America, where they are called ultralights. Our Pegasus XL was a 1984 type, the old faithful work-horse, with an unblemished track record. Below us were scattered huts and rain-forest. I took over the control bar for a few minutes. It was somewhat like a horse's mouth, sensitive to the light touch of one's hands. But I felt most unsafe.

'Check the fuel gauge, please,' said David's voice over the intercom. I leaned out around our extra large fuel tank and saw the fuel level halfway down the clear plastic tubing. When full the forty-seven-litre tank would give us a range of about three hours' flight.

Forest encircled Yaoundé and we came in to make a low pass over the runway, David pulling on the control bar to change our angle and increase our speed. This was the opposite to the light aircraft whose controls I'd been told to push to descend; with microlights you push to climb. A second major difference, of course, was that we flew much closer to the ground, at about 1,000 feet, while other light planes were staying around

6,000–9,000 feet. We could hear them on our VHF radio. English is the language of the air, which helped David who had no French. Our route would be almost totally in francophone countries.

The television crew asked for one more low pass, then we landed and quickly de-rigged the microlight to show how easily the wing can be folded away.

But I must admit, the flying interested me less at this stage because life on the ground had so much to offer. Back in Douala there was a delay because our flight authorisations for Nigeria and Niger had still not arrived. Diplomats in Douala and Lagos were helping me, despite obvious doubts about my sanity and fear of the trouble I might bring down on them. As one attaché put it, 'She doesn't stand a snowball's chance of making it across West Africa.'

It was difficult enough getting around Douala, where the taxis were on strike. The previous night a policeman had shot a taxi-driver who refused to give him a bribe. But one couldn't be sure the killer was a real policeman because people were known to dress up as police to demand bribes. I watched trucks full of soldiers racing in to quash a fight in the street. So while David worked on some mechanical adjustments, I took the chance to revisit a place called Idenao, which had enchanted me when I discovered it twelve years ago. In those days I was on foot, this time Guinness Cameroun loaned me a car and driver.

Idenao lies out to the west beyond Limbe (the old colonial town of Victoria), where beaches adjoin the slopes of Mount Cameroun, and the sand is black, glittering with the mica from volcanic ash. The driver pointed out the lower peak, though the main summit (13,350 ft) was hidden in cloud. The last major flow of lava in 1982 had stopped behind the beach. We crossed its trail, continuing west into thick oil-palm forest. The lushness of the greenery was striking; annual rainfall here is an astonishing fifty inches, the highest in Africa.

Lagoons and estuaries were havens for canoes that plied passengers and black-market products to and from the Nigerian coast, fifty miles away. This region had been part of Nigeria after the First World War, when the German plantation territory was handed into British-Nigerian administration. Now it belonged to Cameroun but it was a sensitive area. Roadblocks were frequent, with soldiers looking for smuggled goods.

Pygmies and Palm Wine

There were three things I wanted to see again. The first was an ancient palm-oil factory I'd loved for its simplicity of pulleys and cogs, fuelled by the screw-pressed husks of palm cone. The Germans had built a narrow gauge railway system to facilitate harvesting, and parts of it were still working when I last visited. Now we saw only wrecked railway carts, tippers and field bogies, overgrown with palm forest. The supports of an aqueduct were still in place, some old water towers, and the swimming pool which the Germans had inscribed with the date they opened it, by coincidence the day that the First World War was declared.

The factory lay derelict and silent, its threshers, crushers, boilers and conveyors all cracked and broken, its roof half open to the sky, at the end of its time. It had been replaced several years ago by a new factory in Limbe, not currently in working order. Recently another palm-oil mill had gone bankrupt because of the economic crisis: it was tragic to think how quickly the plantations could become overgrown and beyond repair. The oil palm, a squat thorny tree, produces football-sized cones of bright red nuts, up to ten cones at a time, which are harvested all the year round as they ripen.

We stopped to drink palm wine at a hut in a forest clearing. The wine seller bade us rest on a bamboo bench while he fetched a nine-foot bamboo tube to show us how he tapped off the wine. One end of the tube is cut into the tree trunk and in twenty-four hours it yields about a litre. The wine we were offered was drawn today, the best tasting, like lemonade. If it's left for three days the yeasts ferment, producing a rather alcoholic drink. Local people claim the high yeast content is good for the eyes. Ants were attacking my feet and I kept brushing them off because some of them bit. Our host said ants were approved of because where you find them you don't find snakes.

The second spot I wanted to find near Idenao was a ruined mansion lying hidden in the palm forest. It had been well concealed twelve years ago, and no one we met at first had any clue where it might be located. We traipsed through the dim dripping forest, avoiding piles of spiky palm fronds, while from the trunks of older trees grew ferns and orchids.

An oil-nut cutter we met eventually showed us the way and told me the German who had owned the house had been one of fifty-eight German nationals with plantations. He had been

27

killed by the Allied forces but his spirit still haunted the place. The pillars of the verandah and the house walls still stood, though they were coated in vines and creepers. But it wasn't the ruin I'd seen before. There must have been several, all equally lost and forgotten memorials to a departed era. I rambled in through the broken arch of the front door, and could hear the oil-nut cutter saying to the driver, 'We fear this place. The spirit is still clinging to it.'

He told us that six years ago a German relative of the former owner had visited the house to pay his respects. No one had told him about the car that the owner had hidden in the forest; almost no one knew about it. The car was a Chevrolet, one of the first ever made. I'd seen it in 1975, where the fleeing German had carefully concealed it at the start of the war. Perhaps he had hoped to return one day. We had to cut our way through to find it. I pulled back the overgrowth and revealed the rusty vestiges of the radiator. The chassis had collapsed but the running boards were recognisable, everything else had corroded to dust. Time had passed.

Two

Palaces and Crater Lakes

Our flight authorisation numbers for Nigeria and Niger arrived at last and we left Douala with Pegasus in the back of a truck since David had mutinied about flying the first hundred miles. His reasons were valid: the rain-forest was no place for a microlight, and with all-up weight we'd be fools to try it; the mountain pass up to Nkongsamba was said to be bad news, giving severe turbulence to stronger aircraft than ours. There was no point in jeopardising the whole trip on the initial leg just for the sake of a principle. So we popped Pegasus into a truck and went north to where the forest opened up, providing emergency landing spaces in savannah. At roadblocks the soldiers asked if our cargo was a missile for firing at the Libyan bases in Chad, but they let us past.

The most convenient place to fly from was Koutaba airport. It looked new and unused; fortunately the runway was open but the buildings had not yet been finished, and in the current economic crisis I doubted they would be finished for some years yet. The place was deserted, and we had to find the controller to file a flight plan, but the man had gone to a local event.

I set off to find him, and the search led down a dirt track in the bush beyond town to a flag-pole where crowds of people were celebrating the installation of a new mayor. All the local chiefs and dignitaries had gathered, wearing their finery. Speeches of welcome were being applauded with clapping, drumming and bugle blasts. Even some of the orators' sentences were punctuated by whoopings and scratched bamboo ratchet instruments. The new mayor was being garlanded with coloured sashes.

Men wearing headdresses of porcupine quills and feathers, chanting and brandishing ornate old long-barrelled shotguns,

29

rushed towards the flag-pole, throwing their guns in the air, catching them and firing deafening rounds into the sky. Others wielded large cutlasses, clashing the blades together as they ran towards the flag-pole.

More dancers materialised, one with a tall wooden mask worn on a raffia collar; their variety reminded me that Cameroun contains over a hundred separate tribes. The male onlookers wore richly embroidered robes and skull caps or tall pillbox hats or a floppy night-cap style; and women sported sarongs and glittery headscarves. A bugler stood beside me, puffing his cheeks and popping his eyes as he blasted out its music. Someone else was bugling with a two-foot length of plastic drainpipe.

An official came to let me know I was in a military area, Koutaba being a military and air force base, and he delegated a gendarme to escort me around the festival. I didn't find the air traffic controller but I did meet the airport commandant, who was very co-operative and also invited me to the mayor's celebration dance that evening.

Despite getting up at crack of dawn we were slow at attaching Pegasus's baggage. This consisted of our two luggage holdalls for clothes, thank-you gifts, microlight spare parts and oilcans which had to be bolted each side of our seats, with the spare propeller tied on top, and survival rations of food and water under my seat. Our sleeping-bags needed to be lashed to the pole between trike and wing, and the fuel funnel, map case, flexible jerrycan, water-bottles and all other loose items had to be securely tied on. Anything coming free would not only be lost, but would most likely be drawn into the propeller and possibly break it. It wasn't until nine a.m. that we were ready. We filed a flight plan that gave us several days' allowance for unforeseen happenings, but we couldn't obtain any meteorological forecast. A large crowd gathered, but all was dwarfed by the massive empty tarmac runway. It was fortunate we had plenty of space since we weighed more than the recommended maximum all-up weight of 192 kilos, 120 kilos of which was David and myself.

'The first thing to remember is the word STAIP,' said David, taking on his instructor's role, despite the staring crowd. 'S for security: now check your helmet and harness are properly secure; T for throttle: check smooth operation on and off; A: all clear around the aircraft; I: ignition. Switch it on, please; and P means propeller.' Then he called 'Clear prop,' loudly and pulled the starter cord.

Other checks followed, the final one being 'Power check on take-off.' We hurtled down the runway with David in control and finally unstuck from the ground, making a slow climb through light turbulence. The control tower kept asking our position, being talkative because we were their only flight of the day. I was straining my ears to understand what they said, but a sudden whump of turbulence sent everything out of my mind. Except for the idea that people weren't meant to fly.

The rough air continued over 2,000 feet so we went on up to 6,000 feet where I was thankful for my thick flying suit and pulled it closer around my neck and over my gloves. Below us were undulating hills of tall dry grasses, and blackened areas burned off by fire to encourage new grass shoots for hump-backed zebu cattle. We saw a herd following its herdsman. Bororo cattle are led, not driven, obedient to the sound of a voice. The Bororo people are not a negroid race, they are tall willowy descendants of a tribe who migrated from the Near East and, on the way, mixed blood with the Berbers of northern Africa. Indifferent to civilisation, preferring their nomadic ways, they had only come this far south to pasture their cattle.

Pegasus was flying well, no hiccups, and David seemed content. We skirted the town of Foumban, though I sighted its triple-arched gateway, and the palace of the Bamoun kings, a negro tribe. The seventeenth-century king, Mbombo, had been famous for his seven hundred wives, though more important was Njoya who built up the capital, the new architecture flamboyantly embellished with wood carving which was an ancient Bamoun skill.

A man of vision, Njoya venerated learning and, long before the advent of Europeans, there were Moslem books and a school where selected boys were educated. In 1895 Njoya also created a written language for his people, a writing of squiggles and dashes called Shumom.

David wasn't interested in visiting Foumban, so I left him working on his calculations of mileage and fuel at the airport outside town and popped into town with a Mobil man engagingly called Mama. Mama said he had fifty-six brothers and sisters. His father had married six wives and now that he was dead, Mama had become head of the family. He knew how to speak Shumom, which his father had taught him.

31

We visited one of his brothers and while they swopped news, I talked with his wife whose hairstyle of twenty-two snake-like braids wriggled above her head and down into one tail. Her shoulder was tattooed with a double-headed serpent, the symbol of Foumban.

At the palace we were met by a contemporary of Mama's, a son of the current king. This king's thirty-two wives had given him 107 sons and daughters. In the portal I found a drum taller than myself, beaten only when a king died. The balconies and main doors of carved wood were also emblazoned with the motif of the Foumban serpent.

The two biggest thrones in the central chamber were the ancient throne of Njoya and that of the present king, made of cowrie shells, formerly used as money in West Africa. It was guarded by elephant tusks and beaded statues of slaves. Above his throne was a photograph of the king who was currently away visiting Europe.

After the palace, I wandered through the artists' quarter, since Foumban has long been renowned for its craftsmen in wood and metal, particularly for the 'lost wax' method of casting bronze. I paused in a workshop to see what was going on: one man was separating lumps off a football-sized wodge of beeswax, another was pummelling clay to make a mould, while a third man sorted out what metal to melt. He had some old taps and bits of tilley lanterns.

The beeswax was fashioned into the shape of a jar and then encased in clay and put beside the forge. The furnace bellows, two goatskins tied at the legs, was pumped by an eight-year-old, the normal age, his master said, for a boy to become apprenticed. Odd-shaped clay moulds were baking in the glowing coals; small ones would cook for two to three hours, large ones for twenty-four hours. The firing would bake the clay mould and melt the wax, then the mould would be turned upside down so the wax drained out and the melted metal flowed into its place. One craftsman was chipping away a mould to reveal a mask, and two men were filing the rough edges of bronze statues.

I continued down the road, stopping occasionally to look at wooden story boards being carved to depict traditional village life, as well as more ordinary items like screens, stools, bowls and palm wine containers. At one stall I was invited to sit down for a quick game of Mbe, a board game played with frinoir nuts. My partner helped me play, and though I never entirely gathered the rules I only lost by a little.

From Foumban our journey should have been one hop to Banyo, 150 miles north. At first we could see a dirt road heading north along a ridge above a river valley, but the sky, which had been cloudless, soon filled with fair-weather puffy cumulus. The only problem was that we couldn't now see enough ground to tell where we were on our map. Ahead the cloud was thicker and billowy, with mountains showing blurred.

The next small town should have been Magba, but we didn't know if we'd passed it or not. David watched the cloud shadows moving to tell him the direction of the wind. It seemed to be quite a strong headwind. Without knowing the wind speed or having any way-point of reference, there was no way of working out our actual speed over the ground; 45 mph in no wind could be 70 mph with a tail wind. No instrument exists to tell us how fast we were actually travelling. Pilots usually rely on met offices to take readings for them. But we flew lower than them and could get no accurate information for our level. In clearer patches we caught sight of the red laterite road again and the shadow of the microlight flitting across the hillsides. It was strange to see it so far below.

According to David's calculations we had missed Magba. But we needed to find it because the engine was consuming fuel at an alarming rate. The normal rate was ten to twelve litres an hour, and we were using sixteen, making it unlikely we would be able to reach Banyo without refuelling.

Just when I began feeling uneasy about the situation, through our radio came a French pilot's voice saying he would land at Magba in ten minutes. David gave him our altitude so he'd miss us and asked where we were. A few moments later he shot past us. 'Magba is five miles ahead. And how is Christina today?'

He was a pilot from Avia Service in Douala where our microlight had been assembled, flying up here bringing surveyors to look at a newly built dam just north of Magba. He landed and turned quickly off the small dirt strip to make room for us. We hit sinking air as we made our approach, the strip looming fast as we plummeted. Only a couple of metres above the ground David pulled the nose up and kept our motor thrusting forward. We skimmed along and made a perfect touch-down.

From the Avia pilot we learned we had been battling a 20

mph headwind, so that a normal hour's flight had taken two hours, and the fuel which should have carried us 150 miles would only have covered eighty. As there seemed little sign of the headwind letting up we were happy to call it a day and accept the hospitality of an elderly Frenchman called Roger who was looking after the local logging camp. Roger had lived in Cameroun for fifty years, and was delighted to have some company. But before bearing us off to an excellent French lunch he set a guard on Pegasus. Last month, he explained, some tools had been stolen and he'd been obliged to call in a sorcerer. A list had been made of suspects, and the sorcerer poured the hot ashes of special herbs on to the list, reducing it to three names. Roger asked the three men to make sure the tools were returned, or else he would have to tell the sorcerer to continue, and by morning his goods were on the doorstep.

Later, while David cleaned plugs and filters, Roger showed me the logging mill and talked about the problems of forestry in an area where villagers still cut and burned randomly to plant crops, and quickly exhausted the thin soil. He showed me iron wood, so heavy and hard one can't hammer nails into it without first drilling a hole. We also looked at some ebony and he explained that the blackness is actually a disease in its healthy greyish wood, and that several types of tree can produce ebony.

Dinner was couscous and mutton with beans and nuts, a Camerouni recipe. The main topic of the evening was how to tackle the flight to Banyo. If the headwind was strong we could fly very low and probably find gentler breezes, but this would, of course, be riskier in the event of possible engine failure. I felt involved but detached. The whole thing was giving me the heeby-jeebies. Perhaps that was only because I hadn't yet got used to the sensation of open-cockpit flight.

That night I awoke feeling restless and went for a walk out under the almost-full moon. Beyond the glow of a bush fire I could hear distant drumming coming in waves, dying out and re-surging again. Birds outside my bedroom window gave me a riotous dawn chorus, despite mizzly air raining dew which dripped from all the leaves. After a hearty breakfast we loaded Pegasus and manoeuvred right to the tip of the grassy runway before turning to take off.

David was worried the wet grass and damp air might lengthen our run. We had already made it longer by being overweight, but the most important factor in take-off is the wind.

'There's not enough wind to help us,' David said, which confused me since I'd thought the calmer the better. 'Until we reach flying speed we run on the ground,' he went on. 'If we could point the nose into a good headwind the airspeed over the wing would be added to our running speed and we'd be lifted off quickly. If you ever try taking off downwind, you'll have a minus airspeed and it could more than double the length of the run.'

'How about landing?' I wondered aloud.

'Same thing, landing straight into wind takes minimum distance, landing downwind it takes for ever to stop. Don't do it, and watch out for crosswinds – they can be hell.'

We raced down the airfield and I clapped David on the back as we lifted off after 150 yards, double the unladen into-wind average. I looked down at rolling bushland, with thickly forested areas where a river's course had once meandered to the east of us. We kept parallel to the river, and overflew a new dam flooding a huge basin of forest. Trees stood stark and bare in the shallow water. The surveyors had said it would take a year or so to fill, but even in infancy it was a big lake.

The red road to Banyo crossed our route westwards. We were flying a direct heading above bush and 7,000 feet up over a range of small mountains. The plateau was grassland and bush, seeming devoid of huts or people except for Bororo with their cattle.

The air grew bumpy and David pointed out something he'd never seen before, a double layer of inversion with a ribbon of blue sky sandwiched between layers of warm and cold air. Both the lower and upper parts were turbulent but we found that by flying along the blue streak the air was calm. We passed east of a mining settlement and nearly two hours from Magba approached Banyo.

Coming from behind Banyo's mountain the microlight was tossed around in wind currents. The airstrip wasn't obvious, being very seldom used and several miles from town. We circled above it to warn a shepherd to move his goats, and came in to land. Seconds from touch-down the turbulent crosswind flipped up one of our wing tips, David fought to steady it, the wing lifted again, he accelerated trying to keep aloft and get level enough to land. Graded one to six, that was a hairy five.

On conventional planes ailerons cope with the problem of crosswinds. I had to rely on David's long experience with microlights and my faith in his ability never wavered, although I realised he needed time to get used to flying with full baggage.

The strong wind made it necessary for us to take off Pegasus's wing and fold it on the ground. Then we decided to try driving the trike frame into town. One is really not meant to do this. The propeller stirred up clouds of dust and we recalled stories of bi-car-ship-planes, but soon the track was four-wheel drive. We only had three wheels, and rather than break the propeller, I let David drive back to the airstrip while I walked in to town in the midday heat.

After collecting water and food I walked back to the airstrip, and rested there while David went to fetch some fuel. Our camp site was under a leafy mango tree, with the trike parked beside. The only disturbing thing was that bush fires were raging to three sides of us, and the wind, still strong, was blowing the fire straight in our direction.

Time idled by, and burned grasses floated past in the air. Feeling suddenly nervous I got up and checked around: the red earth road should hold the fire east of the tree, the scanty runway should give protection from the middle blaze and the length of the runway should keep half a mile between us and the western side of the fire. The crackle of burning grass was stupendous, and coming towards the runway I saw a wall of flame thirty feet tall.

After burning to the runway the fire subsided, and through the smoke came my afternoon visitors, an occasional Bororo herdsman drifting past and yipping to his herd to keep them moving, and a couple of young men in beautiful pink flowing robes who paused and gazed at Pegasus with wonder and delight. They were very polite and saluted me at length. All who came along greeted me with the customary two hands raised, showing their open palms.

By the time David came back the fire had passed by, and at six p.m. the sun set as a red orb and the full moon rose over the opposite horizon. I made fire and cooked supper, and brushed fallen dry mango leaves into a heap for my bed.

This was the sort of travelling I might have hoped for and knew how to handle. My contentment ran high at being back in Africa, despite my apprehension about coming to terms with learning to fly. I hadn't yet tried out the front seat.

At dawn we re-rigged the microlight and took off, heading

around the northern side of Banyo Mountain. I could see where a German lookout post had been, and the route by which I climbed the mountain twelve years ago, a tall rock up which I had chimneyed and the rocks which held a freshwater spring. The summit was higher than Pegasus. We changed on to an easterly course, aiming for Tibati. David was alert for engine splutterings, as he was worried about the fuel he bought in Banyo. It had looked frothy and we'd been warned about people mixing in kerosene, so we stayed high at 8,000 feet to improve our chances of gliding to safety if necessary.

The land drifted beneath us, as if it was unfolding slowly while we sat still in the sky. Hilly undulations were marked by forest and around villages there were patchworks of cultivation. I reached past David's shoulders and took over the control bar for a while. Pegasus flew effortlessly, and it was no problem to back-seat drive.

Suddenly we bounced upwards and sideways. 'It's only turbulence, stay with it,' said David. Fortunately the gusts were brief, but minutes later we hit more. They were hot thermal currents coming up from ground recently burned by bush fires. I thoroughly disliked the sensation and thought the bar would be wrenched from my hands but David helped me each time. As we progressed we caught worse thermal kicks off bush fires still burning. Their downwind side was the trouble spot, and when I could see sky ahead going pale with smoke columns, I gave the control bar back to David. The fires weren't actually devastating the countryside. We could see how quickly the flames burned off the tall dry grass without harming the trees.

After two hours Tibati came into sight with its vast lake spread out beyond. We circled the town and flew out over the lake, a thousand ripples glittered in the hazy light. With the sun behind us we could see down through the water how the main river feeding the lake had built up its banks, all now submerged. A few trees stood half-drowned and some palm trees showed just their circular heads above the water-level. The airstrip beside the town was covered in grass six feet tall, with just two sets of tyre tracks through the grass. A crosswind made me anxious, remembering yesterday's landing, but we touched down beautifully, the wing just clearing the top of the grass.

I found space for us to sleep at the Catholic mission, and we drove the microlight into town along the main road without even taking the wing off, which meant we measured twelve yards wide. The gendarmes entered into the unorthodox spirit of things by stopping all the traffic. Occasionally where trees hemmed in the roadside we had to manoeuvre to get through. At the roundabout we turned right, drove along to the gendarmerie, and parked outside. It would be a safe place for Pegasus to stay.

In the afternoon, while David nursed a headache I explored the lake in a dugout, returning at sunset when the town shore was alive with people pounding their clothes on upturned canoes, and soaping themselves. It seemed a pity the town water supply pipe came from the soapy area, but someone said the system didn't work anyway because the bills for diesel fuel hadn't been paid and the pump no longer worked.

I collected our jerrycans of Super petrol from where Mobil had stashed them. There were six cans, double the agreed amount, because dear Mobil had hit a problem. Their head office in New York had discovered it was against the law to supply petrol for aircraft, they must run on aviation fuel. So Mobil were obliged to give us Avgas. Our problem was that ordinary microlights don't run on Avgas, they use Super (with a two-stroke mix), and although we had done tests to make the microlight fly on inferior fuel, we had no idea how it would be affected by high-octane Avgas which is a much finer and more explosive fuel. Fortunately in Cameroun they hadn't removed our allotment of Super, and we mixed both sorts as a test.

Schoolchildren escorted me back to the Catholic mission. The father ran a school for all children, including Moslems. Open-minded toleration is something I've always admired in Catholic missionaries.

David's calculations told us that the next leg, to Ngaoundéré, was beyond our fuel range. So we agreed that I should hitch up the road next morning with a twenty-litre jerrycan of fuel and he would try to land on the road and meet me. If he couldn't land, I'd have to catch up with him in Ngaoundéré.

I was lucky to find a pick-up truck going to Ngaoundéré whose driver didn't mind stopping in villages while I asked if Pegasus had flown past. 'An aeroplane?' the first ones queried, so I suggested, 'It might look like a motorbike with wings,' and an elder responded, 'What we saw was a helicopter with a parasol.'

In a later village I learned that David had tried to land but some poles along the roadside had made it impossible and he had continued north. Actually I liked seeing the land from ground level for a change, bouncing along the rutted red earth road with dust flying from the tyres. Village huts had grass thatch reaching almost to the ground and the people were tall and graceful. Some women's faces were tattooed and their hair was pulled into bangs over the ears.

The road grew progressively more rutted, and across it scampered occasional troops of monkeys. A bridge had been partially swept away, its replacement half-finished with pillars but no road. We stopped to rebuild a way on to the old bridge using some planks that had fallen from it. They creaked horribly when we drove on to them.

Our next stop was for fuel in a village, delivered in small plastic bottles, being black market from Nigeria. The driver was very dubious about what it might contain.

Just outside Ngaoundéré a military roadblock insisted on searching my luggage. I was carrying a bag of aircraft parts that they solemnly took to pieces. It wasn't until afterwards I realised they were hassling me for a bribe, but I don't approve of bribery and simply co-operated with their search.

My contacts in Ngaoundéré were a French couple, Jacques and Monique Duchene, who helped me find David and kindly offered us hospitality. During calculations for the next leg we discovered we didn't have enough two-stroke oil left, and David was emphatic that we shouldn't risk inferior oil because last year a poor-quality oil had seized up his engine in flight. So I ordered a two-litre can of oil to be sent up from Douala. It would take a couple of days to arrive, and meanwhile David suggested I take the pilot's seat for some flying lessons.

Getting airborne without heavy baggage was no problem; the microlight ran to flying speed and popped away from the ground. We sailed up to 1,000 feet and saw a magnificent volcanic landscape spread out below. I hadn't realised just how many craters there were, but from above the land was clearly pockmarked with them and several held crater lakes.

I was learning to make turns, gentle and steep, using the volcanoes as guide points. The world seemed to spin in full circles around us. The only thing that phased me was when

David demonstrated that Pegasus had pendular stability and could right herself from any twist; he swung the bar and she dived and soared. 'You see the way the wing is swept back with its tips reflexed behind us. This is what gives us balance, enabling us to fly without a tailplane. We manoeuvre by what's called weightshift; when I pull the bar the wing doesn't move, it's the trike that alters its angle like a pendulum.' I glanced up at the pivot bolt, the only real attachment of the trike to the wing. 'By changing our centre of gravity we shift to any direction. Now do a steep left turn around that crater.' I banked, moving the bar away from the direction I wanted to turn, noticing how the trike swung left and this pulled the aircraft around.

'Now dive, then let go of the bar and see what happens.' I complied and, when I let go, the microlight slid back into trim and came out of the dive. It gave me the jitters, but of course David was right and she was steady, as steady as a roller-coaster.

What a view: we spotted two big waterfalls, many dry craters and others which had blown themselves apart, leaving only bits of their cones. It was in the Cameroun highlands in 1986 that a crater had loosed a huge cloud of poisonous gas, killing two thousand people and their livestock. We came down after an hour. The landing was not too bad, though David helped me ease and swing the trike level, but it was better than my evening lesson's landing when a gust of wind caught under the wing, dipping one tip frighteningly close to the ground, while the wheels were still in the air.

The following morning David got bogged down in chores like sticking bands around the plastic fuel line to give us an exact idea of the level in the tank, and recalibrating the oil jug he used for adding the 50:1 ratio of petrol to oil. It was soon too windy for a flying lesson and, disappointed, I stomped off to fill my day with something different.

On the rim of a round blue crater lake many miles south of Ngaoundéré I arrived at the thatched huts of a French couple, friends of the Duchenes. It was a stunning place to live. They kept horses and chickens whose eggs they sold in town. A dog was chasing two cats around under the long fringe of a hut's thatch.

At the lake shore there was an assortment of water craft, and I chose a ride in the makeshift pedalo that splashed water all over whoever was pedalling it. The dog and I sat at the front while we ambled across the middle of the lake to the lip where the lava had flowed out. Under the cliffs it was cool in the mossy shade and looking down through clear water I could see that the lake had no shallows, its sides fell sheer into the depths.

THREE

Blacksmiths and Sorcerers

We loaded Pegasus and flew out of Ngaoundéré, from a happy interlude into a new unknown. We didn't have the range to reach our destination, Garoua, so we took an extra full jerrycan and trusted we could land somewhere to refuel. The volcanoes faded, we headed north and climbed steadily over a range of mountains, and made our last radio report before descending and losing radio contact, flying low to help us against the wind. The tower at Ngaoundéré had said the wind was calm. We'd see if they were right when we got to some cliffs ahead where we'd been warned about turbulence.

From the 3,500-foot altitude of Ngaoundéré we descended into hotlands, a great flat bowl with Garoua at 800 feet above sea level. The plain was dotted with white mounds of cotton; I could even spot the tufts of cotton on unharvested plants. Cotton pickers wearing baskets were working at a leisurely pace. Others were cultivating plots of millet, red millet for making a strong wine, and white millet for food. The villages were enclosed by grass fences. Abandoned and ruined groups of huts, their roofs long gone, stood out as broken rings scattered on the burned ground.

We cleared the cliff without much trouble, and I took over flying for an hour, practising straight flight despite being angled crabwise into the wind. To the west I could see the line of my 1975 journey on horseback. That hadn't been an easy trip: I had run out of water and food frequently, but I learned to survive. The route had been a groundnut smuggling trail and it had been my introduction to horse travel. It felt a world apart yet, just here, crossing my tracks, life felt timeless.

The flying horse motored along smoothly with never a splutter, and I checked our makeshift petrol gauge to see when it was time to come down and refuel. Finding an open space wasn't easy in the bush, but the road to Garoua was good and where the tall verges had been burned back it was wide enough for us. No traffic in sight, we dived down and alighted on the road, and jumped out quickly to pour the fuel into the tank. We had almost finished when a truck came along. I flagged him to slow, and David pulled one wingtip to the ground which raised the other wing high enough for the truck to pass underneath.

Airborne again, we came to a large bush fire and stayed east, though I worried when I smelled the smoke and expected the bumps. Our total flight time to Garoua was four hours, and it was two very stiff, cramped pilots who reported to the airport commandant, to be told our special flight permit was out of date and we could be grounded indefinitely.

My next four hours were spent trying to prolong the permit. My technique is to think positively, to believe in the helpfulness and efficiency of all officials. So far in Cameroun they had been great and, when he mellowed, this one was no exception. He said he would do his best to get authorisation from Yaoundé to renew our permit, but I would have to persuade the military commandant of the province to allow our flight north into the eighty-mile control zone of N'Djamena, the capital of Chad. N'Djamena is right beside the Cameroun border, and Chad was currently trying to repel Libyan invasion forces. France had sent support to Chad but the Libyans were well equipped with Mig fighters and forward striking air bases in Chad, and the war was hotting up. The commandant, however, offered simple advice. We should radio N'Djamena from just outside their airspace to tell them we were not a warplane, then fly very low so that we would not show up on their radar screens. I suggested that no one would shoot down an aircraft marked with the British flag, and he laughed, replying that the Libyans would think we were spies using the flag as a disguise.

Garoua to Maroua, our next point north, would be a short hop, and before heading there I wanted to look around the remote Mandara Mountains, an isolated outcrop of the basement complex rock which thrust up out of the flat plains stretching between Garoua and Lake Chad to form a knot of mountains almost 5,000 feet high. So I borrowed a small pick-up and driver for a few days. The foothills were jumbled piles of rounded grey rocks, with grasslands coloured pink and bleached cream. Some trees were in flower, and some had vultures sitting hunched on their bare branches. We crossed a dry river-bed where people had scooped out water-holes, one of which was being used as a bath by a group of women who ran to hide, perhaps because Cameroun has a law saying all people must now wear clothes. Other women were on their way to a market, wearing maroon red and yellow ochre wrappers, their wares neatly bundled and balanced on their heads. These people called themselves Mafa, though others said they were Matakam which meant 'those who worked hard', and I'd also heard them called Kirdi which meant godless, pagan. Historically a persecuted minority, they had been attacked by Moslem war parties and slave traders, so had retreated to the most isolated parts of the mountains and thus their traditions had been preserved. They were considered too barbarian to bother civilising, so they were left alone and forgotten until recently. Nowadays some development has arrived and their culture is beginning to die.

Tightly clustered hamlets were perched on high ground, their roofs of tall cones like witches' hats. At the top they tapered sharply and were sewn with thatch in cross-stitch, ending in decorative straw topknots. Far beyond them I could see spires of rock in the mountain outlines.

The road after Mokolo was not good, but it had some astonishing scenery: solitary pinnacles sticking up like thumbs, and multi-pinnacled ridges. In Kapsiki village it was market day; the driver and I lunched on sugarcane, guavas, *beignets* (fried balls of bean-dough), and beef chunks covered in crushed groundnuts and pimento, roasted while you waited. The raw beef was crawling with flies, so I asked the boy to cook me a piece from underneath the pile, bearing in mind that David had already been getting attacks of stomach gripes. The boy took out a clean steak and kneaded it with his grimy hands. Really you can't win, but it tasted fine.

The most crowded part of the market was the millet beer drinking area where people crouched under thatch shelters and cradled calabashes of thick grey beer. Some drank in pairs, sharing a bowl. They said it was a tradition and, having drunk with a man, you could not seduce his wife.

We drove on and passed the picturesque village of Rhumsiki, looking for a place where the ancient art of iron-smelting was still being practised. Beside an earlier village I had noticed a clay furnace eight feet high with a spiky-topped façade and crudely moulded human effigy. The blacksmith I visited lived apart from any village, and kept his forge deep in the country-side because, he said, 'No villager would come to my home if the forge was there, they're afraid of my craft.'

Blacksmiths are the only Kirdi who don't farm the land; people fear their magical powers but don't despise them because they are often wealthier than those who till the soil. However, a smith's children may not marry ordinary villagers, only the offspring of other blacksmiths. This one called his son, a seven-year-old, who was also his apprentice, and we walked out to the forge. It was a rough clay oven beside small rocks, with two sunken bowls in front linked to the oven by buried pipes. To the bowls the smith attached two bits of skin and tied them to make airtight bellows. His son took over the pumping while the blacksmith explained how he finds copper in the bush during the wet season, when the rain makes it show up on the ground. He mixes it with other metals to make knives, jars, tobacco pipes and women's bracelets. When we left he killed the fire and removed all traces of our visit.

A few miles from there, as I wandered through a village, I was introduced to a sorcerer. The community had two sorcerers. This was the elder and more esteemed. The villagers would consult him to find the cause of disharmony, domestic prob-lems, a secret grudge, advice about avoiding or getting out of misfortune. Divining was a major function of his job, and people recommended me to ask him a question about my future. There was already a question which I longed to put. The sorcerer told me to sit opposite him and ask him what I wanted to know.

So I said, 'Will I reach the end of the journey I am making without crashing my vehicle and breaking my bones?'

Into a clay bowl of wet sand the diviner placed some broken fragments of calabash, their incised designs representing differ-ent aspects of my problem, and times and events. Around the inside edge he arranged short bamboo sticks for the identity and circumstances of the questioner, added more water and laid some wooden fragments in central patterns symbolising evil and tragedy.

An inquisitive kitten came over and tried to lap water from a dish containing a live river crab. Crabs are believed to be the earthly intermediary of the god, an oracle of truth. The man took the crab, put it in the bowl of wet sand and covered the whole thing with an upturned dish, leaving the crab room to manoeuvre in the dark.

After five minutes the sorcerer lifted the lid, put the crab back in its water, and began to examine what had been disturbed. I stared out over his garden wall to the rifts and upheavals of mountains. I realised that at heart I was still afraid of flying and, because I didn't feel in control of things, had this underlying feeling that an accident was inevitable and just waiting to happen. But the sorcerer saw differently. He said there was nothing to fear. Specifically questioned, he still assured me the journey would be completed without major injury to myself, David, or the vehicle. I didn't really believe him.

Before I left, he gave me a blessing; I stood in front of the bowl, he scooped a little water into a pot-shard, spat into it and dabbed the contents on my toes.

The steed I borrowed for the rest of the day was a small wiry brown pony. He wore a fierce ring-shaped bit through and around his mouth, and his saddle was high-pommelled and cushioned with a red rug. The owner doubted I could persuade the pony to behave, so I growled at it, then hopped aboard and cantered away.

Magnificent scenery opened up. In the breeze I could hear thumping and singing, and on a hilltop I found three women standing in a circle of stones pounding the grains off millet stalks. They used long spoon-like paddles, and said this would be beer millet, later to be winnowed, crushed between stones, and fermented in water.

Further on, I reined in to watch a man chasing a bush rat to its burrow. He dug it out, grasping it by its hairless white tail, and dashed its brains out on a rock before showing me its teeth and large curved bat-ears. The meat is a local delicacy. My horse sidled nervously during the whole incident, and was glad when we left.

The closely turfed hillsides were steep and rocky in places but goat paths were plentiful. This area of Rhumsiki and Kapsiki was only three miles from the Nigerian border, so it was not wise to stray. A woman came from that direction carrying a headload calabash of cheeping chicks. Nearby in another village I watched a man weaving narrow strips of cotton on a home-made loom. He said that within a month he had to finish enough strips to make shirts for an annual festival. This was also the season for grass picking to make new mats for walls and roofs. Leaving the horse to have a breather, I watched a man making a new cap for his roof, interplaiting the stalks and leaving the top as a sheaf of feather-headed grasses.

The late afternoon sun glowed on the pinnacles, turning them redder. By sunset I was nearly back at the horse's home village, and saw a line of drummers and flautists arriving from over the hills. The village chief said they were coming to his clan's celebration and he invited me to stay and watch. By the time I had returned the pony to its stable, the dance was just starting.

Five men with swords and shields approached the onlookers, swords out-thrust, taking turns to make mock attacks on us. Some had long-fringed leather quivers slung across their backs, or crossed sashes of white cloth; women shook rattles and made trilling calls in their throats. The chief sat waving a fly-switch made from a complete horse's tail.

The dance moved stealthily, the chief got up to circle and whirl, his long robe spinning out around him, flapping his horsetail over his head. Old women began chanting fast behind a drummer, some women danced slowly in a line, arms around each other's shoulders, and two of them broke forward bent over, with hands on thighs and vigorously dancing bellies. By now the other women were hopping and skipping, swooping to the ground and clapping. The flute music cried out into the night and the drumming reverberated off the mountains. The finale was a male trio with swords again unsheathed, one with a shield held flat, showing obeisance to the chief and closing with a noble crescendo.

Then my driver of the morning reminded me of the abysmal state of the road we had yet to cover if we wanted to reach Maroua. He had driven quite carefully in daylight but at night he flung caution to the winds. We raced along, bouncing over ruts and rocks until we hit a large sharp one so hard it blew the tyre. Fortunately the pick-up had a spare, but at times, what with breakdowns, roadblocks and security checks, I doubted we would reach Maroua before morning.

Our chore for the next day was a drive north to position a fuel stash for Pegasus's onward journey, and the driver brought me back through very broken mountains where we got a bit lost. We ended up at a mountain-top village whose chief had forty-four wives.

The strangest thing about the village was that none of it was built on flat ground, just contoured to a craggy peak, and there were more granaries than houses. Each wife had two granaries and when I was asked into the chief's compound it was a forest of granaries three times taller than me. They were entered by a notched branch ladder, and only the owner could go inside. Other granary-shaped structures, packed so close together that just one person could walk between them, were the homes of the wives. These had doorholes, marked with circular symbols which were most profuse on that of the number one wife. Each wife had her own tall round bedroom with mud-sculpted bed, and granary-shaped kitchen with clay water jars, grinding tray and flattened utensil-stones.

Deep inside the chief's compound I came face to face with a large bull penned behind a barricade of logs, trunks and rocks, but the way it stamped and bellowed made me wonder if the barricade would survive. The bull was the chief's pride and joy, destined to be sacrificed in a month at the Maray celebration, an important festival of ancestor worship. One of the chief's sons showed me the altar where people prayed before the slaughter, then a room with a double altar, and another with a dead chief's tomb. Few men have the right to sacrifice a bull; but the privilege can be hereditary or become a right if one has already taken part in six previous Marays. Before I left the village some boys showed me how they make toys from millet stalks, cutting short pieces and pinning them on splinters of bamboo to produce intricate toy bicycles and trucks. There was also an aeroplane, looking even less like a plane than Pegasus.

Back in Maroua I had hoped to fly up north to Waza National Park but discovered that we had been grounded. The problem was the lack of an official signature on one of our pieces of paper. I sorted it out at the gendarmerie and prepared for a six thirty a.m. take-off, but was grounded again. Finally we succeeded in getting airborne by nine thirty, by which time the wind was growing gusty. As usual we could get no meteorological information, apart from ground level winds, which gave us little idea what was happening at altitude: a southerly ground wind can be easterly at 2,000 feet.

For the first hour we flew at 3,000 feet, going faster than usual because David had altered the trim. We needed the height, since when we tried to descend we hit pockets of cold air then hot, cold and hot again, making inversions that bounced us around uncomfortably. I was navigating, and it wasn't difficult to pick out the landmarks I'd noted earlier, leading us to a disused sandy airstrip and the hut where I'd left our jerrycans. We refuelled and put the remainder back into safe keeping with the family there, saying that we'd be visiting again in a few days. Then we flew north along a series of ponds linked by cattle tracks. We didn't manage to raise N'Djamena on the radio, our range was not long enough, so we came down low to avoid showing up on the military radar screens. Flying at between twenty-five and 700 feet above ground we sped along, leaving our radio tuned to N'Djamena's frequency so we could listen in case they spotted us.

I hoped we weren't running too much of a risk. I thought of my father who had been a glider pilot in the Second World War, and after D-Day he had flown into the battlefield of Arnhem. I didn't intend to emulate his experience. How would I ever explain it to David's parents if we got shot down.

At Waza we didn't land on the airstrip. There was a flat space beside Waza Mountain which proved adequate, and we pushed the microlight into some bushy trees for shelter. We wanted to see this park, famous for its elephants, from the land and from the air. Few of the roads were open, these flat plains of loamy cotton soil being treacherous for six months of the year, but by car we managed to find herds of horse-antelope, and *damalise*, four-horned beasts with two straight horns and two sticking up sideways. Giraffes with babies sauntered away, warthogs fled with their tails in the air, and finally we spotted some elephants which our guide led us to on foot for a closer look.

For me, the high point of the visit was at sunset when we were sitting by a pond and some jackals disturbed several hundred wild ducks. They flew up, separating into distinct flocks all sharing the same small airspace, groups swooping in different directions around each other.

In the morning we flew over the pond and into the park, past the herds of antelope and giraffes, following sets of elephant footprints that showed clearly even from 700 feet above. Water-holes and wallow bowls were frequent, coloured from milky blue and pale green, to beige and brown, coated partly with yellow-green weed or studded with waterlilies.

Our radio cackled in French. It was N'Djamena air traffic control talking to a French pilot. We kept quiet and descended lower, though it was the Libyan fighters we feared, not the French. Suddenly a herd of about sixty elephants began to stampede at the sound of our engine. We hadn't meant to disturb them but it was a stupendous sight, as we circled to head them back on their original course, then aimed west across the vast burned tract that was meant to keep the animals away from Waza town.

Our intention now was to fly back to Maroua and thence direct across into Nigeria. But first we landed en route to Maroua and swapped seats for me to have a lesson. David wanted me to start making Pegasus bank and roll, doing climbing turns, and diving ones. The boulder-strewn mountains just downwind made me conscious of my vulnerability. After an hour my arms ached, my muscles were clenched tight; the thermals were small but challenging enough for a novice. I wanted to be safely on the ground but I couldn't face the thought of trying to land. It was a relief to let David reach past me and take control of the bar; but even he had a rough time getting us down.

In the afternoon we left the Immigration formalities until last, and it was a mistake. 'You must bring us exit visas. They must be stamped by an office on the other side of town, and we close in five minutes.'

I left David there to prevent them closing, while I hijacked a car and dashed to get the exit stamps. The office was closed but I found a man who agreed to re-open it for me. Then I hurtled back, collected David and the exit visas, and tackled a new problem over David's vaccination certificate which didn't comply with regulations. The doctor was driving away from his clinic but we flagged him down and he also kindly re-opened his surgery and signed David's certificate.

It was midnight before we got to sleep, and at six a.m. we reported to the airport, ready for departure. More official delays kept us three hours, then we took off, but within a few miles developed engine trouble. One cylinder was overheating badly and with heavy hearts we turned back. After landing, David took the motor to pieces. I combed through our luggage, worried by our forty pounds overweight. We had to carry four extra cans of oil, since there would be none of that type in Nigeria, so I pared the rest of our baggage to a new minimum and went to the post office to send the surplus home. There was no brown wrapping paper in the market, only some old cement sacks which people assured me would be just as good. I hoped the postmen wouldn't mind.

50

Arriving back at the airport I found David in a terrible state. He looked so pale and thin and ill, he blamed himself for our inexplicable engine failure, which was nonsense, and for his health which had been rapidly falling apart. The poor man had been suffering severe stomach gripes, backaches, headaches, a sore throat and a badly cut hand. But he never once slacked in his job.

By mid-afternoon the engine was ready to test. It wouldn't even start. David worked on until evening, with no success. I found a friendly family living nearby who let me cook supper for him and offered him a bed. I shared a bed with their children. We should have got up at four a.m. but didn't have the energy until five thirty. We were under pressure because our visas for Cameroun had now expired. By seven thirty the engine was running, but it sounded as sick and ragged as David who I'd just seen doubled up on the ground with stomach pain.

We agreed to let a local mechanic try his skill, despite both of us knowing that we should never let a stranger meddle with an aircraft. But he was good and thorough. The problem was that nothing seemed to be wrong with the engine. David had altered the spark timing then readjusted it, and although he and the mechanic re-dismantled the innards, they still could find no fault.

We tested it and it worked, so David put me in the front seat for a lesson-cum-test-flight. I flew for about half an hour; it was after sunset and the light was fading fast, soon I could hardly make out the aerodrome. But the motor sounded fine. David mocked an engine failure and told me to land. If it had been real we would have ended up in the dirt. I didn't turn fast enough and was surprised how steeply we came down without a motor. An extra nuisance was that our radio was malfunctioning and we had to switch off the intercom between our helmets, so I couldn't ask David for advice or hear his instructions. Even with the power back on, our joint landing was very amateur.

The next morning, it was imperative we got an early start.

The flight plan hadn't been filed, nor had we worked out the route, and our radio system had deteriorated to the point of being almost useless. By taking off his helmet David could contact the control tower on our radio microphone, we received permission to depart, then transmissions ended.

For this flight I took the pilot seat; my take-off run was a hundred yards and we climbed slowly, nursing the engine so as not to strain it. Around the sides of mountains we kept hitting turbulence which made me yelp with fright. In a way I was glad the intercom was dead and David couldn't know how often I squeaked and gulped.

We landed at the disused airstrip where we'd previously left jerrycans, and after a final refuel were ready for our flight over the border into Nigeria. The microlight roared into lift-off, gained a little height, and suddenly it had a total power failure.

There was a horrible silence. At the same moment we were caught in a gust of sinking air and plummeted. David had no chance to stop the fall: we slammed down on to the ground and bounced askew. In an instant David had straightened our line and brought us out of trouble, somehow safely back to earth. We got out and checked for damage. Surprisingly, nothing was broken; our microlight had no suspension on the wheels, but the bounce in the tyres had absorbed the shock. David began unscrewing the engine mounting block, time for another session on the electrics.

By mid-afternoon all was ready for a test flight. But our chances of reaching Maiduguri, our first stop in Nigeria, looked slim and it would have been madness to land inside Nigeria before we reached a place like Maiduguri where we could clear Immigration, as the area was so sensitive we'd have been jailed immediately. Our best option was to offload more weight for this border hop, and after that we could deal with things as they came. So I offered to take some gear and hitch to Maiduguri by road.

After watching David take off and head into the distant blue sky I got a lift to the border with an onion-seller. There were several people in the truck, who he dropped off one by one and then started getting sexy. I deterred him with the all-seeingness of God.

He stopped to show me his onion field; it had an ancient water pulley with a weighted stick, rope and crossbar, worked by hand, raising one calabash of water at a time. His destination was the border town of Kionmatari and he dropped me at the Cameroun exit side.

'We can't let you leave because your passport says you left two days ago,' the officer told me, not unreasonably. 'And your visa has expired.' He suggested I went back to Maroua and extended my visa so that he could correctly stamp me out. I was taken to the boss and allowed to explain my problem. He finally saw my side of things and said I was free to cross the border.

The frontier itself was marked by a heavy link chain lying in the dust. I stepped into Nigeria. There was none of the fanfare I'd imagined on returning to the country of my birth. Just the hot dusty street with black-market money-changers sitting in the shade.

The authorities stamped me in and I found a lift to Maiduguri. After the confined rock-perched villages of northern Cameroun I noticed the spaciousness of these on the plains, their wide yards with big huts, their millet stalk roofs secured in place against the wind by a quilting of tied stalks, and, compared to Cameroun, there were almost no roadblocks. But David, I found, had been arrested.

FOUR

Lake Chad and Duck-Billed Women

Maiduguri airport was big and military-looking; it was not an international airport but we had special permission to arrive there because no international airport was within our range. David was in what they called official detention in a small windowless interrogation room. Our problem was the lack of a vital piece of paper, one that I'd been trying to get hold of for months. It was not enough that we had been issued with clearance numbers by the Nigerian Civil Aviation Authority and by the Nigerian Ministry of Defence, we didn't have it written on their headed paper to prove it. All we had was a telex from the British Embassy in Lagos giving the numbers. One officer said it was a trick.

Some of the uniformed men were friendly, others were very aggressive. I kept trying to calm things down and defuse the situation, but people fired off at tangents, intent on their own power games. They searched our baggage yet again and came to a small bulky sealed envelope marked 'Do not open until 25 Dec'. It was my mother's Christmas present to me. 'Open this,' the officer demanded, so I said, 'No I can't, but you may open it.' This produced confusion and for good measure I added, 'Go ahead, but you're not allowed to say what you see, it's to be a secret.' We kept up the banter for a while and in the end he didn't bother to open it. There was enough else being strewn on the floor.

By late evening we were still in detention. The commandant had agreed to write to the Department of Civil Aviation and Defence Ministry in Lagos, sending the letters with the morning plane since neither the telephones nor telex in Nigeria were working.

When at last we were allowed to go to a hotel for the night we fell asleep in utter exhaustion, until a violent hammering on the door about two a.m. forced us awake. A military chief had come to interrogate us. He grew unnecessarily threatening, grilling me and riling me to lose my temper, but I knew if I said the wrong thing, we would be in serious trouble. Finally he left, warning us not to try and set foot outside the hotel. Anyway, they had taken David's passport and all our documents. David said this had been the hardest day he'd ever had as a pilot.

A vehicle with barred windows collected us in the morning to take us back to the airport for further questioning. In between the bad bits we got some co-operation, managing to clear Customs and get David's passport stamped. Then came a long wait. Late afternoon we were taken to the commandant's office. He was all smiles, our flight authorisation numbers had been confirmed. The twenty-four-hour ordeal was over. He typed a letter for us on military headed paper, giving us special clearance to operate anywhere in Nigeria, except near Lake Chad, elaborately signed and covered in official stamps.

It was a pity we couldn't fly to Lake Chad. I'd never seen the lake and longed to go there. David asked for a day of rest, so I took my flask and a picnic and set out hitching to the lake.

The rough dirt road crossed unending flatness with sparse bushes and huts made of millet stalks. Herds of camels and cattle clustered around ponds which hadn't drained away because the ground was impervious, and a gushing artesian well bore witness to the pressure of the water table below. The Chad basin is geographically a vast flat pan, almost without slope, and the lake is a huge shallow puddle. Non-porous clay, which some well borings show to be over 200 feet thick, lies under the sands. Despite this it's still curious that the lake exists at all: only a couple of rivers flow permanently into it yet it hasn't been dried up by evaporation from the scorching sun and searing desert winds.

The lake is the remnant of two inland seas known as Palaeo Chad, lapping on to Cameroun's Mandara Mountains, Tibesti and the Hoggar Mountains, which receded in arid eras, and was re-flooded by later glaciers to become Mega Chad, 20,000 years ago. Mega Chad, a neolithic site, has shrunk to the present-day Lake Chad, about 140 miles wide, but the low ridge of its ancient shore is still visible. The current shoreline is continually changing, a lake area of 10,000 square miles in the dry season being doubled in the wet. During high winds the shoreline has been recorded as moving five miles in a night. This makes it unsurveyable.

Our road was rutted twisting tracks through deep sand, and the old jalopy surged from side to side at breakneck speed. My fellow passengers had facial tattoos below their cheekbones and five earrings in each ear. Some wore nose rings as well. All their baggage was tied on to the roof, including something that wouldn't stand still. The lake shore inhabitants are Kanuri, descended from the Berber and Yemeni Arab peoples who founded the former Bornu empire in this region. Their arrival had pushed into the floating papyrus lake interior the original lake dwellers, a tribe called So, whose burial urns indicated people of large stature. Local folklore said they were giants. I had already noticed several extremely tall people, some still claiming ancestry from the So.

The other ancient tribe here were the Buduma (Boudoumi) or 'pirates of the papyrus', an isolated fishing tribe whose origins are unknown; they are also large and well adapted to life in the reeds. The Kanuri believed they were amphibious, perhaps because when hunted the Buduma would disappear underwater and swim away.

We continued to Baga, a former habour village now three miles from the shore, and from there I went on by motorbike to a lake-side fishing camp and market, where I hired a small flat-bottomed canoe for the day, and two ten-year-old lads to paddle it. We started off floating east along a wide channel bordered by a long spit of land that seemed to separate the lake into two pools.

Birds waded in the reeds of the shore, carmine bee-eaters swooped at water-level catching insects, while above us eagles and hawks wheeled, scanning for prey. Occasionally we passed a settlement on marginally higher ground, enclosed in thick dry reed walls. The boy behind me wielded a twelve-foot punt pole of palm with a forked branch jammed into the bottom end. He said nowhere in the lake was deeper than his pole. The other lad crouched at the prow, paddling with short sharp strokes. Sometimes the water was so shallow he also poled us along; at one point the paddle stuck in the mud and with a yelp he let go. I grabbed the paddle shaft as it went by and returned it to him, then, seeing some picturesque huts just ahead on a sand-bank, I picked up my camera and took a photo of the boy against this background.

Up jumped a man from under a thatch shelter, waving his army beret and blowing a whistle to summon us over. He accused me of taking a photo of his military post and he tried to confiscate my camera. I played the silly female for all it was worth and it worked. In the end he didn't even take the film.

Waves slapped against the prow, and the wind coming across the lake was cold. These winds cause fearful storms because the lake is quickly whipped up, being so shallow. One puzzling thing about the lake is that one would assume it was undrinkably alkaline. Such a huge expanse of water with little input would normally build up a concentration of natural salts, yet the water is sweet to drink. A plausible explanation is that the reeds and other lake vegetation, like salt bush, absorb the salt from the water.

Some white hump-backed cattle came down to drink. Not the normal zebus, these were large with very fat horns. It's said that the extra airspace inside the horn is a buoyancy device helping the Chad cattle to swim better than other breeds. Cattle here have to swim to reach new pastures.

We dabbled through floating grass, disturbing hordes of insects which swarmed up all around the canoe, making me wish the insect-catching birds would take notice, but they were busy downstream in our wake. The rear boy was humming tunelessly, interrupted only when he cried out that he'd let go of his punt pole. We drifted back to catch it. Later we were questioned briefly by another military patrol. After several miles the peninsula faded back and channels through the labyrinth of papyrus opened up on both sides. Floating islands were formed by knotted reed roots and swollen stems, matted and sometimes carrying a bed of crushed vegetation and sand. Dangling roots usually anchor the islands above submerged sand dunes, but annually when the water-level rises the roots are torn free and the islands float around, sometimes to be commandeered by families to make fishing camps. If the island starts to sink, they just heap on a thick layer of dead reeds to raise its surface.

The lad on the prow pointed excitedly to a plant sticking up above the water beside us with a long dark snake sleeping coiled around it. Further on we passed a dead snake as thick as a man's arm. We paused at various fishing camps and watched fish-lines being re-threaded with multiple hooks, and a man building a new canoe from a wooden frame with planks. Most other canoe traffic was carrying the large twin-gourd floats lashed to a pole on which men sat to fish. The natural buoyancy of the gourds kept them afloat, and the fish caught were conveniently popped into the gourds. We watched a fisherman on a one-gourd float, lying sprawled over it and paddling along with hands and feet as he unhooked his fish-line.

My speedy boys caught up with a heavily laden thirty-foot canoe crammed with people, goats, and bundles wrapped in bright-coloured cloths. I was in charge of the bailing can, a cut-off oil tin, but seepage was not too bad. With a sudden wobble and large splash, the back boy lost his balance and fell overboard. We all laughed. Occasionally we did hit things underwater, sunken canoes, hidden in the brown muddiness.

When the boys dropped me back again on dry land I found a ride to the remains of Kukawa, where the Shehu Laminu, a great sheik and ruler of the Bornu empire, whose wisdom was praised across North Africa and in Europe, had founded his capital city. He had paused to rest here under a baobab tree during a journey and, after reading to the end of the Koran, announced that this would be the site of his capital.

'And the baobab tree is still there?' I asked the driver. I was so disbelieving that he took me to see it. The whole landscape was dotted with baobabs but one was marked as special, its trunk enclosed by a mud wall. I went in through the gate and sat in its shade.

The Shehu had named his city Kuka which in Kanuri means baobab. The Bornu empire is recognised as the oldest Islamic state in this part of Africa. Its people were followers of Mohammed several hundred years before the militant Moslem invasion swept across North Africa. But now Kukawa was just a village. A man wearing indigo robes, a sword and dagger slung from one shoulder, strode past. His face was entirely wrapped in a head cloth, except a slit for the eyes, to protect him from the swirling dust. Shepherds tended their flocks, hobbled brown camels stretched their necks to acacias, running their lips down the thorny branches with relish. Women were driving laden donkeys home from market, and a horseman pranced along on a thick-chested steed. I doubted the scene was much changed.

The empire had been crushed by a deserter brigand who

raised a heap of over 3,000 skulls in Kukawa. Nothing remains of the city except for four royal mud tombs, including that of the great Shehu Laminu. The wood roof which formerly covered them had fallen in and a tin one served in its place. The wind, lifting its edges, made me feel I was not alone.

Back in Maiduguri that night, David had some good news and some bad. The good was that he'd managed to semi-repair our intercom system. The bad was that a different Customs official had been pestering him, trying to re-open the question of the legality of our flight and telling us that Nigerian television had run a news item showing Pegasus under wraps at the airport and saying the pilots were being held for interrogation.

It was infuriating; now we'd have to demand an apology from them to reassert our respectability, or else every petty official in northern Nigeria would be arresting us. Fortunately during supper the military commandant turned up, said we were a hundred per cent in the clear, and there was no need to answer any further official's questions.

Out of the whole experience we made several good friends and I was impressed with their integrity, a rare quality in a country notorious for corruption. Nigeria is also known for arrogance, but I saw little trace of this in the north where people were spontaneously kind to both David and myself.

We planned our route forward through Nigeria and David, who was still looking washed out, suggested I pilot us to Potiskum, 150 miles west, so he started teaching me to draw triangles of velocity for the route. Using the analogy of a boat crossing a river current it became clear that a microlight can be pushed way off course by wind, unless your compass heading allows for drift and you angle the nose against the wind. 'But how much drift?' I asked.

'You have to guess how strong the upper winds might be, and what direction they might come from. It's a bit hopeless without met information but we'll have to try.'

I guessed at a five knot easterly for one option and a ten knot north-east for the second. If the wind was calm, we would not have the range to reach Potiskum. Drawing triangles and using a protractor David calculated time, distance, wind strength and direction to discover what heading we should go for.

At five thirty the next morning we hurried down to the airport, rigged the microlight, and filed our flight plan.

Pre-flight checks completed, I turned along the runway and headed for the very far end. The memory of my last take-off, the crisis of engine failure, was still fresh.

This time was a joint effort, David on the throttle and me with the bar thrust forward, fully out as the white lines flashed beneath, in a touch, out again, then let her climb. Pegasus can't be a she, I mumbled, then decided that her capriciousness and unpredictability were certainly female, and she was beautiful.

'Turn more left,' David called, and I tried to put the wingtip on the horizon but it had become a thick dust-filled blur of harmattan winds, giving me visibility of about two nautical miles. Below was flat sahel with no natural features to use for navigation. North lay a series of parallel sword-shaped seif dunes. The microlight kept veering that way; I couldn't tell if it was due to a crosswind or because our flexible wing batons had got bent. Our speed seemed fast, though by now I knew the normal cruising speed of 45 mph could actually be only 20 mph in a strong headwind.

'Keep to your headings,' instructed David, so I pulled harder against our northerly swing. After one and a half hours we hadn't spotted our first way-point, which should have appeared within twenty minutes. None of the dry streams tallied with our map. Two of my way-points had been military radio masts, 300 feet tall, but I didn't see them in the fog. We did pass a couple elsewhere but I couldn't work out where they were. It didn't seem worth worrying about.

When thermals started rising from the dry land they made Pegasus bobble along merrily like a leaf down a river. It was enjoyable flying. Baobab trees grew more numerous, gradually becoming a spacious forest, their grotesque shapes stretching into the foggy distance. Some had been stripped of bark around their girth, to provide fibre for making string and rope. Debarking the trunk doesn't kill the tree, it makes it grow fatter. The uses of this tree are many: its leaves are cooked in soup, and are reputed to have healing properties when bandaged over a wound; the ripe fruits are edible and the old ones can be roasted; the rind produces a piquancy like chilli, and when blended with oil is rubbed on to horses to kill the ticks.

To conserve power David had turned off the intercom, and as I flew I started singing carols, since we were only a week away from Christmas. Somehow the baobabs went well with 'Angels from the Realms of Glory'.

Lake Chad and Duck-Billed Women

Ox-carts lumbered along a track between villages enclosed by mud walls. Outside each compound were some small thatched platforms, set on legs, which I supposed were where men received their male visitors, since being Moslems they wouldn't want strange men among their womenfolk. It was interesting trying to work it all out, especially one village we overflew which had groups of holes in the ground, many together near a dry stream. I guessed they must be digging natron, a rock I'd seen on sale in markets. Its most common use was to be nibbled with tobacco.

The thermals stopped being gentle, in fact they grew increasingly vicious, and I clamped my thumbs around the bar. At one bad wrench, David came to my help in the nick of time as we nosedived towards the ground in sinking air. It was all very well this learning to fly and handle Pegasus in rough conditions, but I did wish I knew how to make a landing. David had started to teach me about emergency landings but I had yet to make an ordinary one. And at the back of my mind I had the niggling worry that David, being unwell, might one day pass out while flying.

Seeing a big village, we tried again to work out our position, then noticed to our surprise that it had an airfield. 'We'd better land and find out where we are, and probably rest here until the thermals cool off this afternoon,' David said. As we circled we saw a word written large in stones on the ground – Potiskum. We had reached our destination. We must have been travelling at double our normal cruising speed, in the fastest wind we'd ridden so far.

After landing, we tethered Pegasus securely on the lee side of a ruined building and I went off to the town market to buy us lunch of fresh fruit and cooked liver for David; perhaps the iron would bring back his energy. From Potiskum we faced the problem that our route had been planned to go south and take in the Geji rock paintings near Bauchi, then north-west to the ancient emirate of Kano. But according to David's new calculations the latter leg was beyond our capacity. So it seemed a sensible idea for David to fly straight west to Kano and take a day or two of rest, while I made a jaunt by road to visit the Geji paintings.

A man on a motorbike offered me a lift 130 miles to Bauchi. He drove at the usual Nigerian speed of 100 mph and he kept swerving to avoid things that weren't there. He said he had to get to Bauchi to find out if he'd won a lottery. Occasionally his head seemed to be nodding and his body jolted forward as if he were falling asleep. After ten minutes, and a particularly screeching swerve which brought us to a halt, I realised he was drunk. So I offered to drive, he agreed, and we swapped places. Having checked that I could remember how to change gear with my toes, I took off at a decorous pace. It had been years since I'd driven a motorbike, but the road was open and empty and we cruised along until we reached Nigerian speed.

It was great driving across plains of flat pinkish earth scattered with harmattan rose-bushes in deep pink blossom, and grey mounds of rounded boulders. The plateau we were entering had been formed by ancient volcanic activity. Outcrops of granite boulders appeared, some with balancing rocks eroded, overhanging or lodged on a thin neck, and there were several solitary plugs of rock, rising 200 feet like stone hiccups. My pillion passenger seemed to have fallen asleep. I just hoped he'd keep holding on.

People waved with the customary Hausa greeting of a clenched fist, which I returned the same way and with the words 'Sanu, sanuku'. The bike was passed and re-passed by a truckful of horses being sent down south. Due to sleeping sickness, southern horses didn't usually live long, and the northern state of Bornu had long been famed for its breeding stock, while this plateau claimed to be the source of Nigeria's oldest indigenous horse, a small wiry beast used by the early pagan hill tribes. Instead of inventing a saddle they flayed open the young horse's back, roughing it into a thick callous which formed a good gripping pad. Thus mounted they had escaped from their would-be conquerors and kept their independence from Fulani rule by occupying inaccessible hills. But they hadn't escaped the Fulani slave raiders, and the name of Bauchi meant 'slavery'. The town was founded as a slave-collecting centre in the midst of these pagan lands.

It was sunset. My pillion man awoke with a jolt and asked me to stop at the roadside while he prayed. He located Mecca's direction and began his bowing. I wondered if he was asking God to help him win the lottery, or to forgive him for being drunk.

From Bauchi I continued with another ride of fifty miles to a village where I had a VSO contact who had gone away for

Christmas, but had left the key to his bungalow for me with his Nigerian neighbours, co-workers on a nutrition project. I joined them for a supper of *tuwo*, maize-flour meal which we rolled in our fingers and dipped in soup. The soup, thickened with palm oil, trailed long slimy green threads when we scooped it up. Nearby I could hear drumming and women singing. My hosts said they were probably Christians getting into the spirit of Christmas, so after supper I went to find out. The singing was loud, it wasn't harmonious but it rang with exuberance.

Out under dim lights, members of an Evangelical church group were marching in a circle around a solo drummer. Each hymn had a different dance. One involved retreating and advancing in tight lines, while they sang about being soldiers of the Lord; the next had a slow half-step to a tune like 'Silent Night', and the third bounced along with the gusto of 'Jingle Bells'. It wasn't strange to be there, it reminded me of the ten years of Christmases I'd already spent in Nigeria.

Early the next morning I visited Miya, an ancient mud village beside a boulder hill. Some huts set apart on the hill's shoulder were pointed out as where boys undergoing circumcision rites were staying. I was taken to pay my respects to the chief, and sat in front of his palace while elders discussed village business, their voices muted against a background of crowing cockerels, while steam rose from thatch roofs.

An old man was delegated to show me around, starting with the hall of sanctuary. Fugitives were traditionally guaranteed a safe rest here on a naturally curved stone seating area around a sacred wooden post. The sanctuary was also still used for the performance of miracles, and at these ceremonies the post was bedecked with totems. Now hanging from it were several woven circlets, something to do with circumcision. Circumcision usually takes place at four years old, and the boys sleep here until it's time to confine them to the huts up on the rocks.

Although the outcrop is taboo to women the chief gave me permission to climb it. He said it was my risk since the taboo simply says that if a woman ventures there something bad will happen to her. My guide led the way through a jumble of boulders and past a tribal relics hut, on whose wall hung some old sacred forked sticks believed to hold the *juju* ancestor magic to protect property. Above, the hill looked unclimbable, but my guide vanished into a cave and when I followed him I found the cave narrowed back into a short tunnel which opened on to a higher level. He showed me how it could be barricaded in times of ancient war, and the ruined village where people used to hide until trouble had passed. One cleft in the rock held a pond, black but clear, filled by a spring that had never been known to dry up.

We scrambled on to the summit, a great bald dome with an old lookout point. Layers of rock were peeling off in the process known as exfoliation. Looking down at the modern village we could see tall baskets aloft on poles outside some huts. They marked the households whose sons had just been circumcised, the baskets being used to sun dry the meat of cows slaughtered for the occasion.

Descending to the hill's shoulder, my man warned the boys to stay out of sight. Their nine low-walled huts were child-size, though in one were some adult dance costumes and two ceremonial drums. I remembered the taboo after I stubbed a toe badly on a rock, and had to leave and get it taped up.

Fifteen miles on, at Kafin Makadi, I got a bit lost and ended up meeting the emir, a traditional ruler who lived in a 130-year-old mud palace. His bodyguard of old men lounged by the gatehouse, and inside the yard was tethered his white horse. The palace doors were of cowhide stretched over wooden poles. I took off my shoes to enter the impressive throne-room with its four colossal clay arches and other arches at right angles, designed by this emir's grandfather. Light came from small square window holes in walls two feet thick.

The emir was waiting to receive me, sitting on his throne and swathed in robes to make him look fat. Fatness equalled importance: a thin man could not be important since he obviously lacked wealth. In his hand the emir held a horsetail fly-whisk, symbol of status and authority throughout West Africa for centuries. A British trader in the sixteenth century had recommended we sent 'horse tayles most blacke' to Africa as trade goods. This emir was seventy-four years old and had held power for eight years. I asked him how he had been chosen to be emir and he said he inherited the post from his elder brother. Succession was decided by 'king-makers' who went around the village asking people who they would choose.

He wasn't very talkative, perhaps because I was a mere woman. My mind drifted away from him, sitting there in voluminous robes, to the various Nigerian chiefs who had dandled me, as an infant, on their knees. The robe's folds, like bunches of curtains, were ideal for a child to play in and hide behind. A line of children traipsed through the room with enamel bowls on their heads. The emir said they were the offspring of his three wives. When some men in turbans arrived to request his opinion, I thanked the emir for the audience and continued on my way to the Geji rock paintings.

To reach Geji one follows miles of confusing tracks and footpaths. I abandoned the walk and hired a passing motorbike. Its driver was a young Hausa who assured me that his vehicle could cross any terrain. Prickly plants tore at our ankles, we bounced over rocks and ruts and ploughed through deep sand, at a pace slow enough to appreciate nature. Mango trees were in russet flower, laburnums in yellow, and palm leaves were being plaited by busy weaver birds. Guinea fowl blocked the track, too stupid to run away. I was surprised they hadn't become extinct. One lizard we disturbed was stripy black and yellow with a vivid blue tail; another was nearly two feet long, and slithered along a ledge at disconcerting eyeball height as we passed, keeping pace beside us.

Numerous streams ran in sandy beds through black boulders, creating rock pools and occasionally disappearing into the plateau to fill natural underground reservoirs. When these lie in pockets of clay they can store water indefinitely. In a small village where we paused to ask the way, a couple of women sorting millet under a tree had curious lip plugs and I realised I'd stumbled on one of the rare groups of duck-billed women left nowadays.

One woman wore only the lower disc, a hardwood plug, leaving an empty hole above her top lip, while the second woman wore two discs which made both her lips stick out rather like a duck's beak. The slits would have been cut in their youth and small plugs inserted, grooved to hold the lip in place. Usually they leave the discs in when they eat. These women were chewing betel nut, a bitter stimulant which gave them the energy to start filling a millet granary. Their granaries were small with a conical straw hat type of lid on the top. They would hold one year's supply of millet. Bigger granaries can hold a five- or ten-year store. I was invited into the house of one duck-billed lady who gave me a bowl of water from a cool earthen jar. Then we got fresh directions to Geji and set off again.

The paintings were on a cliff beneath an overhang. The

authorities had tried to protect the site with wire netting but the net was now torn open. We scrambled around and found ten crude flat red paintings, some just outlines of poorly drawn beasts that could have been goats or cows. A few yards away, almost lost, was a more skilful frieze of antelope with cast-back horns and forked tails. A final sketch showed a man and horse, much faded. I was glad to have seen them at last, having known of them for years. My biker friend said they had been drawn by descendants of the Nok race, which ruled from 500 BC to AD 200, and that bronze masterpieces of art had also been found on the plateau. Indeed the Nok culture was reputed to have begun smelting metal at the same time as Mesopotamia.

In contrast to that enjoyable day in the bush, the next morning back in Bauchi was totally frustrating. All I needed to do was change some money in a bank. It was the law that tourists had to change any foreign cash into Nigerian naira, but none of the banks wanted to accept my Cameroun money. One refused point blank, the next I tried said they'd run out of currency exchange forms, another said yes, tomorrow, after they'd found out the exchange rate, the fourth apologised that their foreign exchange man was away sick and no one else had the key to his desk, and the last one said they could change my money but they didn't have any naira to give me since all the cashiers had closed early. Africa always wins! I did try the argument of 'How can I get to Kano unless you change some money for me?' and all the people who had been dragged into the dispute responded by pulling out their wallets and collecting the bus fare. Fortunately I didn't need it but what a kind gesture.

I had bread and water for lunch then headed for Kano, using the last of the cash in my wallet.

Kano is a city I've visited several times before, and after the bank I made tracks to some old haunts, the market and the dye pits where mud vats full of indigo were being fed with cloth and stirred by old men. The market I always enjoy because Hausas are great traders, going back a thousand years to when Africa was unknown to Europeans but Kano was marked in Eastern atlases as a trade centre. Merchants still bring gems, silks and incense from far off lands. I bought a snakeskin wallet for David's Christmas present and some traditional cloth to make myself a new shoulder-bag. As I walked the smells changed, sweet to spicy. The old slave vending platforms still had their thick square pillars and wooden slatted roofs, kept semi-repaired by the men who now plied their sewing machines underneath, making beautifully embroidered robes. One man was offering shiny lumps of antimony, each pile a stage more crushed. He said the powdered form can be used to soothe eye troubles.

I found David with some difficulty, staying with kindly British Caledonian airline folk. On the morning we were ready to leave Nigeria for Niger visibility was only half a mile.

The afternoon brought a tiny improvement but not enough. I didn't mind the delay because it was Christmas Eve and I rather wanted to go to a church service. We found an Anglican church, though it was confusing since no one knew the words to the first carol, neither David nor I could find it in the hymn book, and when we did all know the words the organist lagged far behind the singers, while one hearty booming male voice that had been leading the congregation put in an extra line, and stuck behind for the whole carol like an echo. But the spirit of Christmas was not lacking and afterwards we stayed on for a cup of tea.

On Christmas morning we flew out of Kano, heading north to Daura where we would need to refuel before leaping the border. The Nigerian authorities were smiling and co-operative. The only thing I mourned was the absence of the emir's trumpeter who used to ride a great white camel out to salute aeroplanes by blasting his six-foot silvered trumpet. He must have given way to progress. Kano radio tower transmissions were so full of interference we had to get repeats in triplicate. I thought it was our radio's fault until I heard a British Caledonian pilot also request repeats. Their last message to us was to wish us a happy Christmas.

We had feared a headwind but within ten minutes we were so badly off course that it was clearly southerly. At 2,500 feet the wind backed (David said winds normally veer with height, they don't back) but we encountered a south-easterly that sped us along fast. We took turns at guiding Pegasus; the visibility was poor and since there was nothing else to navigate by we kept the road in sight. Our shadow galloped over the flat land, past some small villages and tree-planting projects making windbreaks against the encroaching desert.

At Daura we landed on the road at the far side of town, and drove the microlight along towards the town centre. A car was coming towards us and to avoid it we turned in at the first open gateway, and parked outside the house. The occupants came out, they seemed to think it perfectly natural, but maybe they were too stunned to react. The man was a forestry officer, in charge of the tree-planting projects we'd seen on our way over. He said the trees should be drought-hardy and the scheme was funded by the EEC.

A large crowd gathered to look at Pegasus, and scores of children pushed their way into our host's garden until the mob was pressed tightly around us. I was tempted to throw a fit of screaming hab-dabs. We tried to shoo the crowd out of the garden but there were hundreds more slipping in. Altogether they numbered about four hundred. Fortunately two policemen turned up, and a magnificently turbanned man on a black horse. His robes were of gold and silver cloth, his horse wore tasselled trappings and had a superb long mane. I put the horseman in charge of the gateway, hoping people would fear the horse's trampling hooves, for the policemen were not very effective, and I recruited six more men who managed to clear the garden and put everyone behind the fence, from where they could all get a good view. After apologising to the forestry officer for the invasion, I asked if we could leave the microlight there while we went into town.

We set off walking down the road and a hundred excited children followed us. I felt like the Pied Piper though it had a nightmare quality. The horde kept growing but at least we were peeling them away from Pegasus. A taxi cruised up and we jumped in. The kids mobbed the car, hammering on the windows, and ran behind for half a mile in a frenzied crowd.

In town things were quieter and we strolled over to the emir's palace and the Kusugu Well where, according to legend, Bayajida, son of the King of Baghdad slew the fetish snake, Sarki, and married the Queen of Daura. Their son, Bawo, begat the first rulers of the seven states whose people were the ancestors of the Hausa race. This legend ties in with the recorded history of Kano which tells of the Queen of Daura appointing Takano, the eldest child of her marriage to the serpent-slayer, as the new chief of Kano. Some say that Kano is a shortening of his name. The emir still has the sword used to behead the snake.

In the market the crowds of children became a menace again, getting underfoot and angering the stallholders. We bought food and fuel then, to escape, jumped in a taxi and told him to drive in the opposite direction from Pegasus. After a mile we asked him to make a U-turn and we both hid down along the seat, laughing at our silliness but hoping it would fool the crowd.

There were still about two hundred people waiting around Pegasus. We lunched with our host in rooms strung with Christmas paper chains and tinsel. He admitted he was Moslem but hung the decorations every December because they were pretty.

We prepared for a three p.m. take-off. I shuddered at the thought of controlling the mob safety factor, but the police were good about stopping the traffic, and our wing cleared the heads of the crowd, now numbering well over four hundred, all going bonkers with excitement.

Once airborne I felt safe. We circled above the old town walls then headed for the border. Below us the land became steadily drier with less scrub, and occasional outcrops of round boulders, some bigger than houses. In one village there was a prayer meeting being held but it broke up in chaos when we flew past.

'Welcome to Niger,' said the commandant of Zinder airport when we disembarked. He knew about our special authority, stamped us in with no problem, gave us space to put the microlight in the hangar, and offered us the use of a *case de passage*, a lovely cottage with a shady verandah which served as a government rest-house.

FIVE

Tuareg Country

'This is a good place for a flying lesson,' David announced the next morning. 'We'll go for the first lesson in use of power.' We flew to a small green oasis set in barren surrounds. Its shallow well pools flashed like sequins catching the early light in a geometrical paradise of cultivated squares and neat rows of plants. But the lesson wasn't a success because David and I had a misunderstanding at the start: I'd been called to take a phone call from Mobil in Niamey, and was trying to arrange an extension to our expiring flight permit, but David felt I'd been wasting his teaching time. He yelled at me and then we weren't on speaking terms until later that day.

We did manage another local flight, this time over Zinder itself which was a former capital of Niger. The old town lay within great walls, and we picked out fragmented stretches of them. Among the huts were some enormous boulders, and in the town centre a huge solid rock dome. It had a spring on top, providing the city's water supply, and a couple of children's slides, the smooth rock polished ever more slippery by centuries of bottoms and today used by school kids playing truant.

Belts of sahel and bushland lay in parallel sweeps which we crossed as we flew north. Sahel means 'shore' in Arabic: the border between living land and the desert world. We saw a big herd of camels and goats but they ran in mad bunches when they heard our motor. People ran towards us. Infants ran to hide behind their mothers.

We lost contact with Zinder's control tower. Their last message was to let us know they had radioed Tanout gendarmerie to say we were coming, and confirm they had our stash of jerrycans, and they wished us a continuing happy Christmas. The landscape was now lunar and the sun was sinking fast. We were not far from Tanout, and we could see the road going there. The rutted dirt piste was being rebuilt into an asphalt road on raised banks, to stop it being obliterated by drifting sand. Anywhere on the asphalt stretches would be fine to land. Twilight passed, it felt calm and windless. Finally in the gloaming ahead we saw the buildings of Tanout.

We flew over the town to look for space to land, and opted for the main road at the outskirts. A truck was going along in the same direction as we were descending to land behind it. But it suddenly slowed down and to avoid crashing into it we hopped over the cab, and landed on the road in front. The driver looked rather surprised.

It was a good smooth landing, then we turned off the road and followed a track heading round to a fenced-off road-making camp. This would be a safe place to leave an aircraft overnight. A crowd began gathering, dark-robed men with swords in leather scabbards. Their ranks parted and a Frenchman strode through, the site manager, who opened the gates and the microlight was pushed inside. By bad luck some wellwishers pushed hard on the wingtips, twisting the hang-bracket. This is the main bolt which attaches the trike to the wing, vitally important to our safety. But the Frenchman, Alain, said we could repair it in their workshop in the morning.

A handful of French lived by the site and they invited us to dine with them in their prefabricated house with Christmas paper chains made of polystyrene packing chips sewn on strings. Dinner was a superb meal, starting with frogs' legs in garlic butter.

While David realigned the hang-bracket next day I went for an outing by Toyota with Alain to check on the progress of a well being dug in a Tuareg village. Alain had great affection for the Tuaregs, though he admitted they were not good workers, preferring to wait for handouts of foreign aid. Alain blamed the terrible six years' drought in the sahel in the 1970s when they had lost their livestock and with it their reason for working. They certainly could not conceive of any other form of labour. In the road-making project, only two per cent of workers were Tuareg.

A salt caravan was coming along the track, thirty camels lightly laden, taking just enough salt to exchange for tobacco and tea. Several females had babies at their sides. We stopped near the foot of a long line of cliffs known as the Falaise de Farakh, site of a battle between Tuaregs where thousands were

71

slain in 1917. Heaps of bones were still visible, plus those of animals which had died in interim droughts.

Today a Tuareg group was trying to make a go of settling down. Alain joked with them about it. 'You're always moving your tents, sometimes only a few metres which you say is for better wind protection, but I think it's because you don't know how to stay in one spot.' Of course there are also some sound hygienic reasons why Tuaregs move camp every few weeks.

We were invited into a tent for tea, three small glasses, poured from arm's height for extra frothiness, and given cheese made from goat and camel milk. It had been churned then settled and left to dry in a press of grasses; this batch was moist and delicious. The tea was desperately strong and I was told you are allowed to refuse the first glass but should drink the others, since the first glass is to salute the visitor, the second salutes your host, and the third is for Allah.

Into our tent came a beau with an exquisitely wrapped black turban or *shesh*. It rose to a thin peak in front of a multi-level balloon-shaped top, above a chin and nose-cover conjured out of a clever last twist in the four-yard turban cloth. All the men had daggers tucked into their belts. Women wore heavy brass anklets, long dangling earrings, black scarves looped around their heads, and good-luck talismans around their necks. One man was a maker of talismans, his speciality being small leather squares with a prayer from the Koran written on paper, folded and sewn inside each tiny bag. More prayers, warding off evil spirits, were inscribed on the outsides.

Alain had brought a sack of chewing tobacco as a gift for the womenfolk, who crumbled the dry leaf morsels and nibbled lumps of natron with them to give the tobacco a salty piquant taste. Then they put refills in the tobacco pouches hanging around their necks. Conversation moved to the welfare of their camels, a subject close to any Tuareg's heart. Nowadays they also keep sheep and goats, but don't love them like their camels. Camel's milk forms their staple diet. 'It keeps us healthier than solid food,' one told me. 'You're unlikely ever to find an undernourished Tuareg.' And another added, 'We are connoisseurs of milk and can taste the difference according to what type of leaves our camels have eaten.'

In the evening, women began milking sheep, immobilising them by pulling out one of their back legs while their infants held the animal's head. Lambs were tethered to the communal lamb rope. A girl was sewing a piece of truck inner tube as a replacement for her sheepskin water-bag, but the rubber was cut out in the shape of a skin, including the neck which makes a good spout.

We went to look at the half-dug well which was part of an aid project and the local men were being paid to do the work. Now twenty feet deep, Alain guessed they would have to dig to about 120 feet. I had some doubts about the wisdom of sinking a well in a region that had not offered permanent water. If nomads can only come in for part of the year, after the rains, the land has the rest of the year to recover. With a well, the land doesn't stand a chance and soon becomes a dustbowl.

While Alain discussed the well with his workers, I joined a group of women. They were shy at first but overcame it and took me to visit their friends and an old lady called Tina, the wisest woman in the settlement. Many people shook my hand before we left for Tanout. The Tuareg handshake ends by catching the other's fingers in a flicking motion which gets repeated frequently during the formality of each greeting.

Next morning at five thirty I set off for Agadez, which was where I'd agreed to catch up with David and Pegasus. I travelled with two Tuaregs in a Landcruiser. Dawn crept over the flatness; some small antelope bounded away. The road-makers hadn't reached this far yet and the route was full of holes, deep sand and ribbed corrugations. We got a puncture and stopped in a village to patch it with a bit of a previously blown tyre.

I made one of my hourly radio calls, a blind call using our call sign – 'Golf Mike Tango Lima Golf – this is Charlie Delta calling Delta Yankee, over' – just in case David was stranded in the bush. Then I bought breakfast of fresh hot bread, dried cheese and dates, and drank a calabash of milk which a young boy gave me. He and I sat watching some men load fifty goats into a truck, the big ones first, then the smaller ones to fill the spaces.

From here the land was desert. The sky turned grey and soon we were in a sandstorm. It was mild, perhaps more of a sand wind. I was glad David had flown yesterday and wondered how he had fared. In fact he had done well, flying low to conserve fuel, so low that he admitted twice hitting the wheels against the tops of sand dunes. He had approached Agadez as darkness fell, and didn't have time to stop and refuel if he was going to reach the airport. So he pressed on, and ran out of fuel three miles before Agadez. But he got there in the end and I found him safely at the airport.

Our route had led north for weeks, and we still had one more northerly stage, deeper into the Sahara proper. The desert can be broadly divided into five types of country, known in Arabic as *arummila*, which means empty sand desert; *erg*, being the great dune areas; *keg* which is pebble sweeps and hard sand; *elkidea*, the broken eroded shelf rock; and the mountain areas which have individual names. Of the old volcanic regions the best known is the Hoggar, where I'd been in 1975. Lesser known are the Aïr Mountains, a violently rugged plateau reaching over 6,000 feet, situated to the north of Agadez. Formerly a stronghold of Tuareg bandits, it was reputed to be a harsh, inhospitable place.

I had a contact in the village of Iférouane in the northerly and most wild part of the Aïr Mountains. He worked with a World Wildlife Fund project (now the World Wide Fund for Nature) and I was looking forward to spending a few days up there. The Niger government had only granted my special permit to fly in the Aïr Mountains on condition that the microlight carried full desert survival kit and had a support vehicle, with four-wheel drive. They were a bit stunned that we didn't have one permanently, but we had managed so far, even if that had meant I did the odd bit by land. We weren't after all trying to prove anything or set records. However, since support was now compulsory I had to comply. Thus a Land-Rover and a canny Tuareg called Alagarbit were added to the team.

We sent him on ahead and said we would overfly him en route to Iférouane. The wind was strong but coming evenly down the runway, which made our take-off easy. Lifted by the wind, we were airborne within six yards.

With the wind came sheets of dust, I could taste the grit. Through the fog we could see the smallness of Agadez town, virtually all made of mud and dominated by two Sudanese-style towers, square and tapering, with sticks poking out at angles. The biggest tower was the main mosque.

As we climbed away, on the circuit the airport had instructed, Pegasus began to cough. David cut the power then put it full on, but to no avail, the motor spluttered and wouldn't clear. 'It could be a speck of sand got drawn in when I ran out of petrol yesterday,' David suggested. 'But there's no panic, it's not a total engine failure, we've got enough power to get back safely.'

We were over the town and losing height steadily, but David whirled us in a neat circle and radioed the airport to say we had engine problems. The next moment we saw firemen rushing to their red truck, leaping in and speeding towards the runway, dust flying from their wheels, as David made a perfect touchdown.

We had kept a minimal tool-kit and sent the rest ahead with Alagarbit, so while David started probing around the engine I set off in pursuit of the Tuareg, hoping that he was not already halfway to Iférouane. I got a lift in the back of a truck carrying sacks of yams. It was going to Arlit uranium mining camp, along the road the driver said was called the Uranium Route. We set off into a vastness of wasteland, sand and outcrops of rock shelves scored by wind. At some stone huts we paused to barter yams as long and fat as a man's thigh for a pile of dried cheeses.

A Tuareg in indigo turban galloped up on a white camel and behind him came another on a piebald camel. I asked which was faster, and they argued about it in the harsh throaty language of Tamashek. One spun away in mock challenge, the other overtook him, and suddenly they were racing, camels' necks outstretched, ungainly legs pounding the sand. Someone told me that both were former camel racing winners. The white one forged into the lead but the piebald began to dispute it, neck and neck. Then suddenly both riders turned their steeds and cantered back laughing. The truck driver called his passengers and we moved on.

After about a hundred miles I found Alagarbit, parked near the road, watching the sky and flashing a wing-mirror in his hand. A resourceful man, he had brought a young skivvy with him who was making a pot of tea.

We were just leaving when some German overlanders appeared, looking a bit desperate and saying their vehicle was stuck between rocks in deep sand not far away. I asked Alagarbit to go and tow them out, during which I discovered that they had been looking for a legendary giraffe rock engraving, but they hadn't found it. We pulled their vehicle free and since they said they were going straight to Agadez I wondered if they would take David's tool-bag to him at the airport. They said thanks for pulling them free but they didn't plan to stop in Agadez and wouldn't take the tool-bag.

After they had gone Alagarbit told me smugly that he knew where the giraffe engraving was located. It was a chance not to be missed. We drove across a mile of stone shelf, then down into the sand, squeezing between rock obstacles. Occasionally we had to stop and clear ones which jammed against the axles. The Aïr Mountains should have been in sight but the dust made them invisible. I assumed the engraving would be on a cliff, but there were no cliffs. We reached a low bulky outcrop and Alagarbit said we had arrived.

As I scrambled on to the boulders I spotted a frieze of cattle, small but well-incised, then an equally small giraffe and an antelope as tall as my arm. Looking around I realised that even the rocks I was standing on were covered with pictures. They were chiselled out with a technique called 'pecking'.

Further up in a hidden gulley was a six-foot outline of a man with a curvy shape and four feathers sticking up from his head. Alagarbit told me it pre-dated all the other engravings here. This phase of rock art, called the Roundhead era, began before 6000 BC. The age of rock engravings can be worked out by the patina of the rock which changes colour with age; the darker the chipped lines the older, bearing in mind that carvings on horizontal rocks weather differently from vertical ones.

The Bovid period of the Aïr's art is said to have lasted from 4000–2000 BC, when the region supported herds with ease, as well as elephants which could eat 500 pounds daily. The artists at this time developed their detail and composition. A change seemed to occur around 2000 BC; hippo and crocodile no longer featured, and the cattle herders were replaced by horse-riding warrior-hunters.

As I jumped a ravine I saw two spectacular giraffe engravings, one over fifteen feet tall, the other ten feet, their coats realistically picked out in square markings. It was lovely how the sunlight on the hewn lines threw narrow shadows enhancing the design.

Back in Agadez I learned that David had worked all morning on the motor but hadn't found any dirt, nor possible cause of trouble. He also worked the whole afternoon and most of the night, re-setting the timing. While the engine was open he did a de-coke and freed the piston rings, and said the motor's guts looked remarkably healthy. The basic problem was that microlight flying is still in its pioneering phase. Ours had been designed to use Super petrol, but, ridiculously, international law forbids aircraft to use anything but aviation fuel. We had to use the very much higher octane Avgas which was a completely unknown quantity as far as flying Pegasus was concerned. Our engine was faultless, David's maintenance was exemplary, Mobil's fuel was pure. But we didn't work all this out immediately, which was why David spent so much time searching for non-existent gremlins and advancing the spark. The exact timing was critical but we had no information to go by.

My day became bogged down in administrative details and flight requirements, but I waded through and re-booked Alagarbit for the next morning. We agreed he would wait to see us take off safely this time before following in the Land-Rover.

At six a.m. I walked to the airport, struggling against a fierce dusty wind. David was asleep beside Pegasus in the hangar. He had worked until two a.m. and the engine was ready to test. We chocked the wheels firmly and started the motor. At full power it began misfiring again. It was futile to feel infuriated. David went sadly back to work and I walked to the market to buy us some dates and hot bread, one of David's favourite snacks, for breakfast. The wind was growing steadily stronger, and our flight didn't look hopeful.

After breakfast I went wandering in town. The back of the market was where Tuareg silversmiths worked. An arm beckoned me from the alley into a courtyard, and as I blinked away the dust I saw this was a silversmithy, clearly open for business. Four men were using the lost wax method to make silver Agadez crosses, traditional Tuareg jewellery. They explained that each town or village in this region had its own traditional design, and they showed me a collection of them. They were more like elaborate star shapes than Christian crosses and I liked the three-pronged deep Iférouane pendant the best.

A mile from town I found the livestock market, where there were racing camels for sale, top price about 100,000 CFA (Communauté Français Afrique) which was roughly £240. Watching the black-turbanned Tuaregs haggling round the livestock made me realise how some were as pale as Europeans. Neither Arab nor negroid (in Arabic the name means 'cast out by God'), all Tuareg men wore swords as witness to their hereditary status as warriors and their descent from southern Berbers, a vague term the Romans applied to all those who didn't speak Latin. The Berbers twice succeeded in invading part of Europe, first in Hannibal's time and again during the Moslem invasion of

Spain where their rule lasted from about 710 to 1250. But when the French colonised West Africa with the gun, the swordsmen were outmatched, yet fought bitterly. The result was carnage.

The microlight was operational again and in the evening I had a flying lesson; David wanted me to get the hang of changing pitch. I took off passably into a twelve knot wind. Obviously, such winds are not suitable for novices, but it was quite smooth. The worst moment was my anticipation of doom when David said, 'Give it full power.' We went up to 1,500 feet and began exercises. I had to work out how much power to add to take us out of a downslide, and when I added too much the microlight went into an oscillating movement, rearing and diving. 'Do something about it,' suggested David.

By pulling the nose down one can lop off the top of a rising curve and by pushing the bar forward to flare the wing I could even out the descending ones. And by over-correcting I could cause the whole thing to start again. I glanced down; we had followed a river-bed east and were over a small camp of matting domes and camels. The sun was setting into the dust clouds. My landing was well-lined up, but sinking too slowly, so I pulled in the bar and we zoomed down. Suddenly I realised we were very low, I'd slipped off line, missing the runway. Trying to correct it, we were coming in at a disastrous angle. Once more I passed control to David who of course managed it expertly.

For supper I bought a haunch of goat's meat, vegetables for salad and a melon, and took it to my lodgings in Agadez. Afterwards, a new acquaintance called Sulieman came over bringing tea for me and David. He came equipped with a tea-table, three glasses, teapot, and a charcoal brazier, and he made the whole ceremony more than usually elaborate by starting with washing the dust off the dry green tea-leaves. This gave us time to discuss Tuareg life. He told us about his three camels, and showed me how to tie a *shesh* around my head: the first loop goes right around the head and loosely across the face, the flap is pulled down to form the mouth cover, the rest is banded around from the forehead and twisted to hold it firm. Sulieman's *shesh* was nine yards long; others could be as short as four yards.

He said that if men were in the company of unknown women they usually kept their face covered, not even opening their veil to drink tea, which could be sipped from below its folds. I think this was connected to the belief that the soul could escape through a man's mouth. For him as an enlightened town Tuareg, the most shocking thing about foreign women tourists was their skimpy clothing, and he wished they could know how offensive their mini shorts were to local people.

We also discussed the Paris–Dakar rally which was due to leave Paris on January 1st and would come through Agadez between January 6th and 12th, in two weeks' time. Our route would cross the rally at some point. Sulieman said there were seven hundred competitors and with all their support teams Agadez would bulge at the seams. The room that I was paying 3,000 CFA a night for would be inflated to 15,000 CFA.

The following day was December 31st, New Year's Eve. We were up before dawn and as the light filtered through we wheeled Pegasus out on to the tarmac. David suddenly doubled up on the ground, clutching himself in agony. He said it was the second time this morning he'd been attacked by gripes, but insisted he would be all right. I mentally crossed my fingers and we took off.

We flew up along the west side of the Aïr Mountains, a slight tailwind helping us along. When we reached where I'd seen the giraffe engravings we detoured to try and find them from above. I located the outcrop and we buzzed it low, but although I could just pick out the pictures, their grooves weren't catching enough light for David to spot them.

Beyond, the desert was like a vast beach, the multi-fingered dry rivulets that make patterns on the seashore were here magnified a hundred times. I joked with David about a bucket and spade, and he said yes we had a bucket, a foldaway one he had bought for dropping into deep wells. Small herds of piebald camels and a few Tuareg dwellings set in dry wadis were the only signs of man.

The flying was good, air smooth and wind not strong and we cruised at 500 feet, low enough to stay in the shelter of the mountains. In order to keep tabs on Alagarbit I had given him our second VHF radio and, as agreed, he called us at ten a.m. He said he was chasing us hard, having been delayed by the breaking of a bolt in the chassis, but he was not far behind. He had met some camel drivers who told him they had watched us fly past only fifteen minutes earlier.

We continued towards the junction where the Iférouane road left the Uranium Route, passing a spill of uranium, fluorescent yellow against the sand. But we didn't see a side road, or even a track. Luckily, Alagarbit, driving at a hundred miles an hour, caught up just as we missed the way. '*A droit, tournez à droit,*' he yelled down the radio.

We accompanied him a short way along the track and, since rough mountains lay ahead, we decided to land and refuel from the jerrycans in the Land-Rover. Landing, we were confronted with a howling wind, enough to flip Pegasus upside down, so had to leap into action to get the wing off and secured on the ground. The nose-pin was jammed; David struggled desperately to free it while I clung on to some wing wires and called Alagarbit to hold the other side. Sand and dust whirled up into our faces and eyes as we battled to quick-release the remaining wires. I pushed the trike clear as David hurriedly dropped the wing to the ground, then we all sat on it to hold it down. What a way to spend New Year's Eve.

The next few hours were spent idly in the desert beside a thorn tree, waiting to see if the wind would abate. With dead thorn wood we made fire for tea, Tuareg-style, and a swarm of flies turned up. It's odd that no matter how far you are from anything a fly could eat, they still exist. I wriggled into the sand and lay back listening to the wind roaring through the thorn branches. A noise like thunder reverberated along with a deep vibration in the ground; I reassured myself that it was probably the mining camp at Arlit, far away but passing with clarity through the empty desert.

Gradually the wind lost its violence, though the sky had turned ominously cloudy. If we didn't try to fly out, we wouldn't reach Iférouane, and we'd have an uncomfortable cold night and perhaps in the morning the wind would be worse. So we parked the Land-Rover across the track to break the wind, re-rigged the microlight and took off at three thirty. Getting to Iférouane would be tight but not impossible.

We soon outpaced Alagarbit. He clambered in four-wheel drive up into a line of sand dunes, while we danced over the top, and found a sandy plain where the track split into four ways. The map marked no crossroads there so we followed the most clear-cut until, glancing back, I saw that Alagarbit had turned right.

Once established on the correct route we left Alagarbit behind, but it was worrying that our heading didn't tally with the map. Within an hour we were seriously worried, now deep inside the mountain stronghold, with not enough fuel to reach Iférouane if we'd mistaken the way. It was hard enough to see where the track went; lesser ones frequently branched off, but I suspected they were all alternative routes to the same place. Sunlight dappled patches of the mountains, and made me aware of the vastness and bleak barrenness, and us so insignificant.

David suggested either turning back and trying for radio contact with the Land-Rover, to find out if we were on the right track, or turning off up a random valley to look for another road. The latter idea gave me the creeps; mountains look the same yet different, it would be too easy to get thoroughly lost. And I had no desire to create a search and rescue situation which, if the army was involved, could end up in me being charged half a million pounds. Apart from that, it's always been my philosophy that independence is being able to get out of your own trouble without needing help.

Our fuel gauge showed we had reached the critical point of no return; unless we turned back immediately we wouldn't have the fuel to reach Iférouane unaided. David voted to turn back, and I was in favour of flying on forwards. The main track looked regularly used and was definitely going somewhere.

We came to a magnificent area of tall rock plugs, relics of a volcanic age, now weathered to a lustrous black, a process called 'desert varnish'. The sight was worth all the anguish of the journey.

Suddenly we spotted two jeeps travelling in convoy. We circled and dived down to land in front of them. 'Where does this road go?' we asked.

'To Iférouane,' they answered, 'and it's about forty miles from here.'

We flew as fast as we could, 60 mph, with revs at full power, and calculated that forty miles would take forty minutes. The sun was just setting into a bank of cloud, there would be little twilight. But the scenery was stunning, with wild upthrusts of old cores and sharply defined ridges against the pale gold sand.

'Okay, so it's dark now,' David said. 'In a few moments we'll have to land and camp.' The idea had appeal, the only drawback was that we couldn't really see the ground. Then to my relief I spotted a winking dot of light in the distance. It had to be in Iférouane.

We landed on a great flat gravel sweep beside the village,

81

taxied to the lee of a building and de-rigged our wing for the night. The building had a World Wildlife sign outside, and some children showed us the way to the house of my contact, Peter Tunley, the WWF technical advisor. He welcomed us and suggested we should get celebrating the last few hours of the year.

The project here was due to be officially opened in two months' time. It would contain Africa's largest wildlife reserve under management, which made it the second largest park in Africa, but it did not have enough wild animals to be a game-viewing type of park, this was purely a place to protect the ecology. Peter's work was with ecology and village buildings, which he offered to show me next day.

In the morning I checked in at the police post and learned that our support vehicle had not yet reached Iférouane. I expected he had stopped to camp and would appear later; it would be embarrassing if we had to go and search for him. So David suggested I take a flying lesson. I took off and flew to the U-shaped mountain chasm which is said to represent the bottom pendant U-shape of the Iférouane cross. Above the confluence of three magnificent valleys I began studying how to recover from wing-stalls. One we induced by letting our airspeed drop too low, pushing the bar forward and increasing the wing's angle of attack until the aircraft was forced to stop. It hovered in suspense, juddering slightly, then the nose fell steeply and, far below, the ground stared in my face as we swooped in a deep dive. Microlights cannot slide backwards from a stall because of their design, instead with this type of stall the nose drops and you gain speed until able to fly on normally.

'Now do a stall turn,' David instructed, and I put Pegasus into a downwards twist, then pushed the bar forward until I felt the shudder of the inside wing stalling first, while the outer wing was still flying. The turn sharpened dramatically, as one side of the aircraft stopped flying, and gravity took over, the whole machine started to rotate around its vertical axis, inducing a spin. An aircraft in a spin goes out of control, but Pegasus will simply roll out of a spin, its pendular action preventing the catastrophe. It can of course do spiral dives but they have to be deliberate.

Recovering the bar to normal trim we rolled out right and reverted to a standard glide, floating along over the wide craggy U-valley. The last exercise, a stall while climbing, I didn't do well; my arms ached and my brain was reeling. We decided to leave it for later.

Back in Iférouane, Peter took me to see a building he was getting constructed without the traditional wood or straw, both dwindling commodities in the area. He explained how he was training masons to build with clay bricks and mortar.

'Roofs can be self-supporting if you make a dome, and doorways are strong if you form arches. The skill is in angling the bricks inwards.' Peter's model building was a glorious conglomeration of Nubian arches, window niches, pillars and domes. Even the plain mud exterior walls were not dull; the angles of buttresses, added for structural strength, created a dramatic play of sunlight and shade.

Masons were hard at work shovelling sloppy mortar into wide buckets and passing it to others seated on the walls who slapped it into place between the bricks. Others were turning new clay, and muddy noises filled the air. Peter explained the art of finding the right place to dig for wall-brick mud which should be the consistency of sandy clay, while roof bricks needed more clay in the blend to make them extra waterproof. I was intrigued by the depth of craftsmanship it required.

The plaster which covered most exteriors was a weatherproofing layer since when it rained here, though seldom, it rained hard. Sandy plaster would be washed away, but heavy clay alone was not the answer since it would crack easily in the harsh sun, so it was mixed with chopped grass or straw to bind it.

Peter's driver had an errand to run at a nearby Tuareg camp, so I went with him in his Land-Rover.

The man we were seeking, Ahmet, was camping near the old village of Salufiert which had been here long before Iférouane. Now it was less important since its underground water had declined, while in Iférouane there was plenty. We sat on a rug under a tree and I formed an instinctive liking for Ahmet. His wife had shy dimples, and was pounding some dried tomatoes to add to a cauldron of soup. The pasta we ate with it had come by camel caravan from Algeria.

It was night by the time we returned to Iférouane, but the nearly full moon gave ample light. Alagarbit had arrived, having suffered a flat battery. I decided that he should return to Agadez the following morning, leaving David and me to look for a local vehicle going out when we were ready to leave. Meantime, David wanted to tinker with Pegasus, and I wanted to accept an offer Ahmet had made when he suggested we took his two camels for a trip of several days up into the mountains.

Six

Into the Aïr Mountains

Early morning found me astride a six-year-old slightly skittish camel, while Ahmet was riding a large white *merhari* thorough-bred. We both had bags of supplies and camping gear hanging from the tall three-pronged horn of our typically Tuareg saddles. The prongs were covered with red and black leather and capped in brass. Behind me as a backrest was a flat wooden board, decoratively worked in dyed leather. The bridle was a string threaded through the camel's nose ring.

Our route followed the wadi south, through Salufiert with its strings of garden plots growing maize, tomatoes (nearly ripe), and wheat (young emerald shoots). Some women were cutting down dom palm leaves for new thatch. Ahmet told me the leaves were also used to make string, and the fruit's hard outer shell contained a fibrous, slightly sweet, inner layer which people chewed raw. The kernel could be roasted and mixed either with a little oil, or sugar, and eaten.

Our progress was unhurried. Walking towards us along the river-bed was an unkempt Hausa with a hold-all. He was a traditional medicine man, coming from Nigeria, and he opened his bag to show Ahmet his wares. Out came a leopard skin, used for *gri-gri* magic spells, and leaves plaited with animal hide to help teething infants. He also offered grease of lion against backache, and Ahmet bought some.

At lunchtime he offered to teach me how to bake bread in the sand. We unloaded the camels, hobbled their front feet and left them to browse. Taking six handfuls of wheat flour and a sprinkling of salt, Ahmet added water and stirred it until it became a firm dough. After kneading for ten minutes it was ready to be flattened into a thick pancake and he slapped on a dusting of flour to stop the crust getting too sandy during baking. We had already lit a fire of driftwood and just moved

85

the firebrands aside, to put the bread on the hot sand and cover it with extra sand before laying the firebrands back on top.

While it was cooking he made soup from dried tomatoes. Then we shredded the bread into the soup. It tasted good. My companion suddenly pointed to a family of rock hyrax which had come out to sunbathe, and an eagle that had also spotted them. Birds flitted around us, black ones with white caps and white tail-feathers. 'That's a sociable bird,' said Ahmet, 'it represents the Aïr Mountains and is your first friend when you arrive.' Of some swallows, he said, 'Tuaregs call these the birds of Allah, they live with God in the sky, swooping down for water but never setting foot on earth.'

When we collected the camels I decided to learn to saddle my own, putting the saddle in front of the hump with the girth behind its callus. To mount him correctly Ahmet told me, 'Slide your right leg over the saddle, stand your left toes on the rope until the last instant so the camel can't get up or try to bite you. Now hop aboard and put one foot on the camel's neck to balance yourself.' The camel lurched upward. 'Make him lie down, hiss, ssss, and tug on the nose rope.' He went obediently down, and waited for the clicking 'Kkk' command before rising again.

The afternoon was one of birdsong, flies buzzing, the smell of my camel chewing cud, the feel of his rough furry neck under my bare feet, and the soft scrunch of his soles on the sand. Ahmet's father had been a camel caravan driver with four hundred camels, and he had frequently taken his son with him on trips over the desert to Algeria and Libya. Ahmet himself had been a camel driver for seventeen years. It was only in the last ten years that his family had begun to settle, forced by the drought. His grandfather had been an important warrior who had killed over forty men, Ahmet told me, neither proudly nor apologetically. It was just matter of fact.

Originally the name Tuareg applied only to one group of Tamashek-speaking nomads, but the French colonists misused it to cover everybody. Ahmet's tribe were the only Tuareg people who have a written language. It is called Tifina and looks like dots, circles and lines. Most children in the Aïr Mountains knew how to write it, Ahmet assured me.

Another camel rider joined us for a couple of miles, en route to his family high in the mountains. His greetings with Ahmet lasted over a mile, but neither showed any expression of warmth, for this could be considered disrespectful. Ahmet said that even between brothers greetings should be devoid of feeling. One of the items in their exchange of news concerned a relative who wanted to marry a black-skinned ex-slave girl. His parents had forbidden the marriage.

My camel paused occasionally to bite a mouthful of leaves, which I sometimes allowed, otherwise I waggled my feet to say 'go on' and he obeyed. To trot, you put your left foot down and make 'go faster' noises.

Mid-afternoon we passed a ruined hamlet of stone and shortly after it reached an ancient and revered mosque. One of the few sacred places in the Aïr, it was the tomb of a holy man with thatched shelter outside and a small neatly swept yard enclosed behind a low wall. The place was visited yearly by pilgrims coming on foot and by camel. Ahmet said the guardian of the mosque lived nearby and we might see him later.

We had entered a gorge. Its sides grew taller and rockier, rearing as high as 2,000 feet above us. Down in the river-bed some of the boulders were larger than our camels, and lodged among them were massive palm tree trunks, brought down in flash floods, some wedged ten feet above the ground. Underfoot the river-bed became so rubble-strewn that I wondered how a camel, its head always in the air, managed to know where it put its feet. I said this to Ahmet who replied that the camel sees from afar, calculates the distances to rocks, and works out in advance where to walk. True or not, the camels didn't trip over.

The path took us among palm trees along the bank, then dived in a steep rocky descent to the river-bed. It would be no easy route but there was nothing better available. The thought came that perhaps I should dismount but I decided to stay put and not worry. My camel scrambled down with skips and jumps, as if it was a game he was enjoying more than I was.

For a camp site we chose a sandy space enclosed by trees and rocks; it offered a nearby rockpool, some acacia for the camels, plenty of driftwood, and dom palm trees under which we unloaded. Ahmet expounded the theory that the best trees to sleep beneath are Balanites and Acacia Radian whose tiny leaves preserve more warm air below them than Salvadoria, whose large leaves hold water and are cold to lie under.

Two ravens flapped past squawking. Ahmet called them *kourbot* and said they always give away the presence of an encampment. They would call to others and after we had gone they'd come down to look for scraps. 'They especially love cheese, and will steal it from camps where it's put out to dry.'

The sand was imprinted with baboon tracks and scattered with the remains of dom palm nuts they had been chewing. We hobbled the camels and left them to browse while we walked upriver on foot, past several rock pools, up as far as a natural barrage and a pool which had never completely dried up, not even in the last drought.

I crouched to scoop up some water to wash my face; it was deep and clear. We didn't need to water the camels, though I learned that it's not simply a question of water stored in their tissues; camels can also raise their body temperature so that they neither suffer the heat nor do they sweat. Some other desert species found here do the same, such as the oryx and addax.

On the way back to our camp we heard a lot of baboons barking. Here they are now an isolated species, cut off from any other environment since there is not enough food or water to enable them to cross the surrounding territory. The two types of monkey found here are not marooned, because they can eat different types of food, so can reach the outside world.

It was after dark when we went to visit the mosque's guardian at his home. We didn't have a torch and the river-bed was a mass of boulders, but the moon was full and it lit the gorge in dramatic tones of black and pale silver.

Dogs rushed up angrily barking and I stayed casually behind Ahmet. Then we came to a riverside clearing with a line of three fires burning at the front. By one was an old man and woman, at the next a solitary young boy, and from the third a man came to greet us. Ahmet explained to me that the family belonged to the grandmother, now aged about eighty. She was ten when the French army made war on the Aïr Mountains. In those days she wore animal skins and didn't believe the French could conquer her people. Her son, whose wife had died of old age, and the child of her grandson, showed four generations here. The man and Ahmet exchanged greetings and we were offered a bowl of cold water and a calabash of fresh warm milk. The man went around behind the fires to pick up something and returned, a black-robed figure carrying a small white lamb. A long knife flashed in the moonlight.

'*Kai, kai, kai,*' said Ahmet to him, gently refusing the gift, and he looked at me so I shook my head, the lamb was too young to die. Thankfully bleating, it rejoined its mother, and instead the family presented us with fresh cheese and dried goat's meat.

An hour later we wandered back to our camp and made a fire for brewing tea. Ahmet talked about nature's balance. 'I do believe that whenever we disturb the balance, the land has to change. The signs pointed to tell us that the land could not support all our livestock. Perhaps we caused the drought by keeping more herds than we needed. Some men had a thousand camels, some only had a few hundred. But our livestock was our wealth, seldom used for meat or sold. The lesson is clear, keep only what you need. I myself now only keep two camels. But few Tuaregs see it that way.' He sighed and added, 'Everything has a function, even the desert. Without the protection of the desert's dryness we would have been overrun with locusts. It's a natural barrier.'

I wriggled my toes into the sand by the fire to warm them, and my friend laid some strips of dried meat on the embers to roast. Around us the palms made fan-leafed silhouettes, and the moonshadows moved slowly over the stark gorge. In the night I woke several times hearing odd noises, which I assumed must come from our camels. The wind was chill and although we kept the fire going all night, I was glad to have the camel's saddle rug as an extra blanket.

When I opened my eyes at dawn the air was clear and cold, and the sky turning deep blue. Ahmet was already starting to bake bread, first flicking some drops of water on to the hot sand to see by the sizzle if it was hot enough. We had a long day ahead.

During the morning's ride we saw a troupe of red monkeys playing in the rocks ahead, and other bigger grey monkeys on a stony ridge. In an open sandy part of the river-bed Ahmet showed me how the Tuaregs' camels dance: 'You ride into the centre, Christina, make like you're playing tam-tams, that's the role of the Tuareg woman in the dance.' He began urging his camel to trot in circles around me, pulling in its nose rope and drumming his feet on its neck to make it prance.

The climax of the performance was when his camel dropped to its knees, shuffled slowly towards me, then stretched its head out flat on to the sand in submission. 'In the proper dance you'd be sitting on the ground, he would lay his head on the

89

tam-tam of the best woman, and she rubs his face and he is content.'

For the return journey we retraced our steps downriver then changed route, cutting across on to a plain. The wind was strong and full of dust. We stopped at some huts at midday for tea and shared the remainder of our supplies with them for lunch. In the afternoon the wind increased, dust thickened, and the sunlight put haloes on the furry outlines of our camels.

We rode back into Iférouane, pausing to see Pegasus on the way. Unfortunately there was no sign of David and the wing had been tossed by the wind on to something spiked. The sailcloth of the undersurface had a rip over a foot long.

The morning of January 4th was spent sewing up the rip in Pegasus's wing. We cut a nylon strap off a bag and glued it under the rent then I sewed it into place. The glue kept grunging my fingers together and made flies stick to my hands. I had to use pliers to pull the needle through, but the difficulty was that, being part of the wing which had an undersurface inches from its top layer, I couldn't sew from both sides. While I was working, a raven landed on the trike cover and began pecking holes through at the engine. The holes didn't matter but I wondered what he was after.

Peter's masons needed supplies from Agadez, so he would send his Land-Rover and this could be our temporary support vehicle for the journey back. The programme was flexible, fortunately, since David was not at all well. It worried me that he might not be fit for piloting. He wasn't seriously ill, just way off form with very low energy, moving in a slow dream. He was still getting agonising bouts of stomach cramps and had all the symptoms of Ghardia, for which I had some medicine in our kit in Agadez. Often we had joked about the way I looked after him like I've looked after my travelling horses, trying to keep him fit and strong, watching and not pushing him too hard. This time I resorted to saying meanly, 'If you were my travelling horse, I'd sell you.'

After a final day of rest we left Iférouane. From the moment of take-off the sky was beautiful, a clear deep blue with no wind, and the mountains standing out in stark ridges and isolated cones like witches' hats. Bathed in sparkling early sun, it was magic. The air was exceedingly chilly. When the sun warmed the ground and made inversion rise, hiding the mountain bases, their shapes floated high above the pale sea of sand like black varnished islands in the sky.

We saw many crown tombs, some in clusters on low summits, some on shoulders and shelves, some in natural basins. These were generally a mound of stones surrounded by a stone circle. The smallest was about four paces across, and the largest perhaps ten paces. The fanciest ones had arcs of standing stones. Probably these were the pillars which act as 'supports for the soul'. But I wasn't sure if the graves dated back to the horse-riding invaders of 2000 BC or to the cattle-herding tribes preceding them.

Several of the burial mounds had been opened. We could see this because the middle would be an empty sandy spot and I wondered what the robbers had found. And because of the way that even small fragments of the outer circles were visible from the air, we also sighted half-buried tombs in the process of disappearing beneath shifting sands, or ones that had lain hidden, now becoming uncovered. Beyond one large cluster I saw some fast-moving dots which may have been ostriches. Altogether it was a stunning flight. We wove between and over the peaks, following faint tracks in the sand, past where we had landed to check our way, and through the desolate stretch where we'd thought we were lost. Finally the summits faded as we turned down the last main stream-bed and across a broad valley into the desert. The rocks flattened out, sand took over, with patches of many crescent-shaped dunes.

Once over the flat desert we put on speed, both of us pulling together on the bar to make Pegasus fly faster. Ahead we could see a duststorm. I remembered David saying, only a few days before, that at any sign of blowing sand we should land and tie the microlight down. It was clearly blowing hard, and we would have a very difficult job on the ground, but it wasn't too bad in the air and we decided to try to hop over the storm.

Duststorms in the Sahara can be big but most are localised; this one looked to be only half a mile wide and less than 1,000 feet deep. We got on top of it but then it seemed to grow and we were forced to try outrunning it. We ran as it grew. We were both still hauling on the bar, the air became dense and gritty then clearer; we had managed to leave it behind.

Naturally we had lost all idea of how far we had come along the road which we could see to our left. When we were well clear of the storm we landed on the road, refuelled from our spare carry-tank and flagged down a vehicle to ask how far we were from Agadez. Seventy miles, still quite far.

The visibility was again fabulous, much better than on our way in; this time we could see the massif of southern Aïr and the way it rose out of the desert. Then as we reached the end of the barrier and emerged from behind its shelter we hit swelling gusts and thick clouds of dust blowing up from the ground. Conditions deteriorated by the minute.

About fifteen miles from Agadez we ran into a gigantic duststorm. At first we tried to jump over it but it was 4,000 feet deep and when we climbed over that level we encountered winds so strong we weren't moving forwards. On higher levels the winds would be yet stronger. 'We can't make it like this,' David called. 'We'll have to fly low and deal with things,' and he eased off the power into a descent.

Immediately we entered the storm the jolting started. It was rather a horrifying descent, the nose rearing steeply one instant then diving sharply down. We tried to maintain a height of 700 feet, and made some progress. Glancing at the altimeter I noticed it was waving like a pendulum. A gust caught us, sweeping us downwards at 900 feet a minute. Unpleasant, but David was doing well. The next sinking gust moved so fast our altimeter went off the scale. My stomach plummeted and my knuckles were clenched. I held tight but nothing felt reassuring.

'Can't we get out of this?' I suggested.

'It would be very tricky if we tried to land,' David pointed out. 'This wind would flip us over. But we can't be far from Agadez. If we can get there we can taxi straight into the hangar. We'd move faster if we went lower, and I think that's what we've got to do, but it's going to be rough.'

I loathed the idea. If only we could land and let me walk to Agadez, anything rather than continue in worse turbulence. But I gritted my teeth and said I would hang on. We descended, the wind was less strong but the bumpiness was horrendous, moments of calm followed by sharp sudden wrenches that made David fight for control while I closed my eyes and prayed.

At the lower level the grit and dust were thick in the air, visibility so murky that we could get no idea where Agadez lay, though we had to be close because we passed a radio mast. We battled on, sand got in between my teeth, and the smell of dust filled my nostrils.

It made me recall how the gods of Mount Olympus had

knocked Icarus out of the sky for daring to fly. But I encouraged myself by remembering that it was Athena, goddess of wisdom, no less, who helped Bellerophon catch and tame the legendary Pegasus, after it had sprung from the blood of the gorgon Medusa when Perseus cut off her head. Bellerophon rode Pegasus to kill the fire-breathing Chimera. I wondered how they had coped with turbulence.

Four hours after leaving Iférouane we spotted the outskirts of Agadez. I didn't dare feel relieved until we were safely on the ground. The fire truck came rushing out, understanding a problem. The wind was diagonally across the runway and blustering, though as we turned into the final leg of our approach its direction momentarily backed and gave us a straight line.

Thankfully we dropped on to the runway before it could change, but it needed the remaining strength of both of us to hold down the wing as we taxied over to the hangar.

The commandant of the airport was in a miserable mood, normal for him, and when I went to pay up our landing fees he gave me a hard time. He was determined to find fault with David and me. He tried accusing us of not keeping to our flight plan, he claimed he'd received no message from Iférouane's gendarmerie, which they swore they had sent, and each time I proved us innocent he would cast in his mind for other ways to put me in the wrong.

Our meeting dragged on for hours. I wished I could think of some small point he could score against me that wouldn't matter, so saving his face and letting me leave. Finally he thumped his fist on the table and said he was charging me an extra 40,000 CFA (nearly £100) as landing-light fees for a day when I'd had a late lesson and landed after sunset. I pointed out that the landing lights had not been turned on, and he said they should have been.

In fact the controller had asked if we wanted landing lights and we'd said no thank you. The commandant retorted that the man had no business asking our opinion, and by regulation the lights should have been on, therefore unless I paid up he would fine the controller the same fee. During the confrontation an aircraft arrived, bringing an advance party involved in the Paris–Dakar rally, and since I didn't want to get caught up in the rally, which was racing south-west, I opted to put into action the second of the special permits I'd been granted. So I paid the nonsense fee to the commandant and filed a flight plan to leave Agadez the next day.

My special permit allowed us to fly west over the desert to the old salt workings of Tegguiddan Tessoum. It specified that survival gear and ground support were compulsory, and Alagarbit agreed to organise one of his men to drive the Land-Rover to the salt village, carrying some fuel cans for us. We would all make an early morning start, and the microlight would meet the Land-Rover in Tegguiddan Tessoum in the afternoon.

We took off and at full power the engine hiccupped. David quickly said his foot had slipped off the pedal but we both knew that wasn't true. It was *déjà vu*, but this time we didn't turn back. Picking up the dirt road west, David suggested I used the trip as a navigation exercise. It didn't look difficult because the track would always be visible and the map showed some wadis and hills as good way-point landmarks.

'Make sure you read from ground to map,' David warned. 'Look first at the ground, see its shapes and then try to locate them on the map. If you do it the other way round, it's misleading because it seems to fit.'

Our maps weren't the best anyway. The Niger map was already twelve years out of date. I supposed there was no demand for air maps here.

'These are a lousy scale, too, as ONC air maps go. We should be using 1:500,000,' David pointed out. 'This is double that scale.'

It didn't look to me as if bigger maps would be more use. There was so little shown on these, I reasoned a bigger one would just have larger blank spaces. At least some tracks were marked. But David was sounding the warning note again. 'The worst thing you can use in navigation is roads. They're always confusing, and in this case none of the routes created in the last decade will be marked on our map.'

A strong tailwind helped us along, and our time to the first way-point was thirty minutes, whereas I had calculated for forty-five. So I adjusted the sums to produce new overall timings, and reckoned the total flight time should be about one and a half hours.

The desert sped underneath us and the landmarks were in the right places. Yet we didn't reach Tegguiddan Tessoum.

There was nothing but empty desert and after the one and a half hours were up David started having qualms. The track still led straight ahead, so I felt sure I'd overcompensated in my sums and we would arrive any moment. But as time ticked away David began insisting that something was wrong.

Finally we turned back to a one-garden oasis we had seen and landed on the sand to ask the way. The men pointed in the direction we had been going, so we re-embarked and David apologised for doubting me. When we took off the engine spluttered and lost some power, but climbed enough to continue, though it coughed a couple more times as we rose.

Thermals were starting to bounce off the sand in a lumpy way; a sharp one flung us almost sideways to the horizon. The desert got bleaker. Within fifteen minutes we were both aware that our heading was not right, we were now flying north towards Algeria.

Our fuel was running short and obviously if we went too far into the emptiness we would not be able to fly out. David recommended turning back to a group of three Tuareg tents we had just spotted, but the wind was pushing us along so fast it took surprisingly long to get back. I couldn't really believe I'd blundered; usually I'm good at navigation.

When we descended near the tents I watched one terrified woman snatch up a shawl and cower underneath it on the ground, and another ran to hide in her tent. After we had landed a man approached, bringing a rug for us to sit on, and he said that Tegguiddan Tessoum was due south, we'd overshot it by far. The direction he pointed out showed no tracks, and since he spoke no French we couldn't ascertain how far it might be. The Tuareg bade us sit while he gathered firewood and made tea, and during tea we discussed how to tackle our problem.

It seemed best for David to stay and keep an eye on the microlight since the wind was rising, and I could head out on foot towards the salt village to find our Land-Rover and jerrycans. I was just getting set to leave when out of the blue came a jeep, crossing from Algeria with a family of Arabs. They made room for me to squash inside, and since they weren't following any road I remembered to take compass readings so I'd be able to get back again. But after ten minutes the vehicle broke down. The father was sure he could fix it, although it would take time.

In the distance I spotted a camel caravan, walking in a mirage as if wading through silvery surf. They were going to Tegguiddan Tessoum to pick up a load of salt in exchange for millet. So I accepted a lift with them, riding on a lightly laden camel. The rocking pace, slower than Ahmet's camels, was matched by the tuneful humming of one of the men.

It was now two p.m. and scorchingly hot. I nibbled on some dates. Before leaving the tents I'd had some spoonfuls of yoghourt and dates in a thick sweet gooey mixture, which the Tuaregs there had presented to David, but dried dates were easier trailfood. The ground was a maze of dried cracked clay, a desert of crazy paving. I looked back and tried to memorise the route. But the flat horizon went in a full circle round me without any landmarks. Tegguiddan Tessoum was not yet in sight when a motor echoed from behind. It was the Arab jeep. I abandoned the camel and drove into the small mud village oasis.

There was no sign of Alagarbit's Land-Rover, so I walked along some dusty narrow lanes and stopped at a bakery. The shopper in front of me was using salt-cakes to pay for his bread: two for each loaf. All supplies here could be bought with salt, and other people came here with their local produce or goats to purchase salt. The value of salt blocks changes as one moves away and by southern Niger their worth can increase tenfold. Salt blocks that reach the market of Kano fetch even more.

While I was munching fresh hot bread the support Land-Rover arrived. Directing the driver where to aim across the desert, I began retracing my tracks, but there were innumerable other fresh prints leaving the village. The driver kept asking me if I was sure we were going the right way. After some miles I had to reply, so used their own inscrutable response, 'Insallah.'

Half an hour passed and just as I was about to admit to having failed, we saw Pegasus's wing ahead, dead on target. David and I refuelled and took water, then I sent the Land-Rover back to Agadez, since from here on no more ground support had been required by the authorities. Also, the driver was a rogue and we were better off without him.

David had made camp beside the microlight, a socially polite distance from the three widely spaced tents; he needed to rest so I went visiting our new neighbours. Their tents were made of tiny pieces of brown leather sewn together in an intricate patchwork, supported on poles and held steady by guy ropes.

Facing away from the prevailing wind, the open front was twelve feet wide, and in the mouth lounged four women who giggled shyly when I joined them. For conversation we discussed the size of their world; I named some places, and if they'd never heard of them they looked blank, but if they'd been there they would nod and touch a finger below one eye. Then I showed them my postcards. One woman tapped the Queen's horse and made a horsey neigh, which made all the others fall around laughing, so I told her she was right. My presents of tea-leaves, tobacco and earrings met with the women's approval. I always carry plenty of such lightweight commodities as thank-you gifts.

Making visits to the three tents, with the women accompanying me, I found the second tent contained long fringed bags and camel decorations, and two camel saddles, well tasselled. The camp had five camels, and as the sun sank low they drifted in from their day of browsing. At sunset each woman in turn knelt down beside the tent to pray, making me think how seldom I saw women at prayer, perhaps because the men are flamboyant about it and the women are tucked away indoors. I sat outside the third tent with ten very young lambs, not currently attached to their tether. They hopped around unsteadily; one jumped on to another's back and they both fell over in a tangle of legs. They bleated, calling their mothers who seemed in no hurry to return to the camp. A boy on a donkey herded them in at a gallop, scattering the twenty-odd sheep which had already gathered. The boy stopped to say hello and he beckoned me to ride another donkey, so I borrowed a rug for its back and rode off to help round up the sheep. On the way back I picked up a week-old lamb which had strayed, and tucked it under my arm until we reached camp.

After reuniting it with its mother I joined Pegasus and David, and moments later a man brought us a bowl of fresh warm milk. We cooked supper from our supplies and settled down for a peaceful night under the stars. Small dead twigs on the fire gave enough light to write by, and the night was luminous despite the lack of moon. I fell asleep to the sounds of camels grunting and the Tuareg women drumming on their tam-tams around another fire.

Dawn was very cold. We bought a bowl of fresh warm milk which went well with our coffee. After packing up camp we cleared stones off our chosen runway, scraping down the

97

roughest bits, and did a ground test of the engine to see if it was going to cough. For this I leaned my weight against the nose, while David moved the throttle to full power. It spluttered. I decided not to suggest I pilot this leg.

It coughed again on take-off, then was fine and we sped away across the flat desert. We followed my tyre tracks of the previous day, and after half an hour we could see the small oasis of crumbling mud houses. Beside one hut sat the camel train of yesterday, waiting to be loaded with salt.

From our height we could also see the salt pits; dug in a basin, there were countless small round pools of amber, ruby, green, and crusty brown and white.

We touched down beside the oasis. There was no vegetation, the well was salty and my baker friend added that it wasn't very clean, although they usually drank it. Salt water was believed to be good in moderation, but he said we'd be better off buying water from the barrel of an Arab merchant, costing a bar of salt or 40 CFA (10p) per litre. We stowed our luggage at the bakery, and after tea and fresh bread my friend took us for a close-up look at the salt pits.

We climbed the enclosing banks, which were actually low mud walls moulded on to a bed of rock, and went down among the acres of pools. Several salty springs came up into ponds detectable by their green hues. A few people were at work, each family owning a group of pools. One woman was watering a patch of the ramparts which were re-used continually in the salt-making process. The baker explained that chunks of muddy sand had to be sprinkled with salty spring water for a week before being transferred into one of the larger shallow pits. After a final dousing with salt water the liquid mud was poured into pools as small as one foot in diameter. Clusters of tiny pits were like sequins catching the sun. The darker red pools were saltier than the amber ones.

Evaporation brought a salt crust within half a day, if hot, and I watched a woman who was flicking heavy drops of water from her calabash on to the crust, breaking it. The crust fell to the bottom. She said she'd do that every time a crust formed, until the salt lay thick on the bottom and the water had all gone. Another woman was emptying a pit, sweeping the brown-coloured salt into pans which she carried away to dry, weaving a course among the pools in a time-old way with the pans stacked on her head. The salt is dried in traditional oblong pats, and at a hut where we stopped on the way back a man showed us how he first makes an oblong base of salt which dries for a couple of days, then loads the base with a second layer of salt crystals, smoothing and curving it with his thumbs. Lastly he puts a dent with his index finger in the middle, to mark the salt bricks as his product.

The people of this locality, though in Tuareg lands, are not Tuareg, nor are they sedentary vassals of Berber descent, nor a Hausa slave caste from the south. They are called Azawaren, their language is entirely different from other local tongues, and they don't even herd animals. Possibly they derive from a left-over colony of the Songhai peoples from Gao in present-day Mali.

In the afternoon some gendarmes arrived in Tegguiddan Tessoum, looking for us since no one had told them to expect strange visitors. Their boss, the chef de poste, demanded our passports and said he would keep them during our stay in his territory. I said no. Refusing to agree to demands isn't wise, but I believe that my passport belongs to the British government and no one has the right to take it away, not even for a day. I became stubborn, and he became furious.

After a sparky clash of wills we looked for a compromise. He offered to send a radio message to Agadez to check out our credentials and I said yes please do. The answer must have been all right because the chef de poste suddenly dumped his suspicious attitude and became mellow. Actually he grew rather likeable and humorous, and kindly said we could stay at the government rest-house when we reached In Gall, sixty miles to the south.

In Gall was his headquarters, and our next stopover. I would be the pilot for this stretch. The firmest sand for our runway was the impacted Land-Rover track. It had a bend in it but we hoped to be airborne before that. Take-off was hairy because the engine began spluttering at the wrong moment, I couldn't unstick before the bend, but after curving round we did lift off, then had a partial engine failure as I tried to gain height. In the nick of time it seemed to recover, so we carried on flying, but for the first seven minutes it was doubtful and we wondered about aborting the flight. The air was surprisingly turbulent and once the bar was nearly wrenched from my hands. David ticked me off and told me to master it, so I gritted my teeth and hung on in there.

Pegasus wasn't only choking on full acceleration, the rpm gauge showed erratic readings of less power than usual. 'Where would you land if you had to?' David's voice rang in my mind, though I wasn't sure if I was hearing it internally or through the helmet's intercom. The rolling desert hills, grey and pale gold, were unsuitable. The many dry stream valleys had outcrops of darker sand or rock, with greeny-gold patches of dried grasses. In the soft light it seemed a lunar world. We could have landed if we had no choice, but so long as the engine kept going and the winds didn't bat me out of the sky, I had to keep flying.

An hour had gone by. My arm muscles ached, I wished I was elsewhere, and for long intervals was only conscious of Pegasus's nose rearing and diving through the currents; I couldn't see where we were going, the dust fog had reduced visibility to the appalling, but through it I could just make out the faint blurred track that I was determined not to lose. Neither David nor I spoke. He said afterwards that other students would have been moaning and wailing. It was an evil flight, I hated every moment, and by the time we finally reached In Gall my arms ached miserably and my mind felt frozen with terror. I never wanted to fly again.

Seven

Dinosaurs and Road Racers

The chef de poste at In Gall, Alhaji Sidibe, lodged us in a delightful house and brought us a delicious dinner of four courses: soup, goat roasted in herbs, couscous with mutton sauce and ending with milky rice pudding. Sidibe said that twenty years ago all this area was forest and vehicles en route to the salt village used to cut their own paths through the thickets. His job, apart from administering law and order, was to lead people through this extended time of hardship. He was a Peul, whose family name dated back 1,400 years to when Islam came to West Africa: one of Mohammed's caliphs was sent to spread Islam in Guinea, he converted the emperor who asked the caliph to stay and teach the Guinean people. He settled, married the emperor's daughter, and they had four sons; the second son founded the Sidibe clan.

The following day Sidibe took me for a drive into the desert to show me his vegetable garden where two gardeners were tending and irrigating some seedlings. I teased him about being a nomadic Peul and needing to employ gardeners to do the agricultural work. But he assured me he had planted everything with his own hands.

'We must all start learning to do new things,' he said, 'and when I look at this bare earth, and look closer, I see how the shoots are just beginning to emerge.' And he pointed proudly to some minuscule cracks in the earth where seedlings were breaking through.

Back in In Gall, David was depressed. He had spent the whole morning taking the carburettor apart for the umpteenth time and cleaning the fuel system, but still the motor coughed. I reminded him of his own consoling maxim: 'It's better to be on the ground wishing to be in the air, than to be in the air wishing to be on the ground.'

Sidibe saw me wondering what to do next and suggested an outing to a place he'd crossed on a recent hunting trip, where he'd seen some unusual fragments of bone. He hadn't stopped for a proper look, but he wanted to go back there, so we climbed into the Land-Rover and headed out into the desert.

The sand was very pale and overlaid with purple stones and mauve dust giving an airbrush effect. We hoped to be able to find the right direction by following Sidibe's previous tracks, where the drifting sand had not already covered them. We passed a line of ancient cliffs, and another craggy range lay ahead, looking as if they could once have been river banks. Fossilised wood in this area was witness to the vanished trees. Sidibe pointed to some low mounds that were speckled with white, and when we reached them I saw they were fragments of huge bones. In low heaps almost entirely covered in sand, there were over ten separate mounds, each one made of many bones like crumbled skeletons.

Sticking up out of the top sand was an outsize leg bone. Sidibe and I crouched beside it and began carefully scooping away the sand, uncovering a four-foot-long thigh bone as thick as a tree trunk. At the top was a knobular joint and at the bottom it was flared. Below the sand was dry clay, which had been shallow mud when these creatures lay down to die.

There wasn't a shadow of doubt that these were dinosaur bones. Nothing else could have been four times taller than an elephant. Dinosaur bones have been found before in the environs of Agadez, and some miles south of Agadez my map marked a 'graveyard of dinosaurs', but people said nothing now remained there because the locals had plundered the site for saleable bits, and tourists had taken souvenirs until only tiny fragments were left. The last major find of a complete skeleton was twenty years ago, and it was now in a museum.

Another patch that we investigated had a leg bone almost twice as big as the first we had exposed, measuring over six feet long, though it was broken in the middle. From their position in the mud I doubted they had died of thirst when the water receded away and neither did they have the aspect of desperate search or fleeing; they were too big a group. Looking around I counted numerous distinct patches of bones and undoubtedly more lay just out of sight. The most recent theory is that a long spell of cold weather prevented cold-blooded dinosaurs hatching their eggs.

Dinosaurs and Road Racers

Before leaving we covered the bones with sand, to protect them from the sun and sand winds, and from the hands of collectors. Obviously, from the undisturbed state of the dry mud we were the first to discover these bones and I felt stunned with the thrill of it but also with fears for their survival should the site be discovered.

Over supper that evening, Sidibe and I talked about the possibility of an international group from university paleontology departments being invited to uncover the site with proper care. We agreed to do what we could to get it conserved.

Pegasus was back on form again. I wanted David to fly her out to see the dinosaurs, but the next day had a fast gusty wind and thick dust fog that made it impossible. Each day the winds and dust grew worse, even the early mornings were gusty and unflyable. But there was pressure on us to get back en route, our permit was expiring and I had to get it extended again. For myself, I'd temporarily lost my enthusiasm for flying. It had gone with the horrors of the last flight. I felt sure I'd get over it, but was inclined to keep my feet on the ground for the next short leg of our journey. I would move on ahead of David. Without me, he would be lighter laden and able to fly in less good conditions.

I found a lift going thirty miles out to meet the road west from Agadez. It was early morning and the weather was strange with streams of sand blowing low across the road and gradually obliterating it. Visibility closed in, blotting out the dark hills. The driver said it could get a lot worse. We reached the junction and stopped at a hamlet where my ride ended. The wind was now howling along full of dust. I wrapped my sarong like a *shesh* around my head against the storm, and kept only one eye open at a time since it quickly filled with grit. Vehicles occasionally went past, they came racing through the dust with their headlights on; I tried flagging them down but didn't think they would stop for such an image.

The vehicles were uncommonly numerous and I realised I was seeing the advance guard of the Paris–Dakar rally. Several were competitors who had already dropped out, others were support teams, and one French back-up team pulled in to give me a lift. We headed south-west. I was going to stop at a small town called Abalak to check on Mobil jerrycans at the gendarmerie.

While the storm outside the car rocked and howled, the Frenchmen told me about the rally's progress south over the Sahara as far as Agadez, and the tragedies to date of three deaths. Two had died yesterday as competitors grew more reckless with fatigue. A Range-Rover had rolled off the road and a truck had hit a pothole too hard. The men said it shot up in the air, smashed down and exploded. But most drivers were lucky and their accidents were not fatal; one of the luckiest was a mechanic sleeping quietly in his tent which was run over by a car. Out of a starting number of over 600, there were now about 300 still competing. The first to reach Agadez had been the motorbikes: men who let their bike fall to one side while they fell the other, already asleep, too tired even to get into their sleeping-bags.

The rally would leave Agadez the following morning, coming along this same road and, visibility permitting, I wouldn't be able to miss it. I hoped David wouldn't pick that moment to be flying in fog and trying to land on the road.

The Frenchmen paid no attention to the world passing outside. Even when the storm cleared they sat chain-smoking Gauloises. Two were asleep in the back, one was reading a novel, and the navigator had his nose buried in the map. No one glanced out of the windows.

In Abalak the gendarmes were charming and helpful, and the fuel was in place. I checked out a possible good landing area and left a message to be radioed to David in In Gall, adding that I'd decided to continue on another sixty miles to a village I'd heard about, which was confusingly called Tabalak. My next lift was in a minibus already holding nineteen people. My neighbour's face was tattooed with arrows and zigzags, and the man beside him had concentric circles on his cheeks and narrowly spaced parallel lines on his temples.

The village of Tabalak had enormous charm, sitting on the fertile bank of a long blue lake, with sand dunes coming down to the lake shore. To reach the lake I walked through a primary school yard, and the head teacher said I could camp there. In the market I met a horseman and asked if I could hire his horse for a couple of days. It was a neat black stallion, small but strong and, after letting me try out its paces around the market, the owner agreed to my scheme. He would leave the horse with me for the rest of the day, collect it at sunset and feed it extra well to be fit for the morrow.

Dinosaurs and Road Racers

So I set off on horseback to see where I had come to. My mount, for lack of a name, I called Blackhorse. His bridle seemed too long and the bit, far from being snug in the gap behind his molars, was hanging between his front teeth. But he was used to it like that. He had a red blanketed saddle with raised pommel and back, and a swinging jogging pace. He was nervy but not hard to control.

The village people looked to be a mixture of Peul and Tuareg. Being on horseback I could see over the courtyard walls and watch Peul women pounding millet in chunky old wooden mortars. It might have been an invasion of privacy in Surbiton, but there's no such value as privacy in Africa, and anyway when they saw me they giggled and squeaked, returning my wave.

One belle I noticed particularly because every now and then she clapped her hands while the pestle pole was on its upstroke, taking her hands off just enough to prove her rhythm. She had a lovely hairstyle of many plaits along the crown descending into ear bangs, a muffy bun bobbing above her forehead, and bunches at the back. I asked her if she could clap twice on the same stroke, which amused her companions, and made her concentrate and go for the two-clap. First she built up a strong beat, then made a double clap followed by another in the next stroke.

The style of granaries had changed since Nigeria. In Tabalak they had big spherical pottery ones, sitting on legs, which were topped by conical baskets. The huts were round or square and made of mud or millet stalks. Three men on camels came past at a trot, the camels' heads bobbing at every step, and I felt happy to be on horseback which, to me, is by far the best means of transport.

We passed more women at the village pump. When a goatskin bag was full the woman slung it under the belly of a donkey; that way it couldn't fall off. At the lake shore fishermen were setting poles and thick lines of hooks, carrying them balanced on their heads. Canoes wove through water now lit by the setting sun. The shore shelved slowly on a sandy base and Blackhorse waded out in a rather determined way. I wondered if he intended lying down to roll in the lake or just having a deep drink. After stabling the horse for the night I sat back in my school camp site listening to gentle waves on the sand, the chirring of crickets, wind rustling in trees, and the bubbling of a billycan brewing tea.

The head teacher stopped by to make sure all was well, stayed for tea and shared his worries. Last month he had taken a second wife because his first one was no good. She kept running off home and made his life a misery. He had divorced her some time ago but she then insisted on coming back, only to give him a hard time. 'She was never like that when we were courting, but when we married, she changed.' He hoped that by marrying another, the first wife would come to her senses, though for the moment she was insanely jealous. The new wife was a honey; she brought me a dish of their supper of millet porridge and fiery fish soup. When I tried to turn off their paraffin stove it wouldn't die. The second wife tried it too but it stubbornly stayed alight, so she threw a bucket of water over it. 'There, that's put it out.'

I washed in the lake, disregarding any thoughts of the water-snails which carry bilharzia, irresponsible maybe but I'd already got dormant bilharzia from my last African trip, so now refused to take it as seriously as others. The water was cold and refreshing, though it didn't take me long to fall asleep that night, so comfortable was I in the sand.

Early next morning I set off on Blackhorse into the huge sand dunes north of the village. They rose about 150 feet; very golden and with a scattering of air-potato plants. On top of the first range of dunes I came to some hamlets of grass huts. Blackhorse pranced at the sight of another stallion being saddled, and the men called to ask where I was going. 'Around,' I answered, sweeping my arm in a wide gesture across the landscape. Beyond all those dunes the land flattened into a plain with hills in the far distance.

The next settlement we came to was newly built, made from stalks of millet, the weight of the huts' thick roofs resting on a ring of posts around their thatch walls. Each roof had five or six stepped tiers of thatch, bound at the top into a knot. Some were still unfinished, though the granaries were ready, sitting on legs of rock with their forked branch ladders in place. It was odd to find it unoccupied.

Beyond here the countryside held small thorn trees and bleached grass. Herds of camels and goats wandered randomly. Underhoof was sandy and Blackhorse bounded along. The wind was picking up, a most chilly wind and I rather wished I was wearing my flying suit and gloves. Apart from being cold, I noticed how the dryness of the air was cracking the skin of my hands.

Dinosaurs and Road Racers

About four miles later we circled around on to the high dunes again and went along the crest. The lake was long to the horizon, its opposite shore arid desert, gold with a blue sash, and on this side was the road, with two trucks racing along it. I had almost forgotten about the Paris–Dakar rally. The trucks roared past, neck and neck, filling the road, and as they reached the village they blared their horns but neither slackened pace. Their wake of dust blotted them from sight and I watched other race traffic rocketing towards us.

It came in spates and surges, and during a lull I edged Blackhorse down the duneside nearer to the road. Three trucks appeared, all vying to overtake, and I spotted a motorcycle in their midst. Klaxons blared and suddenly I saw the motorbike slide off the road into a pit of sand. The trucks were gone in a whirl of dust. The rider struggled to his feet and shook off the dirt, but couldn't seem to shift the bike which was half buried in sand. Here comes the cavalry to the rescue, I thought, and kicked Blackhorse into a gallop.

In a moment we were beside the bike and, using Blackhorse's tether which was coiled from my saddle, I managed to make the horse pull the bike free. It was still in deep sand in the pit but the rider said it could make the climb and, without pausing to say goodbye, he leapt on the bike and roared away.

That left me astride Blackhorse who was pelted with sand and frightened by the noise. He fought for his head so I let him run, putting a safe distance between us and the noise. After six hours I was nearly back at the school; it was time for a midday break so I bought a bale of dried grass for Blackhorse, which he carried, taking bites out of it as he walked.

In the afternoon I rode east along the dunes and into a dry river-bed, chancing to meet the *gri-gri* seller from Tabalak market carrying a hyaena's head. He showed me how it was empty inside but with the skull and skin still intact, and he said it could be used to cure diseases caused by demons. Later I came to a village where the women had intricate facial tattooes like railway lines and bunches of metal loop earrings starting from the tops of their ears. They took me to their well to replenish my water-bottle while they filled their goatskins. One more gallop then we'll take a break, I thought, and turned back towards Tabalak.

As we sped over a slight rise Blackhorse suddenly jammed on the brakes, skidding to a halt. I clung to the pommel and fortunately the saddle didn't slide over his neck. The cause was a carcase, a recently dead young donkey lying with its neck twisted and mouth shrivelled back, leaving its teeth bared in a snarl. The carcase didn't smell, it was already dried out. Blackhorse had sensed not smelled it. Later, as I rode through Tabalak again, the roadsides were still trembling from the rally which would continue all day. Most families had forbidden their children to go outside, it would be too easy for them to get killed. Someone said there had been another accident in the rally, a support aircraft flying in murky conditions, unable to tell if the land was rising or falling. The pilots weren't killed, although their plane went nose first like a dart into a dune. A car with rally stickers pulled off into the school yard, and out jumped David. I rode up and he said, 'D'you want the good news or the bad news first? The good news is that I'm alive, the bad is that the microlight is a little bent.'

He had taken off from In Gall in a strong wind and within thirty minutes Pegasus was coughing badly. The motor's rpm dropped one-third of its power then recovered for two minutes and dropped again. David had managed to limp up to 5,000 feet and at the junction with the Agadez road he'd seen a sandstorm. This was the same tempest I'd been through the morning before. David said there were two helicopters flying along above the road, 2,000 feet below the microlight, probably containing officials and press of the Paris–Dakar rally. The road was hogged by race traffic. The storm reached out, the helicopters were grounded a moment later, but David stayed high. When he tried to turn back it was too late, the wind was stronger than Pegasus. Descending, he saw the sky clag in ahead, and knew he'd got to land.

Racing trucks on the road made that a no-no; he chose an open space then turned to land into the wind. 'I landed like a crow on a gate-post.' He looked like he'd been through quite an ordeal. He said his touch-down tracks were only three yards long and the instant he stopped he'd begun de-rigging. A dozen Tuareg tribesmen helped him, and most of the wing batons had become bent in the process. That problem was one we could easily fix. But now we needed to devise a new plan of action. Sandstorms and dicky motors were not an acceptable combination.

It was January 13th; we set out to rescue Pegasus, travelling in the back of a truck which carried spare parts for army vehicles, and a full load of passengers and baggage. At the first stop ten men and one fat sheep were also hoping to board the truck. They all squashed in and there were grumbles and protests as the men's swords caught on other people. Most were young bucks in robes, *sheshes*, swords and daggers. David and I had found space to sit on a heap of tyres with our feet perched on a gear-box. We watched the land grow drier, the trees more dead, the grass more withered, leaving empty shifting sands. There were settlements every thirty miles, their mud walls almost surmounted by drifting dunes.

At Abalak the truck picked up additional cargo of firewood and six goats. David said we were like war refugees, rattling across windswept wastelands in a battered truck, and me wearing a German army donation sweater wrapped around my head against the cold gritty wind. At the lunch stop we bought barbecued goat meat and tomatoes, and poor David slashed his hand on his knife but we managed to stop the bleeding eventually. He was also suffering from a terrible sweet tooth and lust for toffee. I'd stashed some away for him but he yearned for it continually. He was still looking stressed and pale though in general his health seemed to have improved.

When we arrived back at the microlight, David began checking the wing batons, and nearly all of them needed reshaping. Fortunately we had a paper pattern. In the evening there should have been a calming of the wind, but it didn't relent. What a godforsaken place we were in, a few mud hovels and a couple of camels. The wind could go on for many days; it had already been blowing for a week.

An empty truck stopped at the junction and I went into negotiation with the driver. With the helpful muscles of six men we lifted Pegasus into the back of the truck, and thus managed to hitch-hike with the microlight. The driver agreed to drop us when he turned off this road, not far from the town of Tahoua. Daylight faded in the fog and night took over.

How we were going to find another six strong men to help us unload at night was a problem I decided not to worry about. Sure enough at the junction where the truck left our road we found enough people for the job. We put Pegasus down in a dark space beside a lean-to millet-stalk shelter and a padlocked mud building, and made camp there. The house looked abandoned but our noise produced its sleepy occupants who were too dazed to say more than '*Sava*, you can sleep here,' before going back to bed.

The morning brought disappointment: Pegasus's motor wouldn't start. There was no spark, and when we opened the magneto it was full of sand. So I bought some firewood and made coffee while David cleaned things up. No success, he needed a tool we didn't carry and a workshop where he could take everything to bits.

Mid-morning an army jeep arrived; the authorities had been informed about us and wanted to offer some help. An army truck was despatched to bring us into Tahoua. It didn't have an opening tailgate so the microlight had to be hoisted eight feet up and over the side. The passengers of a minibus with a punctured tyre all helped.

The truck dropped us at Tahoua airport and the commandant bade us welcome. Our flight plan was hopelessly out of date but no one was upset because one of the three messages I'd sent by radio had arrived.

While David opened the crankshaft, and examined Pegasus's entrails once more, I decided to take the opportunity presented by the delay to explore what appeared on the maps as a vast empty space to the north-east with one track through it to a village called Tchin Tabaraden. It would be possible to get there with traders going to the weekly market. One thing which interested me was the chance of meeting Woodabe cattle herders, famed for their face-painting and tribal male beauty contests.

EIGHT

Blank on the Map

On the first evening I reached the hamlet of Kao and spent the night in the hut of some young Peul men. They were the local veterinary force, which enabled them to retain their tribal links with cattle. Over our shared supper they discussed their work and one of them told me how cows tied in with their creation myth. His name was Sambo. Well, I thought, somebody must genuinely be called that somewhere in Africa.

'The father of the Peul race was an Arab, the mother was Berber – there are many theories but this one is most favoured by Peul historians.' Sambo was a natural story-teller, his voice taking on the melodious note of a bard or griot. 'The couple bore twins, in Guinea by the sea. One day a cow became visible in the waves and when the twins lit a fire the cow approached. When the flames died the cow retreated. Each time they lit a fire the cow came nearer, it adored the fire. The twins used the fire to lure the cow from the sea, lighting it further and further away until they had taken the cow home for domestication.

'We Peul firmly believe we brought the cow into this world, and that all cattle are descended from the sea cow. Our cows still come automatically to fire and love it. Every evening when a Peul lights a fire in the *doudal* [corral], the cattle come to stand by the fire in order of seniority with the lead bull closest to the flames.'

Sambo paused and the other young men added comments, saying that their cattle brought them to Niger. Unlike that of Tuareg warriors who conquered through the sword, the Peul invasion of West Africa was a peaceful infiltration of pastoralists in search of grazing. As strangers they paid pasturage dues to the people in whose lands they roamed. 'But we are Bororo, the purest Peul, untainted and therefore superior. One major difference is that our beliefs are animist, while the ordinary Peul are now Moslem.'

Sambo took up the tale again, talking about how some Bororo lost their own language and customs as they migrated. The words began to flow over me as tiredness stopped me understanding them and I just listened to the flow of tones. The men talked deep into the night, though they curtained off a bed for me at the end of the room and I fell asleep to the murmur of their voices.

Next morning I gave up my front seat in the truck to a woman and baby, and scrambled up on top of the full load in the back. It was sacks of *trotot*, crushed groundnut, cooked and dried in balls, hard and knobbly to sit on. I perched on the edge, a precarious position since there was nothing to hold on to, and the man behind me kept jabbing his elbow against my back. The truck hurtled along, swaying on the badly corrugated road, but it was worse when it raced down dips to cross rough wadis and bounce up the other side. No handholds and only one foothold wasn't enough and I searched for a second point. Feeling around I was helped by a young dandy who offered his hand from the other side of the truck; I grasped it thankfully; hands across the ocean, fine, but hands across the truck was just as good.

The sacks had holes and we left a trail of *trotot* along the road. No one spoke French, they spoke Hausa and Tamashek, or Fulbe. But I'd been learning some essential words of Hausa so I got by. The foggy sky grew darker ahead, the men saw it and began to retie their *sheshes*, already pulled loose by the wind.

On arrival in Tchin Tabaraden I went to be checked in by the gendarmes and managed to hire a horse from one of them called Hamidoun. I wanted to visit the hamlet of D'Akarana, about fifteen miles away, right in the middle of the empty part of my map. It wasn't certain I'd find Woodabe people there but undoubtedly would see Peul clans.

In the duststorm I had to use my compass, heading northeast, but unsure exactly where D'Akarana lay. It wasn't long before I was lost. Black stony mountains opened around, and my horse, which I called Blackhorse II, picked his way carefully. Herds of cattle loomed through fog and vanished. The day began heating up. I found the track to D'Akarana amid copses of calitropis or air-potato trees which were so old their bark was gnarled with long fins running the length of the trunk.

112

Blank on the Map

An armada of donkeys was coming along the track, laden for market, and guided by women in black with headloads of calabashes decorated with incised designs in white. The sun broke through the fog, revealing blue sky and high cirrus puffs. Blackhorse II grew hungry and started snatching mouthfuls wherever the land was not grazed bare. I gave him a half-hour break, but it was quite tricky to re-bridle him because, being a feisty horse, he wore a three-pronged bit. This was the cruellest bit I'd yet seen and came complete with a metal ring around the tongue and chin.

Near D'Akarana I reined in at an encampment of six brown Tuareg tents. A family invited me for tea, already brewing. As I sat down some young goats bounded up and jumped over the tea brazier. The women shooed them away. Here they wore black and white embroidery, and some lovely pendant silver earrings, necklaces with silver dangles, and local crosses.

Arriving at D'Akarana I stabled Blackhorse II in the school-teacher's compound, and was introduced to his family who asked me to stay. An old camel driver came over to enquire why my country hadn't sent his people the foreign aid to build a cement-sided well. In 1984 most of their livestock had died from drought; yet the people were still merrily chopping fire-wood. Two schoolboys took me to see the current village wells, forty-foot holes in crumbly sand; quick to dig, but they didn't last because their sides soon caved in. Each herdsman had his turn at the wells at an allotted time of day. A big herd might be given an hour, while a few beasts would merit ten minutes.

Then the schoolboys took me for a walk into low undulating hills dotted with stunted thorn trees. At one we stopped to guzzle *ajin* berries. The boys shook the branches to make the ripe ones fall; they were like small wrinkled cherries with crunchy sweet skins.

We went on to a camp to see three baby camels, whose mothers I later learned how to milk. To make them stand still for milking the man hooked one of the camel's front legs around the other, ingeniously immobilising it. Each camel gave a frothy bowlful, and was rewarded with a weekly treat of salt. They gambolled around him when they smelled it, almost falling over him when he knelt down to crush the salt.

On the way back the boys stopped to knock down a one-inch crystal of gum arabic from an acacia tree. They gave me a piece to eat; it smelled like glue but I remembered hearing that

113

aborigines in Australia could live on it for days. Inside the crystal was gooey, not sweet nor with any taste except of glue, and it stuck to my teeth and gums, and made me think people probably did live on the stuff for days just trying to get it out of their teeth.

Back at D'Akarana I made sure that Blackhorse was watered and fed. A camel was also visiting the compound. Its rider was an old sage, respected for his poverty; he wore a ragged *shesh* only two yards long and had no blanket. We drank tea in a room outside the courtyard gate since no men visitors were allowed inside the yard. I drank my tea extra hot, trying to melt the sticky gum off my teeth.

Next morning I learned that the Woodabe were at present only twenty miles to the south at a hamlet called Oduc Two. To get there I would have to pass through Tchin Tabaraden again, a pleasure since I enjoy markets.

Before I left D'Akarana the boys refilled my water-bottle; too late, I said no thanks, seeing how muddy their water was. It was a day of wind but with a clear sky not blowing dust, except for the puffs wafting ahead of Blackhorse's hooves. After about ten miles I stopped and gathered firewood to make tea. Nearly noon, I lunched on bread and dates, and offered a hunk of bread to the horse. He slobbered on it and left it, not knowing its taste.

A man turned up silently on foot. He carried a three-foot wooden bow bound with bark strips and stubby arrows, and he stood looking at me, so I judged it time to ride on. Tchin Tabaraden village was deserted. Everyone was at the market whose main attraction was the livestock. I counted at least a hundred camels, plus their young, 200 sheep and goats, fifty donkeys, and a horse that Blackhorse wanted to fight. A man trying out a camel careered past out of control, much to the amusement of the crowd. I kept meeting friends from D'Akarana, and others who came up to shake hands. If one says anything funny or clever, you get an extra hand slap. Then I returned Blackhorse II to his owner, Hamidoun the gendarme. He said there was a gendarmerie truck going to Oduc One which could give me a lift.

They dropped me, as agreed, and pointed the way to Oduc Two, several miles to the east. It was late afternoon. I set off walking across a plain and into hills of dry grass. There were some big herds grazing, and occasional tents in the copses.

Blank on the Map

At dusk I wondered why I hadn't yet reached the settlement of Oduc Two. In the still air I could hear millet being thumped and I followed the noise to a camp whose occupants pointed me in the right direction, and a bit further on I was accompanied by a Bororo leading a herd of ten cows. Finally I reached the Oduc settlement where the headman, a maribou, or wiseman, called Kidik, bade me welcome. He was ending his supper and gave me what remained: millet dunked in gravy, and some meat on bones, but I couldn't find a soft spot to dig my teeth into.

Various people visited his straw shelter or *hangar* that evening to talk and ask his advice, and women peeped in at me from the darkness outside. Some of them were Woodabe, recognisable by their hairstyles and thin oval faces with long chins. All wore talismans, being more animist than Moslem. The Woodabe men were fine looking and proud of their beauty. The *pullo* (marriageable men), who hold annual beauty contests and poetry recitals, said their next event would happen when the rains came, as dictated by 'the Woodabe Way'.

'The Woodabe Way' is known as *pulaaku* and comprises three factors: *seemtende*, the humility and reserve in daily life which produces good behaviour and co-operation; *hakiilo*, meaning carefulness and wise decisions, manifests itself in exercising common sense, in attention to the cattle, finding out from others about migration grazing; if men lose their cattle it is because they have lost *hakiilo*. The third quality is *munyal*, the ability to be patient and endure troubles, whether they be major crises or the daily domestic upsets of polygamous marriages, or sick cattle.

More men arrived and sat down to talk to the maribou. Their language was said to be particularly hard to learn and understand because the words change sound according to the flow and poetry of the sentences. I asked my neighbour about the Woodabe beauty contests and he described a dance called *Yake*, where young men paint their faces with ochre and stand trying to be noticed by the young women. They use their most seductive expressions, pulling long faces and popping their eyes. He gave me an eye-rolling and teeth-flashing demonstration. As for beauty aids, they will use black kohl to make their lips look thin, pale yellow ochre on the skin to lighten it, and shave their hairline back to show off the forehead. Pale lines are normally added to emphasise the length of the nose, a long nose being most desired. But, as with our own beauty

115

contests, looks are not supposed to be all; a man's charm and magnetism must also come across.

Another speciality of these people is their herbal medicine and before the men left I asked if they knew where I could buy some Badaadi bark for David, as it is reputed to relieve stomach cramps, or Sotoore leaves which might work, though normally they were used to ease labour pains.

On the evening air I could hear the singing of women doing their chores, while others sang to their children sitting around camp fires. The dark gentle hills had many flickering camp fires, and it became easy to tell where people had hidden their camps in woodlands; all the little fires showed against the black night and were like a reflection of the sky with its brilliant patterns of stars.

The maribou gave me a straw hut to sleep in. Its doorway was a three-foot hole with long fringe against the dust. I didn't close the straw door, and an assortment of goats, chickens and guinea fowl kept coming inside. My skin felt dirty and my muscles saddlesore, and the night wind blew through the straw walls, but sleep came to me quickly.

My breakfast was *boule*, porridge of millet and milk, no sugar, and the milk was sour like yoghourt. We passed the bowl around in order of politeness, me first then the second guest, and lastly the maribou. He had been head of Oduc Two since it was established as a permanent settlement in 1984; his people had begun learning to grow crops but this year they hadn't planted because there wasn't enough rain. Their well was twenty-five feet deep but didn't have enough water for irrigation.

Leaving the settlement, I picked up the distinctive pattern of my own shoe-prints and followed them back into a dry stream-bed and out across the plain. Only a couple of other footprints were new and although I lost the trail where a herd of goats had taken it up, the direction was obvious. The wind began blowing dust, but it was a tailwind and comfortably pushed me along.

Towards me came a group of *pullo* and some women, all larking about and laughing at something. The only man who could speak French was hard to understand but they seemed to be going through the horseplay rituals of escorting a young bride to her future home. One man sipped from a bowl of milk and blew the drops in the bride's direction, others held sticks for giving her a symbolic beating. A bride is taken to the husband's mother, who taps her with a stick of *abuhinia*, the tree of blessings. The bride spends two days with her mother-in-law in quarters taboo to men. Then she goes home for a last week before moving into her husband's shelter and her hairstyle changes to a style called *beekteedo* which means 'reconciled'.

This girl was first cousin to her future husband, a popular link because it safeguarded their cattle herds and protected their prized facial features from outside influences. Looking at the young men, all of pure blood, I noticed their faces were indeed somewhat identical.

Two miles passed and finally through the fog I could see fat shapes of granaries and pale lines of straw huts: Oduc One. I sat by the corrugated road and waited for a lift. Dust rained so hard on my diary that the biro kept clogging in it.

A truck came along and stopped for me. It was carrying a load of firewood to Tahoua and there was room for me in the cab. We were halfway to Tahoua when, on a downhill stretch, a front tyre burst and the truck went out of control. We skidded over an embankment, cracked down heavily into a gully beyond, smashed out over the top and kept going, while branches and trunks of wood from the back of the truck came like battering rams straight through the cab window. Another jolt sent us sprawling, then we rolled to a halt. Fortunately, I had kept my head down, but my left arm, with which I'd clung on to the driver's seat, ached painfully. The shoulder felt wrenched, but if that was the full extent of my injuries I was lucky. We had all been lucky, no one was badly hurt and I thought of the rally truck which had exploded when it hit a gully. Our possessions were scattered all over the ground and I found the driver's watch twenty paces away.

Another truck gave me a lift back to Tahoua, where David was also suffering, though at first I didn't realise and nearly went bonkers at him. He said, 'Right, let's fly on. Can you be ready in half an hour?' So I threw my packing together and then noticed he had not yet washed up his dirty cookpots, nor packed his gear, nor the tools. Clearly there was no point in hurrying. He said the visibility was now too poor for flying, contradicting this a moment later to offer me a flying lesson. 'With a wrenched shoulder,' I retorted, 'no thanks.' So he did a test flight, and the motor conked out again. Life wasn't meant to be easy.

I suppose David found my energy maddening when he was so below par. I used to bully him for not drinking enough water. This is one of my foibles; by drinking gallons of good water daily you can cure a lot of stomach problems; there is no better medicine for them. David tried his best to get well, but he wouldn't stop working. He was up until four a.m. then he slept for two hours and was up again, having had a brainstorm and taken the engine to bits. The worrying thing was that he still couldn't locate a fault.

This was the day of the presidential visit to Tahoua. The old president had recently died and his successor, President Ali Saïbou, was newly installed. It would be the most important day Tahoua had seen for years. The airport had been washed and polished, national flags hung from trees and a new wind-sock had been erected. We were breakfasting by the fire truck shed, with Pegasus dismantled, tools and filters spread on the fire engine's wide running boards which made a particularly convenient table. But the firemen arrived at six thirty a.m. to shine their vehicle. By seven a host of drummers had also arrived and began warming up, pounding until the air vibrated.

Soon there was a stream of traffic, bringing people with klaxons and bugles which they blew as they drove along, six truckfuls of soldiers and dozens of cars. They all poured on to the airstrip. The president had not yet left Niamey but the crowd was already in place. I stoked our fire for another cup of coffee, and David worked on. The morning air was calm and would have been ideal for flying.

The drummers' rhythm increased dramatically and an instant later we heard the roar of a jet. It touched down in swirls of dust and when the president disembarked the crowd cheered, the military saluted and there was an inspection of the guard of honour. We stayed discreetly by the fire station, not wanting to attract attention. Then with a wailing of sirens ten motorcycle outriders escorted the presidential car into town.

Our next hop should have been west over empty bush country to Fillingué, then on to Niamey, the capital. But David was now so demoralised by our flying difficulties that, ever mindful of the need to get us both to the end of the journey in one piece, he preferred to take a safer, more southerly, loop where help would be at hand. So, as we had done before, I shuttled our fuel reserves by road, relying on hitching lifts and catching up with David at the roadside. We met up that night at Nkonni and slept under Pegasus's wing. In the morning I was woken by a Fulani on an ornately tacked horse who stopped to look at us, then trotted on. Next came a man leading a cow which wouldn't pass the microlight. This was followed by a herd of goats, people on bicycles, and camels laden with hay. It was time to get up.

David flew off solo again, while I took our remaining jerrycans forward by road. I found the mircolight this time on an airstrip just before the town of Dosso, where we had crowd problems. They coughed and scuffled and kicked up the dust. 'Zamna [sit down], zamna the lot of you,' I said sternly, waving my hands at the ground, and, like a magic spell the ones in front of me sat down. I moved around the circle doing it again. It was like conducting an orchestra or calming an ocean.

David was busy changing the propeller, the other having been chipped by a stone. It was mendable with Araldite but wouldn't have dried in time for an afternoon flight. From Dosso we decided that both of us should fly, all-up weight, but when we took off from the dirt strip the engine started coughing. We struggled to gain height, lost power and came down fast. It was a simple landing, but it was a blow to our journey. I felt we were getting more used to engine failures than to normal flights. When we got to Niamey, we promised ourselves, we would sort out the microlight once and for all.

So David flew off solo towards the capital and I set about finding a lift on this last leg from Dosso. It proved surprisingly difficult, but when the director of Mobil in Niger, Daniel Trevidic, heard I was marooned in Dosso, he came out to collect me himself in an air-conditioned car. He also gave me the run of his office to get our paperwork up to date. He could not have been kinder.

Meanwhile, poor David was having new difficulties. Because our radio frequencies were out of date, he hadn't been able to raise Niamey control tower and, knowing that the President's plane was due in any time, he couldn't land at Niamey without reporting in first. So he had landed in the bush three miles from the airport and was soon being given a hard time by the police, the fire brigade and the military who viewed him as a suspicous character. Our baggage was emptied out on the ground, and David's lack of French made sending messages to the airport control tower or to Mobil difficult. The questioning got very irrelevant, but finally the military took pity on him and over four hours later David flew in to Niamey airport, breaking the new propeller on the way when a string came unknotted from the pannier sacks and caught in the blades. Landing, he faced another barrage of officialdom. I was relieved to see him at last. But he was not having a good day, not plane sailing!

A call came from President Saïbou's office. The president presented his compliments and wished to receive us in his office at midday, to talk about dinosaurs and microlights. Dear Daniel Trevidic lent David a shirt, tie, trousers and shoes, and his wife Marlene dressed me in her chic skirt, blouse and shoes. We both felt a bit absurd. Before the audience I found time to zap into the museum and look at the size of the dinosaur on display there, *Ouranosaurus Nigeriensis*, said to be the first dinosaur to be shown in an African museum. I was pleased to see it was a mere infant, compared with even the smallest that I had seen in the desert.

The president's office was inside the army headquarters and I wondered if he was a frightened man hiding in a military bunker, but Daniel Trevidic said this was not so. He still occupied his old office as chief of the army and had expressed no wish to transfer to the pomp of the presidential palace.

I was a little nervous at first in case my French led me to commit a fault of protocol. The president, dressed in military uniform, shook hands with the three of us and ushered us to armchairs. I soon realised he knew and cared about the empty quarters of his country. Pointing to the map on his wall he showed me various spots where dinosaur skeletons have been discovered. He even knew the locations of fossilised trees, and when I indicated the site of the bones I'd seen he said he was pleased but not surprised.

He had been president for two months, and was already well liked and respected; he believed in pushing his administrative officials to increase agriculture and to recognise the importance of the land. Our audience lasted half an hour and as it finished I remembered to compliment the president on the honesty and kindness of his people; then he thanked us for reporting the dinosaur discovery and wished us a safe journey.

There is an interesting postscript to our dinosaur discovery. The bones belonged to a four-legged camarasaur, the first one to be positively identified in Africa, and some have now found their way to the Natural History Museum in London where the experts reckon that alive our specimen would have measured about sixty feet from snout to tail. Its thigh bone was five foot six inches. The Museum also discovered, mixed in among the bone fragments, two new species of coelacanth, the prehistoric fish which still exists off Madagascar, and a new species of small crocodile and turtle.

That evening Marlene Trevidic gave me something I had always longed to possess – one of the legendary black stones of Central Africa. Warm to the touch, and about the size of a sweet chestnut, the stone is used medicinally to draw poison from bites by snakes, scorpions, spiders, centipedes, bees, and wasps. It also draws abscesses and ulcers by sticking to the wound and absorbing the poisons into itself. Afterwards it can be cleaned in milk and re-used. Its powers were discovered by Belgian monks in Zaire many years ago, and they have kept its source a secret. I later learned it is fossilised charcoal on the way to becoming jet, but still with active charcoal properties.

We didn't actually try it on Pegasus, but the next day we discovered the root of the mechanical problem that had dogged us since Cameroun. It was not any fault of the engine which, as David had thought, was working beautifully; it was that we didn't know how to adjust the motor to run on Avgas. We had done tests before leaving England to see how it ran on low octane fuel, but we'd never reckoned on Avgas whose octane is a very high 110-130. So we guessed what adjustments to make since, to our knowledge, microlights have never run on such high octane, and we ordered a box of extra hard spark plugs.

As days trickled past I noticed a marked change in the weather. The chill had gone out of the night air and the mornings were merely cool. The hot season was beginning and would increase rapidly over the weeks until temperatures reached fifty degrees. If our journey didn't get a move on, we'd be roasting in the desert.

Before we left Niamey we appeared live on Niger television, flying in from the airport to land in the hippodrome. I was happy to do this to thank Mobil for being such a magnificent support, but the crowd that gathered was terrifying and, the moment we came to a halt, they all surged enthusiastically forward like fans mobbing a pop star to touch and grab at our wires and even try standing on the lowered wing. A thousand hysterical people were so entranced with us that we feared we would soon be torn to bits. The camera man and sound recorder were knocked flying but the determined interviewer kept talking, and David and I feared for the survival of our machine, if not our journey.

The episode ended ridiculously. We managed at last to get a clear take-off space, but then David realised he had forgotten the new radio frequency for Niamey airport, and he would be unwise to go on without it. So I got out and told him to take off immediately, while he had the chance, and I would race him to the airport by car with the ever helpful Daniel Trevidic and our spare radio, ask the tower for their frequency, then relay it to David. All in all, it was another exhausting day.

NINE

The River of Rivers

We finished preparations to leave Niamey and head north-west up the Niger River, whose course we could follow for 150 miles to Gao in Mali. We thought this stage would be simple because the prevailing easterly winds would help us along and it should only take two days to reach Gao. Dawn was murky but Pegasus stood ready, baggage well strapped down, so we said an affectionate farewell to the Trevidic family and the Mobil team, and motored out towards the runway. David radioed the control tower for wind information and they responded, 'Wind thirty knots from north-west.'

'What!' David shouted. 'Please repeat winds.' They said it again, and we queried it a second time, unable to believe they hadn't made a mistake. They insisted they were right, so we stopped outside the met office and turned off the motor.

The met chief hurried to us with a weather chart. 'Although, as you see, the whole of north Africa is having normal easterly winds today, there's a spiralling pulse on Gao which is funnelling the wind down the Niger valley. The river valley from here to Gao is the only place affected by this pulse.'

The hub of the trouble was firmly placed over Gao. Wind speeds there were reported in excess of forty knots, and the sand kicked up by the storms was expected to be blown along the Niger valley for several days. I was speechless, the word unfortunate wasn't large enough.

We decided to go for a test flight to see how bad it was. We hadn't flown fully laden since the last spate of engine failures, and today we were overweight by about fifty pounds. Pegasus took off effortlessly and soon we were 800 feet above the runway, not that it was easily visible in the quickly deteriorating visibility. We could just pick out two old wrecks of passenger aircraft on the ground, one with a snapped wing. The river was a vague blurred ribbon. It would have been folly to go on.

I voted to take the risk and try, wanting to leave city life, and reasoning that the wind at this low altitude wasn't as bad as we had feared. My vote was immediately vetoed by David who pointed out that regulations forbade flight in such poor visibility. There was no need for argument, I'd appointed David to teach me how to behave as a responsible pilot. We landed and I untied my overnight bag. But I wasn't feeling patient and reasonable and, much as Niamey had been fun, I needed space and wanted to be back in the bush.

Leaving David and the microlight in Niamey I took the dirt road north-west to Ayorou, a village a hundred miles further up the Niger. At the last minute I stuffed a flare gun and some coloured flares in my bag so that when David did manage to fly upriver I could let him know where to find me, and also indicate the safest ground to land on.

The route to Ayorou was rutted and sandy. To my surprise, after nearly an hour the dust-laden air cleared revealing pure cloudless blue sky. It was a pity I couldn't tell David. The sun made the tall regal silhouettes of fan palms and spiky acacia stand out darkly against the pale sand of the river's broad flood plain. Outcrops of greenish rock overlapped each other in clumps alongside crumbling mud villages. The other road traffic was horsemen, camels with robed riders, and women with buckets balanced on their heads. The play of shapes in the open countryside made me feel free again.

At Ayorou I was not far from the Mali border and it was the chief of the Customs post who organised his soldiers to find and clear a makeshift runway and installed me for the night in an empty part of the government rest-house on the river shore. A soldier fetched a tin bucket of river water for my washing, another brought a kerosene lamp, and the rest helped string up my mozzie net, with much laughter at its lop-sided shape.

While I ate supper in the market I could hear drums being warmed up for some evening celebration. Two men with talking drums under arm sat at the next table, using their arms to squeeze the rawhide strings at the thinnest point of the drum's narrow waist and rapping the drumskins with a short curved stick to produce the whooping note-changing rhythms that relay messages.

I followed them to the festivities and found a crowded garden

124

The River of Rivers

where two large dumpy drums and another yet bigger one were being beaten so hard and fast the leaves on the trees were shaking. The leader of the talking drums began to dance and the crowd fell back as he pranced with bent knees and sharp kicking out movements, turning and twisting in circles in a semi-squat, his robes trailing behind him yet never tripping him. A woman in tight bodice and sarong stepped into the cleared space and crouched down in similar fashion, dancing with a long scarf between her outstretched arms.

Their circles crossed and re-crossed, the drummers pounded and marched, at every fourth step twitching a foot out with a sideways hop. The dancers' circles tightened and the drumbeat grew frenzied, drumsticks ferociously near breaking point, moving so fast I could only see a whirring blur. In a crescendo of percussion the dancers collided. They lay for a moment sprawled on the ground, receiving the crowd's applause and beckoning two women who took over with a new dance, hands on wriggling hips, bellies quivering in a continual ripple of motion.

They began an odd slithering pace sideways, propelling themselves by sliding toes then heels across the ground without losing contact and using a thrust of their hips to move them along. As they danced they made a sibilant noise, hissing with concentration and effort, a strangely primal sound. When they slid away from the lamplight a group of ten Tuareg women stepped forward, clapping and at each beat jerking their chests, while a couple of turbanned men moved in a fast shuffle-stamp, slim and lithe. The women's bracelets jingled as they chanted and the metal jewellery in their hair caught the light; the men paired together for an effeminate yet dramatic dance, which involved brandishing their sheathed swords.

Now one man crouched, transferred his weight on to his hands and began kicking his feet under his palms, lifting each hand in the nick of time, Cossack-style. By the minute the performance grew more spectacular. The other man followed suit, swirling his legs one side then the other, as his repertoire warmed up. The first did a quick forward handstand, touching his forehead to the ground, then bounced back into his crouched dance.

It was the most skilled display I had seen for months. Each group of dancers had their special style; the Djerma were mostly wriggling girls, led by talking drums; the Tuaregs used no

125

tam-tams, only the fast drumming of their feet on the hard ground.

I moved around to different vantage points and by the closing stages was near the chef de poste's family who invited me to go with them to yet another traditional party just starting on the other side of the market-place.

This was a Malian festival, and after some formal speeches of welcome the Malian men made a line opposite their women-folk and began a slow stately swaying, arms undulating with intricate wrist movements, as they approached the facing line. Dark graceful shadows were cast on the mud wall by a pressure lamp, the men topped by prayer caps, the women with long kaftans. Several had beaded calabashes which they threw into the air making the beads and seeds rattle, the height of each toss creating the rhythm. Slowly the lines came together and passed through each other. One man's elegance was slightly marred by outsize yellow plastic galoshes.

The only drummer was seated on the ground using half an upturned gourd that he slapped with his hands while hooking one foot under the bottom to let the sound woomp out. Some-times he raised his other foot on to the gourd to change the tone. When he warmed up he began to bounce around, whirling the gourd round his head between beats. I was fascinated by how skilfully he could flick up the gourd, pass his foot underneath to the other side, drumbeat, then lift his foot back over, beat, foot to the other side again, and not lose time by even a fraction.

People began sticking money on to the dancers' fore-heads, signalling the end. I pressed all my coins on to the drummer's face; they stuck easily in his sweat and he was soon as pretty as a Christmas tree. On the way home the chef de poste asked if I intended to spend the next day looking for hippos.

'Of course,' I improvised. 'Where should I look?' He suggested trying upriver by canoe and warned me that, if there were baby hippos around, their mothers would be aggressive. When angry they could bite a canoe in half.

In the morning I breakfasted with a family from Tchin Taba-raden who were also camping at the rest-house. They knew me from my journey with Blackhorse II. Breakfast was millet porridge, warm, milky and sweetened, excellent, washed down with tea. We could already see a variety of canoes on the river so I wandered down to the shore and began bargaining over possible rates for hiring a small one.

The result was a flat-bottomed plank canoe manned by two teenage boys with punt poles, plus their infant brother with a bailing can. We set off upriver beside the bank, though where the river broke into channels around islands the young men altered course alongside the islands. I sat in the middle of the canoe on a crossbar, sometimes using a spare paddle to help us along, but at first the current against us wasn't strong, and the water was shallow enough for the boys to punt with ease.

The water-level was dropping, now being midway between the flood and low-water seasons. My companions said this year the flood hadn't been deep and they hoped that the river wouldn't stop running by dry season, as it had done in a previous year. I could see how quickly the water-level was going down by the red moss on partly submerged rocks which was brown and brittle where the rock had been long dry, and still red for several inches between that and the current level.

Yellow flowering creepers trailed out across the water from the sandy cliff banks, which also sprouted clumps of purple morning glory. A flock of wild ducks took flight as we approached, scuttering along just above the river. In the shallows there were herons, white egrets and large black-headed birds with long curved beaks. I scanned the clear blue sky for the more colourful wing of Pegasus, but there was no sign and I wondered if David was still fog-bound in Niamey.

We entered a faster stretch of water, wind ruffled its surface into waves and spray came over the canoe's sides. The youngest brother bailed idly with a squashed tin can. The older boys punted strongly. Up one rough channel, fighting the current between rocks, the canoe began slipping backwards; I sat tight, wondering if we were going to swing sideways and capsize. With a grinding of wood we jammed on to a rock; waves surged angrily around the canoe. The boys tried to push us backwards but we were stuck fast; they strained and levered with their poles, I hauled on my paddle and the infant did his part back paddling with a broken blade. The planks beneath us groaned and to my relief we slid downstream off the rock. Then the boys steered out midriver and we headed up a chute where water poured over a small ledge. Clearly our pole and paddle power wasn't going to get us up the fall but as we closed in to the rocks beneath it the boy in the prow jumped out on to a

127

rock, taking the bow rope and, while we paddled furiously, he hauled us up the chute. Once above it he hopped back in and we continued upriver, by now soaking wet.

Six miles from Ayorou we reached Firgune, a village divided between the river's left bank and a picturesque island. Beyond this the water grew deeper and my boys were punting with the tips of their twelve-foot poles. Most of the other canoes were going downstream to a market, carrying cargoes of straw, mats, yams and tomatoes; the canoe girls had coins decorating their braided hair. A couple of sixty-foot canoes went by belonging to nomadic fishermen who plied the river between Mali and Nigeria. Their whole families lived on board and they sold their catches to villages along the way. Some villages specialised in smoke-drying fish for inland consumption. The best fish here was the capitaine or Nile perch which the boys said could reach a weight of 200 pounds.

My canoe was now surging along. The youngster had fallen asleep and I took over the bailing. Hours ticked by. I asked the boys if they knew the date and they agreed it was probably February 1st, which was my birthday. What a lovely day for a birthday; we threaded between grassy isles and sand-banks, enjoying the glorious tranquillity of river travel.

We peered into inlets, looking for hippos, but were not rewarded. The river grew rough and rocky again; my companions resumed their punting but the pole ends kept losing their grip on the river-bed and it was hard to keep control. The boys' faces grew more urgent as we suddenly swung broadside to some rocks. We had been joking about how often their canoes capsize and they'd assured me it was rare because they were almost born in canoes.

'Hippos,' they both called out and I scanned the river but could only see rocks. 'Let's go closer.' With a roar two hippos erupted from the water nearby. Their great mouths gaping wide, they lunged playfully at each other, locked jaws, tussled, let go and sank from sight. Then their heads burst out of the river again, as they grappled each other once more, the hippo equivalent of arm wrestling perhaps. What amazed me was their vast size and strength as they reared out of the water, crashing together, sending big waves that poured over the canoe sides. We were close but could easily have escaped if threatened.

'Plus des hippos,' called the boy in the prow and gestured

128

wildly up ahead at grey lumps, still to me looking no different from the rocks around them, and it wasn't until they moved that their shapes became clear. None of the rocks was a rock, they were all hippos, about twenty of them. Their heads were resting on the water's surface, and eight were snoozing with their muzzles lying on the back of an outsize hippo. Some babies frolicked and wallowed near their mothers, but it was a male that got agitated and came at us.

We retreated to the river-bank. The male calmed down and went back to sentry duty, swimming to and fro between us and the herd. The rest weren't worried; they yawned, showing great pink mouths and tusk teeth, grunting and oinking like giant pigs, hissing air and snuffling water. I wondered if their great fat shape was somehow inflated with air to make them float well; the ones I'd seen before on land were thinner with loose wrinkled skin, not tautly swollen like these.

The midday sun was beginning to cook us on the river, and we headed back towards Ayorou. I had to bail for most of the way since what had been a little water bubbling through a crack in the plank by my feet was no longer seeping, it was flowing strongly in. But we poked a bit of rag in the hole and my bailing kept pace with the leak.

The river near Ayorou was thick with canoes heading for the market. Up until only fifteen years ago Ayorou market had been famous for its slave sales. Captives were marched north from central Nigeria, particularly around Bauchi, by slavers like a notorious Emir of Potiskum, and sold to join slave caravans across the desert.

I arrived at the market-place feeling famished, so my first priority was to buy kebabs, sweet potatoes and radishes which I devoured before setting off to explore. There were great piles of pinky-yellow pumpkins, baskets of scarlet tomatoes, yellow plaited straw mats, black soggy balls of something used in cooking sauces, and brick-orange lumps of clay in round pats with holes, which were used for the interior decoration of homes by newlyweds. It struck me that the sellers of each commodity sat together so they could keep an eye on the competition.

I felt a tug at my skirt and saw that a goat had taken the hem of my skirt firmly between its teeth. It wasn't willing to let go, despite coaxing and the bystanders were laughing fit to burst.

So I sent a small boy to buy a maize cob, and offered it to the goat to make him open his teeth. This succeeded without even tearing my skirt. People carried on laughing as a donkey was led over to be loaded with a heavy sack; it simply looked at the sack and lay down defiantly. It was pulled to its feet and loaded, then it sat down again.

Firewood was being sold by women with ornately plaited hairstyles. One sported pieces of wood along her crown to hold her hair up like a crest. Many wore their plaits beaded and coin-studded. Their skin was very black and their clothes black and embroidered. I asked one woman how the coins were attached and she showed me how they are glued on to thread which is woven into the plaits. These were Bello women and former slaves. She said independence was all right but it had been unpleasant getting used to harsh reality, having to fend for oneself, never knowing where the next bit of food was coming from.

In the peak of the afternoon heat I retired to the rest-house, took a bath in the river and later sat on the river-bank to watch the shoppers heading home by canoe. Those who'd bought camels or donkeys and lived across the river had problems. The idea of putting a camel or donkey in a canoe seemed ludicrous when they could swim. But their new owners assured me it was too far to swim. As if to prove it, two cows were persuaded to swim, and one suddenly turned upside-down. Men quickly jumped into the river, righted the cow, re-tied the rope to her horns and towed her tightly beside the canoe into the sunset. The river glowed like liquid gold.

There was still no sign of Pegasus and David, but I knew they could arrive anytime until nightfall. I wandered over to where the chef de poste sat holding judgment. People with grievances sat on a bench; most of the conversation was in Tamashek, though the innocence and outrage were in universal language. During proceedings I discovered the date was only January 31st, not my birthday until the morrow.

In the twilight I recognised the sound of a motor and I jumped to my feet. The chief also rose, abandoned his court and hurried to his car. We could now discern the microlight's wide wing fast approaching. I grappled in my handbag to find the flare gun kit. When I triggered the flare nothing happened, just a dull thud. On the fifth attempt it detonated with a fearful bang that stunned the ears of everyone around. The red trail went high and David turned to circle, he'd seen it. Now we had to drive fast to the chosen landing site before it got too dark for David to see the bushes, though already we needed the car's headlights in order to pick out the track.

David kept circling at about 1,000 feet. I hoped he'd spotted the car's headlights and would use them as a guide. Three Bella women on donkeys were blocking our path. Two donkeys moved aside but the third stopped across the middle of the track and wouldn't budge. The woman jumped off its back in embarrassment, she pulled its rope and yelled but it still wouldn't move. In desperation the women pulled the donkey forward by its ears to let us pass.

We screeched to a halt at the landing site and, using both hands, I managed to fire the second red flare to say 'land here', while the chef de poste put the headlights on full beam to indicate the longest open expanse. Pegasus came in to land, touching down fast and heavy, and only just stopping before some trees.

Although in theory the flares were a good idea they also told the whole of Ayorou that something was going on out here. Empty bush was transformed by hordes of people running, robes flowing, boys leaping over rocks, racing to beat the yet more enormous crowd running behind them. The chef de poste was fortunately good at mob control and we were able to park Pegasus in a nearby cattle corral.

We left Niger next morning, watched only by a man with five camels, and gained height slowly above the river where I had canoed the day before. I could now see the frontier post across the great sandy track to the north, and it made me think how normal travellers have to put up with frequent military roadblocks and being hassled for bribes. We were lucky to avoid that caper; my experience of dealing with soldiers had so far been very pleasant, for which I was thankful.

The actual border was not marked, or I never saw it. We flew along the river, its island-studded width tapered into a narrow stretch; there were a very few small spots of cultivation, the sahel grew dry and meagre, just sand rolling desolate into the river. The Niger's total length is about 3,000 miles, its history also long, being mentioned by Herodotus the Greek historian, and later by Pliny in Rome. Ptolemy, the second-century geographer, confused the issue by mixing the Niger and the Congo. The name Gjer M-ighere in Berber means 'river of rivers'.

Shapes of bends provided our way-points. To the first one we flew low to conserve fuel, being in a headwind; David was pulling hard on the bar to increase our speed. To the second, an equal distance, I piloted and got there faster: I found the strain of pulling rather tiring, so I relaxed and the extra power not being used for speed gave us lift, taking us by chance at 2,000 feet into a more favourable layer of wind.

The river looped away temporarily to the east and we aimed for a straight line course across the bend. Visibility was poor but half an hour later when we rejoined the river I was spot-on course, a great improvement on my last attempt.

We had crossed from Niger into Mali, the only change a profuse number of tall anthills. I pointed them out and David answered, 'Let's go back to Niger. I don't want to stay in a country that's got giant ants.'

The eastern river shore rose into cliffs several miles long. The land was sparsely inhabited; we saw one group of nomads' tents, big oval domes of pale woven straw with bands of dark brown. A man on a donkey, riding along the cliffs, spotted us overhead and simply slid off the donkey's rump. He stood transfixed, staring up. The donkey walked on unconcerned. When I glanced back, the man was still standing staring at the sky while his donkey plodded into the distance.

We refuelled on the clifftops while we had a chance of a reasonable landing space, then followed the river, wide now, flanked by massive lagoons and patterned with sandy isles. Underwater sand dunes added to the beauty. There were squares of cultivation beside some small villages and as we overflew them we saw they had barrages and dykes to retain water for irrigation.

We debated how far we might be from Gao. I noticed a large village in the dust-haze and we studied the map to try to work it out. Then David happened to glance right and said, 'Good grief, we're passing an airport.'

That was Gao. We could easily have missed it. We called up the control tower but got no reply, and when we circled we saw that it was empty. The airport had a hangar and a good Russian-built runway. The wind-sock showed a strong cross-wind and, since the place seemed deserted, we landed on the apron.

TEN

Kings and Slaves

The place I wanted to look at first in Gao was a monument dating back to when the city had been capital of the ancient Songhai kingdom. It enclosed the tombs of several kings and had been built at the close of the thirteenth century. The first monarch buried here was the founder of the Songhai empire, Sonni Ali, who transformed the small unimportant kingdom into a powerful empire. Somewhat cruel and ambitious he was nevertheless a strong leader.

The founder's successor was ousted by a full-blooded African lieutenant who became known as Askia the Great, one of the most respected rulers in African history. He expanded the empire still further, organising proper government which was firm but humane and charitable. He also improved agriculture by sinking wells and controlling the encroachment of desert. Under Askia, West Africa came to a peak of its commercial and cultural glory. In 1528 he was overthrown by his unruly sons, who banished him to an island in the Niger River, to live in misery and degradation. His was the tomb I'd come to see.

The tomb was a rough pyramid of clay with lots of wooden branches sticking out of it at random. As to why these were there, the guardian said he didn't know, the tomb had always looked like that. We climbed a spiral stair, hot mud under my bare feet, since we'd had to leave our sandals outside, and crawled along a short tunnel to reach the top, where the muezzin makes his call to prayer. From the top we sighted a giant red dune on the far river-bank.

Late afternoon I had a flying lesson, having now reached a total of twelve hours under instruction. The strong crosswind on the runway made it unsafe for me to do the intensive touch and go practice David had intended, so I took off diagonally across the tarmac into wind and began learning how to handle

133

low-level turbulence and wind gradients. Friction against the land affects the wind up to about 2,000 feet, and as the aircraft rises from the ground its nose gets pitched up steeply by sudden gusts catching under the wing. Whooshing upwards, I was always tempted to cut back on power but David insisted I kept full power until 300 feet. 'You're in a gust, the extra airspeed will go in a moment and you'll be flying so slowly you'll stall. And you can lose 300 feet height in a stall.'

With my landings the effect of wind gradient was more hairy, making me think I was going fast but once through the gradient the microlight suddenly lost momentum. The nearer the ground the slower the air. I felt Pegasus sink rapidly and tried to compensate by pushing her nose higher, but this made her wing begin to stall. 'Pull on speed,' David ordered calmly, so I accelerated and tipped our nose down. 'Speed comes from your angle,' he said. 'You can handle it without the throttle. Now get it right.'

Despite my mistakes I was enjoying the lesson. It was a lovely evening, wind strong but smooth. The sun set and the full moon rose the same size and luminosity as the sun behind the haze. This day, I had subsequently discovered, was actually my birthday. The boys in the hippo canoe had been ahead of themselves. But I didn't feel the need for festivities that evening. The flying had been a celebration in itself.

The following morning I had another flying lesson. David was determined to make me master the moment before touch-down, so we did pitch control exercises. This meant flying low, at about two feet off the runway, trying to keep the aircraft wing level, which is less easy in a seven knot crosswind, and at an even height while David added and cut back the power. Added power, and I had to stop Pegasus climbing by pulling the nose down, cut power and keep her level by pushing the bar out until I could feel her wing give us lift. We raced along at 45 mph, trying not to touch down, the motor surged and idled, never constant. I really had to concentrate. Only once was my reaction wrong and we dragged a tyre, but David seemed pleased and I found the exercise great fun.

Afterwards I flew us north to have a closer look at the great red dune of Gao. We went upriver beside the town and out over the islands. The red dune was about 150 feet high and shelved steeply down into deep water, dwarfing the canoes on the river. I levelled out and followed its long ridge, a sharply-defined wavy line with pink sand in the sunlight and red in the shadow, quite unlike any other dune in sight. On return to the airport I made a very poor landing, my excuses were a strong crosswind and our radio which wasn't working well.

In the afternoon I wanted to leave for Hombori, the next leg of our trip; visibility was good, the wind was light though unfavourable, but David was making bull-headed remarks about our fuel range not being enough to get there. I couldn't see that it mattered if we didn't get there. What was wrong with the idea that we might have to land and find fuel? Tongue in cheek I assured David that there were plenty of fuel stations along the way.

Our first take-off was aborted because our battery charger was interfering with the rev counter. Our second was fine, though there was now no chance of reaching Hombori before nightfall. Night flying is forbidden to microlights which are bound by visual flight rules. We flew across the river and west into a vast empty sea of dunes, the *erg* type of desert. As far as the eye could see in every direction there were golden dunes, enclosing white sand basins. From our height we could pick out their different shapes, some in parallel bars, some crescents, some horseshoes.

Pegasus purred along; we hit a few big thermals but they weren't violent and we used them to increase our altitude. An hour into flight I noticed some dry ponds in the dunes but no proper villages until we had been flying for two hours. 'Where are those petrol stations you told me about?' David asked, which made me laugh and wonder if he had really believed me.

Daylight faded, the sun lit up some puffy pink clouds, and the desert beneath us changed hue. I took over the control bar for half an hour to give David a rest and a chance to try and work out our map position. The dunes were now slashed with white stripes, and far to the south were some black hillocks, though the map didn't show them. Darkness came, we flew on. We passed a village by a lake, and decided not to land there because of the crowd, but the land was almost too dark to see and the desert didn't seem to offer shelter.

However, the tarmac road showed up in the starlight and made a good runway. We landed on it, intending to branch off and make camp nearby. Too late we realised that the road was built on an embankment against shifting sand, and the sides were too steep for Pegasus to be able to pull off. Then suddenly we saw a truck coming towards us without his lights on. We also had no lights and were in his way.

Quickly we braked and with the propeller still running I leapt out into the centre of the road, flashing my torch and trying to make sure the truck driver knew he'd got to stop. David lifted one wingtip to full height, I shone the beam on it, and the truck slowed. Then in low gear it crawled to go underneath the wing. The wingtip scraped on his cab roof. I was afraid his load would be taller and would bend our wing, but luck was on our side.

Soon after that we found a reasonable slope off the road and just hoped we would be strong enough to push Pegasus back up the bank in the morning. Our only other problem was a slight fuel shortage. Fortunately we did have two gallons of water, so I built a fire and began cooking supper. A car came along and stopped, bringing some Frenchmen who had crossed the desert from Algeria and had enough spare Super petrol to take us on to Hombori, sixty miles away.

The night breeze was chilly and I stayed wakeful since if the breeze grew we would have to jump up and de-rig the aircraft. Sand started blowing, getting into my eyes and ears, so I put the mosquito net over my head and listened to faraway sounds of camp life carried on the wind.

Pink stippled clouds marked the dawn. When we pulled the microlight back on to the road, our only spectator was a young lad on his way to look for a camel. His expression was as if he was seeing a spaceship. When he went home and told his family what he'd seen they probably wouldn't believe him. They'd say, 'That boy's always been a dreamer.'

We took off nicely into wind, Pegasus coughed a little then recovered, and we picked up a fast north-easterly wind.

Below us the desert continued, rockier to the south, while to the north a vast area of *erg* was speckled with occasional bushy basins and a few dome huts, herds of goats and camels. One dry marsh-bed had a dense pattern of wells, supporting a village, and where a ridge of dunes rose into a long barrier there were enough wells for a string of small villages.

'What on earth is that?' I wondered aloud, staring at a huge cloud-coloured shape with straight sides and flat top, sitting in the sky ahead of us, but higher than Pegasus. As we got closer, it didn't become obvious, it grew more like a weird pale rectangle, motionless at about 3,500 feet, although the ground was now obscured by dust haze. It took us many awestruck moments to deduce we were looking at a mountain. Slowly its base became visible through the haze, a tall cone of grey tumbled rocks topped by this massive pale cliff-sided plug. What a wonderful sight it was.

'There's a pinnacle in the sky beyond it, and another,' I called as we found ourselves entering a fairyland scene of tall pearly peaks and spires. We circled, swinging around to enjoy the view. On the flank of the flat-topped mountain's base I spotted a village, well camouflaged, made of disorderly grey stone. 'Why d'you think they live up there rather than down on the plain?' David asked.

'I suppose they've always lived there. It would have given them protection against slave raids, but nowadays, unless there's a spring, it would be a long haul to get water.' Then I added, 'Where do you think we are?'

A moment later we saw a small town on the plain which David said should be Hombori. There was no sign of its airstrip, so we dropped down on to the road just outside town and taxied along a track to park by a collection of mud buildings. It was his turn to go and find the fuel which Mobil had deposited for us at the local gendarmerie. I sat in the shade of Pegasus's wing and talked with the local people. Two of the women had pale skin and a wide black-stained area around their mouths, plus the tribal scars of three short lines behind their eyes. Some darker-skinned women had braided their hair in fat wodges: two side braids, one at the back and one at the front, with a flap over the forehead, and two straight double horns bound with shiny black thread, coming from above the ears and pointing forward and down. It made them look like Amazons in battle helmets, especially those with nails and sticks poking from the coiffure, and leather straps across the forehead. I told them where I came from and asked them where they originated. While we talked a boy plucked melodies on a one-string guitar. Some infants came over to their mothers but when they saw me they screamed with fear and ran to hide.

Eagles were circling over the pinnacle peaks. A man named the mountains for me: La Main Heureuse de Fatima (the Happy Hand of Fatima, who was the daughter of the prophet Mohammed), Mount Hombori, and the Hill of Barcouchie. David came back with two jerrycans of fuel, saying there was

137

a third still at the gendarmerie which we'd have to think about sending on, because our next fuel stash was out of range. Since we had all day to resolve that problem we went for a walk up Mount Hombori.

We found a track leading to the stone village I'd spotted from above, a steep rocky climb, foot and animal traffic only. As we emerged on to the mountain shoulder we passed through a natural passage between tall eroded pillars of rock, then arrived at the village. The narrow streets were confusing because some seemed to end at doors, though the streets went through them. Other alleys went into tunnels under two-storey homes. The best building was the old chief's house with small round windows and scalloped parapets. The mosque had a tall conical tower with bits of wood sticking out, like Askia's tomb. We were being plagued by children demanding handouts, so we nipped out the back of the village and along the mountainside to a promontory where I'd noticed some curiously eroded rocks. The only people we couldn't shake off were a couple of teenage girls, partly because the well-endowed one was busily propositioning David and he, not understanding a word she said, kept replying, 'Okay, *bon, très bon.*' When I translated what he had agreed to, he looked aghast.

Reaching the rocks we found them to be worth the trek: some were waisted like an hourglass, one was a pure tall cone nearly twenty feet high, and another was an upside-down cone balanced on a tiny neck. From there we bypassed the village and scrambled downhill from rock to rock. Back in Hombori we bought lunch of kebabs, bread, tomatoes and dates, and while David went off to find the village water point I tried to organise sending our spare fuel can a hundred miles ahead to Douentza. At the gendarmerie's roadblock I found the police chief sitting under a shady tree with fellow officers eating lunch. They insisted I join in and chew a rib of goat, which was delicious, followed by rice and sauce. They ate with their hands in a scoop shape, and the chief explained how each type of food requires a different hand shape: you splay your fingers to make a fork, use the palm of your hand to roll rice into a hard ball, and you should flick the food into your mouth, not slide it in off your fingers; for spaghetti he demonstrated how he twists his first two fingers in a double twirl with one slightly bent to entangle the pasta, rather ingenious.

All outbound vehicles were obliged to stop by the gendarmes, who called me when one was destined for Douentza. The driver agreed to take my jerrycan to Douentza gendarmerie, and the chief gave him an officially stamped note so all would be in order.

Mid-afternoon, back with Pegasus, David was working on the engine and we managed to make the adult audience sit down quietly, though their expressions were like people watching a circus act. Their children were playing in a row of empty forty-four gallon oildrums, heads popping up and down like Ali Baba's forty thieves. Everyone was beautifully behaved when we prepared for take-off; they heeded my warnings of the danger behind our propeller, and someone asked if they should lie flat with their heads covered. 'No, that's not necessary,' I answered, 'but you must all stand in one group and hold tightly on to your children.' Out on the road we raced into lift-off and were soon airborne, but at 200 feet the motor suddenly lost power. 'This is ridiculous,' I muttered to myself, and gripped the seat frame as we wumped downwards. David fought to make the aircraft recover, but to no avail. We hit the road, a fast but good landing. Thank God there was no traffic. Without wasting time we hiccupped back along the road, stopped for David to change the plugs, and tried again.

As we left the ground I remembered that I'd unfastened my seat-belt during the plug change, and I fumbled frantically to re-fit it, knowing what might happen if the engine failed again. But this time we rose cleanly, and circled to wave goodbye to the gendarmes and the villagers, who rushed back into their group to wave at us.

Our route continued beside the pinnacle mountains until they ended, then we followed a marvellous dark fault line of rock, four miles long. The rock was gently sloping with great loopy swirling lines which at one stage formed a complete and multi-banded circle. It must have been quite a squeeze to cause that. The map told us to expect more mountains. We knew they must be getting near but the air was very hazy and we couldn't see them. My nerves began to jangle, I was not used to mountain flying in fog.

By the time the first of these mountains loomed visible, we were close by it, but I forgot about my anxiety and wanted to fly between its twin spires 2,500 feet high. Together with a tall ridge they looked from the air as if they had once formed part of a circle, and the raised plateau they sprouted from was also circular, and then, as I gazed around the landscape more broadly, I saw that this huge ring was part of an even greater round formation. Sedimentary rock had been fragmented by wind. The mountain layers were one milliard, two hundred million years old, from the pre-Cambrian epoch which came before the separation of Africa from the South American continental shelf.

Next came a table-top mountain, gleaming in foggy sunlight, growing from an empty desert. It was followed by a lone pinnacle, cracked in half; we soared around it and over the top. We decided to land somewhere pretty when daylight began fading. The mountains on the left ended and a sheer massif rose on the right. Being on the lee side of it we either had to gain a lot more height to stay above its turbulence, or come down low into its protection. We opted for the latter, but as we entered its influence the microlight started getting badly jolted. Suddenly we were pulled to within a few feet of the ground, then the wind calmed and we steadied, puttering along at ten feet. Severe gusts brought us up to one hundred feet again and pushed us to race alongside the cliffs. They were still sheer with occasional broken bluffs and splinters hanging out, breaking away inexorably. One fallen rock was the size of a two-storey house. Among other giant boulders in a cove were some nomads' tents. What a glorious place to live.

We knew we had no chance of reaching Douentza so at ten minutes before nightfall we popped down on to a road and drove over the sands until we found a suitable place to camp beside an anthill and a fallen tree, which we hoped would act as a windbreak. To protect the microlight, we detached the wing and tied it to the base of a tree.

Some Peul nomads turned up from their tents beyond the next headland and I bought a bowl of sheep's milk from them. Supper of desert survival rations, dehydrated stew and rice, was delicious when you're hungry.

During the night the hot wind grew worse; forceful gusts with moments of absolute stillness in between, the surges getting stronger until they had the violence of a storm. Large bits of grit pelted along in the blowing sand. My sleeping-bag flapped wildly and the microlight's wing, despite being tied down, fought to fly away. Fiercer and fiercer came the gusts swirling off the cliffs. A full moon had risen; the line of head-lands in the cliffs looked magnificent. In the early hours David took out some of the wing batons and he slept on top of the wing to hold it down. The noise of the wind rose to a howl. Gusts blasted in excess of 60 mph. I kept thinking the storm would slacken, that it couldn't get worse, yet with each passing hour it seemed to find a new strength.

By dawn's light our camp looked like a disaster site, an unfinished disaster, for the wind had not abated at all. We completed de-rigging the wing, then tried to eat breakfast, an emergency pack of cereal, though the bits blew off our spoons before we could get them to our mouths as we huddled under a rock with our plates.

When a Landcruiser came along the road we flagged it down and left Pegasus being guarded by a Peul nomad while we went to Douentza in search of fuel. Our one jerrycan was safely at the gendarmerie but it was not enough, and since Douentza had no petrol station, the gendarmes directed me to the black-market fuel sellers. Our main worry with buying black-market petrol was that during its clandestine journey from Nigeria it may have been carried in cans that previously held diesel oil or other things that could upset our engine in flight.

We also bought food and, while passing the gates of a Save the Children project, we met a warm-hearted and spontaneous Englishwoman called Fiona Patrick. She looked at our dishevelled state, heard our tale of adventure, and welcomed us with great hospitality to her home. Retiring there for a wash and a cup of tea, I asked Fiona whether Save the Children was still facing a crisis in Mali. She explained that during the 1984-5 drought the organisation had supported ten child feeding centres, distributed seed to farmers, and set up health clinics. There had only been one doctor per 25,000 people. The infant mortality rate had been the world second highest, with half the children dying before their fifth birthday. Immunisation has been the key, and since many villages were only accessible on foot, Save the Children used patrolling vaccination teams with good success. That programme had now finished, though the centre was still responsible for a couple of clinics where children received daily feeds of porridge.

A separate aspect of the organisation's work was trying to improve the famine warning system in Mali. The country was one of the poorest nations, with four-fifths of its terrain being desert or semi-desert. But it had benefited greatly from foreign aid and, according to another project worker, had become very

141

clever at pulling in aid, and played one scheme off against another.

Aid would be necessary here into the foreseeable future, because Mali was simply not viable as an economic unit. It didn't have the resources to be able to stand on its own feet, and this, coupled with its harsh climate and terrain, meant it might never be able to do so.

In Douentza itself I noticed little of the wind we had encountered by the cliffs, and was told that area was infamous as a wind-trap. We would have to seize the earliest chance to rescue Pegasus and fly out of there. Soon after midday we began hitch-hiking. Early in the afternoon a van stopped, with space for just one of us. I suggested David should go since he could rig the microlight. After he had left nothing came. An hour later a young man walked past and greeted me, '*Salaam Aleikum.*' '*Aleikum-na Salaam,*' I replied, then he added '*Adieu,*' and '*Bon voyage,*' so I said '*Xiexie*' which is thank you in Chinese.

Eventually I got a short lift on a camel, but I wasn't getting anywhere fast and this tempted me to stray from the road when I came to a mountain and high up could see caves, natural mouths in the fault lines. It seemed a good idea to climb up to them. A young boy appeared as I started to climb; he scrambled up beside me and said he'd show me something, which I guessed might be rock paintings.

We rose above tree level; I still kept an eye open for any traffic but knew I wouldn't miss a lift because against the rock I'd hear the reverberation of a motor miles away. The rock being sedimentary had ample crevices for footholds but was very crumbly. The child reached a ledge and a moment later I joined him on it, not realising it wouldn't hold both our weights. As it collapsed beneath me I scrabbled at the rocks with my fingers but failed to get a grip. I fell a short way and rolled safely on landing but must have hit something since blood was coming from my mouth.

The boy was now stuck on the remainder of the ledge, his return cut off. Having ascertained I was not really injured, just bleeding above one tooth, I looked for another route to direct the child down. When he reached ground level he took me to a man in his village who I gathered was some kind of dentist. He cleaned me up and crushed some herbs to hold against my gum. During this he said he was Dogon from a village on the plain near Bandiagara; his normal work was filing girls' teeth to points, and although pointed gnashers were considered a bit old-fashioned by the girls here, in other villages they were still popular. He gave me a chewing stick, bitter tasting; local people use them instead of toothbrush and toothpaste.

The boy rushed in to say a vehicle was coming. I waved it down and found it was the same Landcruiser and driver that had given David and me a lift into town that morning, and though it was fully loaded, the driver made space for me. Since it was already evening, everyone helped me scan the skies for Pegasus. 'But don't look for an ordinary aeroplane,' I said, 'look for a helicopter with a parasol.'

After all that, David and I managed to miss each other. I suppose it had to happen some time and we only met up again after we had both separately returned to Douentza.

It was lovely to spend a relaxed and civilised evening with Fiona Patrick. She had been operating in the small hospital. There hadn't been enough light to do the operation required by the patient, but she had found several kidney stones so removed them instead. She said one of the problems of her work was that local people believed all European doctors could perform miracles. Fortunately, if the miracle didn't happen they were fatalistic. I'd also noticed how people assumed all whites were doctors, bringing their sick babies to me, or their wounds, their gummy eyes, and bellyaches. They refused to believe I carried nothing more potent than malaria pills and Tiger Balm, not that the latter wasn't a superb cure-all and I frequently let them rub some on their aches and pains.

We slept on mattresses on the mud roof, and woke before dawn when the muezzin began calling people to prayer. Fiona lent us a jeep to take us to Pegasus, though it soon became clear that David didn't know where he had landed, and we drove round in embarrassed circles for over an hour before finding Pegasus. I wasn't seriously worried; it had to be somewhere; you can't lose a microlight *and* an airfield, and in future David would no longer be able to tease me about my navigational errors.

Once reunited with the aircraft, there was time for me to have another flying lesson. Circuits and landings: my take-offs were no problem, but I didn't understand the importance of doing tidy circuits and I seemed always to mess up my landings. I would get to within two feet of the ground then realise I didn't know what to do.

143

'Why can't you teach me to land,' I pleaded with David, but he said you can't tell someone how to do something that is done by feel. Every landing is affected by different conditions, your speed, weight, wind strength and direction, you've got to feel it all through the contact of your hands on the bar.

So we chugged around doing left-hand circuits at 500 feet over open desert country with lovely mountain outlines in the distance. Turbulence was negligible but growing. My first landing wasn't bad but that was only by chance. The second was poor: we fell from several feet up, hit the ground with a terrible thump, bounced and took off again. My third was equally bad. I wished I knew how to get it right.

David introduced me to a Tuareg called Abdourahaman who had been minding the microlight overnight. We took off our shoes and were ushered into a spacious straw-thatched *hangar*, carpeted in rich eastern rugs. On the central carpet sat an enormously fat man, his size showing his importance, all 25–30 stone of it. This was Chief Marouchett Agdbossa of Inhabou, one of the most powerful men in this part of Mali. He was visiting the Tuareg camp run by Abdourahaman's father, a slightly less fat man. We sat on the rugs behind the chief while he finished a mid-morning snack of roast mutton. Tea was brewed for us, though first we were offered a thirst-quenching drink of water from an attractively carved wooden bowl with ornate metal handles. A dozen other men sat around in the *hangar* and we talked to the one or two who could speak French. One was a servant, an ex-slave. Slaves often had more education than their masters, since Tuaregs disdained schooling. The other servants, sitting at the far end of the *hangar*, were distinctive for their black skins and negroid features. Abdourahaman explained that in the days of slavery, which were only fifteen to twenty years ago, even slaves could have slaves of a lesser caste.

'Slaves, or servants as we now call them, who have spent all their life with a family, are not downtrodden or exploited. The head servant usually holds his master's purse-strings, he is in charge of the spending and is entitled to buy what he needs for all the servants.'

The work of the fat chief's servants, apart from being at hand to help him stand up, because clearly at that weight he couldn't do so without the support of several men, was doing all the camp chores and running its daily life. Tuareg women were not allowed to do any form of work.

The chief, who had now finished his snack, rocked around on his rolls of flesh, lounged backwards against a leather cushion and joined our conversation. He said that it would be degrading for a Tuareg woman to cook or clean or do washing; her role is to stay in the women's tents and she may only leave if she and her husband are moving camp. In that case she rides inside a closed 'tent' on a camel's back and is reinstalled in her usual tent at the new site. I looked out at the women's tents of stitched brown goatskin, drawn up at the sides to allow the breeze to cool the women, who reclined lethargically on light-wood beds.

Women are not permitted to drink water, they may drink only milk or tea. This might sound sensible since it prevents illnesses from impure water, but it's less healthy when you remember that fresh milk here is often rife with tuberculosis. At marriageable age the girls are fattened to make them attractive; for fattening, the chief recommended lots of milk followed by butter and dried meat, washed down afterwards with very sweet tea.

What struck me as really absurd was when he said that a woman may never speak to more than five categories of men during her whole life – her father, her brothers, her husband, her sons, and her husband's sons. If any other man speaks to her she is forbidden to reply. I couldn't resist showing him a postcard of Queen Elizabeth, pointing out that Britain's greatest chief is a woman, while our country is governed by the second most important woman, Margaret Thatcher.

The chief's expression was aghast and he sent some words of sympathy to David. Unfortunately David was feeling too tired to take part in the conversation and was lying down with his eyes shut. Without understanding French, it must have been boring for him, and a blow for the chief, since for a Tuareg it's an insult to have to speak to a woman. But I couldn't help that, and just concentrated on amusing the chief and keeping his interest in our talk.

On the subject of Tuareg men and work, he explained that Tuareg men were raised and ingrained with the idea that it's shameful for them to do any work or make a living. The main problem with this is that, having lost their wealth of herds in the drought, Tuaregs are now very poor but many are so proud they refuse even to look for work. 'What could we do anyway?' a man asked me. 'Why should we carry loads for another man? We can't do menial work, and we can't gain money by stealing because a Tuareg never steals.'

'Other tribes are born to be gardeners or agriculturalists, and others to be traders,' Abdourahaman's father said. 'The Tuareg métier has always been livestock.'

'And now it's gone,' the chief groaned. 'The Tuareg race is finished; our history has been written and now we are finished – *fini, tout fini.*'

My heart went out to them. But it should be said that 'all gone' was a relative assessment. This group were left with about five hundred camels, plus the cattle and goats they had recently begun raising. I decided to change the subject before everyone started wallowing in self-pity. 'What about marriage?'

The chief perked up and said that Tuareg men may only marry Tuareg women, they want no cross-breeding for they are the élite and all other tribes are below them. Unlike Moslems who can have up to four wives, the Tuaregs take only one wife, for which they used to pay about twenty head of camels. And while eastern Moslem women wear the veil, Tuareg females do not; they have the right to choose their husband, and many clans still maintain a matriarchal society with the ancestry passing through the mother's line.

'When you see black-skinned Tuaregs they are not real Tuaregs, even though Tamashek is their mother tongue. They simply are one of our dependent races whose language was lost when we enslaved them. Our true colour is like the desert sand.'

'How long has your camp been here?' I asked, and was surprised to hear that it had only been established two weeks previously. So I asked if there were problems of inhabitants being unwelcoming, since they had brought all their remaining livestock into an area where grazing was already poor.

'Douentza was originally ruled by Tuaregs, before the French came and pushed us north into the desert. Now we've come back to our own territory, and we have as much right to be here as anyone else. When we ruled Douentza the Peul people lived high in the mountains with their cattle, trying to stay out of reach of our slave raids. My father would say, "Let's go and catch a few more slaves today."

'Now that slavery is banned, many of them have come down

to live on the plains. Like us they've brought the remnants of their cattle herds, but it's not their land. Most of the people already here when we set up this camp are all refugees too.

'My own camp,' Chief Marouchett went on, 'is to the north behind this mountain range. It's also a new location, my servants there are trying out some vegetable gardening.'

I could see lunch being carried to a tent beside the *hangar*, and the camp chief went over to serve it out. His role was to give food to everyone, starting with guests, then menfolk, children, women, the servants, and lastly himself. If nothing was left, he would go hungry. He piled big chunks of mutton on to a series of trays which were brought into the *hangar* by a parade of servants.

The Tuaregs shifted into groups of four to six men, cross-legged around each large tray. In my group was Abdourahaman, David, two elders, and the fat chief who managed to find his appetite again. After the mutton we received a bowl of rice and gravy, and a dish of pasta and potato. It was tasty and we were growing adept at eating with our hands.

Having eaten, I sat back against a beautifully worked leather bolster, dyed in five natural colours, with long leather-tasselled fringes. Our companions began chewing tobacco; one used a half and half mixture of tobacco with powdered charcoal, another chewed a mixture with millet and natron powder. They said it's not nearly as addictive as the tea they drink. This was the cue for a final glass of tea, then I thanked everyone and gave the camp a present to cover their hospitality. It was time for us to fly.

ELEVEN

The Inland Delta

By four fifteen we took off, unsticking easily, and flew over to buzz the Tuareg camp. To our surprise, and in our honour, the great Chief Marouchett came out to wave. I had doubted I'd ever have the chance to see him on his feet, and wondered how many servants it had taken to accomplish it.

We also overflew Douentza to wave to Fiona and the Save the Children crew before continuing west along the mountain contours at clifftop level. These cliffs, at 1,800–2,400 feet altitude, were smaller than the range we had followed to reach Douentza, and different in that every available cranny was terraced for cultivation. Well camouflaged among immovable rocks were hamlets of stone huts, and on top of the plateau I spotted some derelict villages. Other formations in the rockscape were yet older, particularly the pre-Tuareg crown tombs which showed up so well from the air.

The mountains tailed off and we were above semi-desert, vast tracts of empty sand with patches of scrub and woodlands of baobab trees. Visibility was not very clear but we had a good tailwind. We nattered away about nothing in particular and from time to time I took over the controls while David did calculations. After one and a half hours we saw water. 'It's a mirage,' I joked, 'next you'll be saying you can see lakes full of water.' Soon the lakes came into sight, mirroring the low sun as we moved along. This was the beginning of the inland delta of the Niger River which, here in Mali, spreads into a 10,000 square mile maze of seasonally flooded basins and streams.

Our next destination, Mopti, had no airstrip shown on the map, the nearest being ten miles away at Sévaré. This was easy to locate because it was the crossroads of four routes: to Mopti, Bandiagara, Douentza, and the main road towards the capital, Bamako, about 500 miles west of us. We called up Sévaré's

148

control tower but received no answer, except a hello from a light aircraft above us at 6,000 feet.

The runway was a mile long, well-surfaced, and David demonstrated a perfect landing, making Pegasus float in and kiss the ground. We parked outside the airport building which adjoined the control tower and I went to look for someone in authority. The airport commandant hurried over. He seemed inclined to be hostile and complained that he wasn't expecting us. 'What!' I exclaimed, 'do you mean that Mobil didn't tell you? I admit we're a few weeks late, but the delay is due to such a lot of wonderful experiences, especially here in Mali.' The commandant gradually mellowed, lent us his car and chauffeur so we could go and buy supper in town, and unlocked the airport terminal for us to use as a camp. Its spacious hall echoed emptily when we spoke, and it offered showers and loos that were the cleanest I'd seen in any airport. We took over the Customs and Immigration side of the hall; I spread my belongings over the douane's table, while David's gear covered the passport and ticket desks. It felt absurd to be making ourselves at home in a spot one usually associates with hassles and crowds and impermanence.

The commandant's wife sent me a thermos of boiling water for our morning coffee, then we climbed into the microlight and went flying. This was Pegasus's one hundredth flight. I spent it doing an hour of landing attempts but none of them was any good. I still tended to lose concentration at the vital moment, three feet above the ground, and come down with a frightful bounce. But I enjoyed the moments when at 500 feet one cuts off the power and makes a gliding turn in towards the runway with the wind whistling under the wing. Descending steep and fast, wing level, I would flare it in a quick check at fifty feet, and again at twenty-five feet, staying on line, keeping speed, eyes far ahead, but from the corners of my eyes I would see the ground rushing at me. Then I'd freeze.

So we did a pretend landing at 1,000 feet but that was no problem because I knew the ground wasn't there. David's next resort was to put me through a pitch control exercise, racing along three feet above the runway while he accelerated and cut back on the throttle. The crosswind didn't make it easy and I hit our wheels on the ground a couple of times which made him mad. He was even madder later because on my last touch-down attempt I did everything totally right until the final instant when, predictably, I forgot what to do and we plummeted like a stone. At the end of the lesson we swapped seats and David flew us to Mopti, since I had to do some journey administration there and seek out a contact.

Sitting on the bank of the Niger River with an ancient system of canals and dykes to protect it, Mopti is called 'the Venice of Africa'. We flew along the town waterfront and admired its mud buildings, especially the very pretty mosque with arched and fluted façade. There was no suitable landing space so we came down on a path between dried-up rice paddies. It was very rutted and poor Pegasus got badly jolted. We stopped quickly, I hopped out, and David took off for Sévaré again just ahead of a large crowd who were running excitedly towards us.

The crowd escorted me into the town as if I were a returning hero. Fortunately they left me in peace when I reached the post office, and I waited for them to disperse before I came out again. Then I tracked down a contact, Richard Moorehead, Field Director of the World Wildlife Fund's activities in the delta. By a lucky chance I found Richard in town; he was normally at Youvarou, a village sixty miles into the delta, and I was delighted when he said that he had indeed been expecting me at Youvarou, and had even sent some jerrycans of fuel there for us.

At sunset I hitched back to Sévaré. It was a hot night and we rigged our mosquito nets outside the terminal for coolness. We were woken soon after dawn by the fire truck going for its daily warm-up. 'Just think,' David called from his mosquito net, 'all over Africa at this very moment, fire trucks are warming up in remote airports and waiting for planes that almost never come.'

By seven a.m. I was doing Pegasus's pre-flight checks. I was now growing interested in flying, more involved with it. Time had been needed to settle into this journey, let alone learning to fly, but now at last I felt at ease with the trip, and began to take pleasure in anticipation as I ran through the checks: CHIFWAP, another of David's helpful little mnemonics: 'C, controls full and free.' I pulled the bar and waggled the wing to within a foot of the ground. 'H, harness and helmet, mine are secure, check yours,' and waited for David's reply before continuing. 'Instruments, altimeter set, clock running, engine temperatures coming up properly; fuel, on and sufficient, fuel cap on, key stowed; wind, horrible; all clear on the runway and in the circuit; power check on take-off.'

In the first half hour I did at least six circuits and landings; the initial one was super, though it took so much concentration I got the shakes in my feet. But from then on it was fine. At least that was my opinion, though David rightly criticised me for untidy circuits and late conversion at landing which meant that I had waited until the last moment to flare my wing and round out the touch-down. What thrilled me was that I had begun to feel how to land, and I felt safer in the air than formerly because at last I knew how to get back down to the ground.

Without warning as I hurtled along at full power into lift-off, the motor spluttered and one cylinder conked out. It wouldn't revive, but there was no alarm since we'd hardly left the ground. We limped the plane back to the apron and had a look at the plugs. One of them was fouled, classically carboned with a black line across the spark gap. If that had happened just five minutes earlier flying around a misshaped circuit, I'd have been too low and too far away to reach the airstrip. It made me realise why good circuits are important, and why I needed to get them right. David said my next phase of training would be 'Power failures in the circuit'.

We cleaned the plugs and screwed them back in place, a slight risk, but they should last us to Youvarou. We worked out a straight line course since no other route offered us a better chance.

Beneath us were round islands in dry empty sand, each isle capped by a hamlet with a distinctive arched mosque. We flew over the Niger River and entered the vast inland delta but it wasn't the lakeland I had imagined, it was a parched clay marsh. This side was higher lying and most of the floodwater had by this season drained into its northerly reaches, leaving only a few small lakes and isolated loops of streams, cut off in dotted lines. The River Niger went away to the east and another big river meandered to our west. I had been expecting to see lots of people growing food and using big irrigation schemes, not just empty wilderness.

For once we had a good map. At 1:500,000 it was twice the scale of our previous maps, out of date certainly, but at least it had plenty of detail to navigate by. One minor concern was that it was illegal to possess such maps in Mali. All large-scale

151

maps had been banned when the military government came to power.

We crossed a raised tract of dense bush and beyond it an area of parallel sand bars. One large lake lay across our course but we found some friendly thermals to give us the height to cross it. David reminded me that a microlight must stay within range of emergency landing ground, but pointed out that where the lake shore receded, we should have the option of gliding back to shore. Actually it was quite hard to tell where the lake ended because the water was invisible beneath weeds and lake grasses that seemed to cover most of the surface. Channels through the grass had been pushed open by canoes, making straight line water paths which glinted in the sunlight.

On the flatlands beyond the lake we started seeing herds of livestock. I counted twenty-eight in the space of three minutes. Now the waters had subsided the delta offered grazing, until everything dried up again in the hot season. I remembered learning that this period brings vast herds of Peul cattle in migration from the northern deserts into the delta.

Near the confluence of several minor rivers a village came into sight and we decided it must be Ombolori, with Youvarou village just beyond. The latter wasn't printed on our map but Richard Moorehead had marked it on for me and he said there was an airstrip. We overflew Ombolori but beyond it was nothing but sand, scrub and rivers. 'He definitely said it's just beside Ombolori, and on the same river-bank. Let's try it again.'

Above Ombolori we swooped down for a closer look and all of a sudden we saw a faintly defined runway, its white markers obscured by sand, and we realised that although to Richard there were two villages, Ombolori and Youvarou, from the air they appeared to be only one big village. Having attracted attention with our circlings we landed on the airstrip, and hordes of people came rushing at us.

'Get out quick! Get out, mind the propeller! You've got to find us a safe place to park,' David yelled, near to panic as the mob, hysterical with excitement, bore down on us. 'I'm taking off right now and I'll pretend to have gone. In twenty minutes I'll be back.'

There was a walled yard nearby with iron gates but they were padlocked. Richard had suggested parking the microlight with the Land-Rovers at the World Wildlife's administrative building, and although he would be away for several days he said

152

all the staff would be helpful. I found the WWF office on the river-front; the gates were open but no one was there, it was long after office hours. However, there was space for Pegasus if we de-rigged the wing, and the hard sandy river shore would do fine as a landing strip.

The microlight reappeared, the crowds ran back to the airfield and I ran down to the beach, madly waving a white shirt to catch David's notice. He landed on the beach and we hurried to unload the baggage and dismantle the wing before we got mobbed. The crowd arrived within five minutes and it was a nightmare because, no matter how often I made the front rows sit down, the back ones kept jostling forward to pull the wires, hit the propeller with sticks to try and make it turn, and someone was pushed over on to our poor fragile wing. David was going nuts with worry.

Luckily some of the WWF staff arrived and soon we were ready to try moving the folded wing, the trike and the baggage to the shelter of their headquarters. They gave us the *case de passage* to stay in and organised people to carry the luggage. Four men picked up the wing, and two more were assigned to help David push the trike through the soft sand at the top of the shore. I dashed frantically around trying to prevent baggage going astray, and make sure our helpers didn't heave against the propeller blades, the thin fibreglass pod, the motor, carburettor, or air filter, none of which was designed to withstand such enthusiastic assistance. We wheeled the trike at a walk, but for the deep sand we had to run at it and the mob went mad. Everyone wanted to help push; they grabbed hold of every part of the engine, shoving, pulling, fighting over it all, and shrieking with eagerness.

When the microlight was finally stashed away David and I retired to the *case de passage*, overcome with tiredness.

At Youvarou our journey was pleasurably delayed while we waited for new spark plugs, and for confirmation that an unlabelled tin in the WWF store was really our two-stroke oil. Also I had to sort out our flight authority for Mauritania, which kept assuring me that no stamped and numbered piece of paper was necessary. But every other country had insisted and I felt sure that we should be in trouble arriving without one. 'It's easier travelling by horse,' I muttered darkly as I sent out HF radio messages via Mopti to Bamako, asking Mobil to send telexes for us.

Meanwhile, Jamie Skinner, a bird life specialist with the WWF, took me with him when he visited the village of Akka, one of the oldest in the delta, with its multi-arched weatherworn mosque. While Jamie and the village head man had men-talk I went for a wander. There appeared to be three types of inhabitant: the Peul cattle people, the Bozo fishermen, and the agriculturalists, mostly Sonrai (formerly Songhai), who also kept a sheep or two in pens stall-fed by the house. In one house I visited a small quantity of rice was spread in the corner of the room, a meagre enough harvest. The farmer said the millet harvest had been just as poor. In the yard of a Bozo house I watched men repairing fish traps.

On the way back to Youvarou Jamie showed me a particularly interesting grass which regenerated itself here by chance and was now being enthusiastically spread around by the local people. A sprawling unruly thick-stemmed grass called burgu, it had existed in a lake somewhere else in the delta and its virtues were not discovered until a clump broke loose and was washed up outside the hut of a man who happened to press its notched stem into the damp ground. Later he noticed that each notch had grown fresh roots and was producing succulent long blades of grass. Each fully grown stem was two to three yards long. Now the grass covered acres as villagers joined forces to plant more. They sell their harvest to people with stall-kept livestock, after which the land is grazed by nomads' hungry herds, and the grass even helps the fishermen since, when these lands flood the burgu is a good place for fish to reproduce, and the young fish can find food in the roots.

I saw the whole growing cycle in operation when I visited a Peul collective who were laying wet grass stems all along the soggy mud shore at right angles to the water, then trampling in the notches with their bare feet. It was muddy work, oozing and sloshy.

The collective's eldest man showed me the strip they had planted the previous week further up the shore when the water's edge had been at that level. The grass looked poor because it was taking root not sending shoots, while the section behind it had a few new blades, and the part done a month before looked great, with drying cracking mud and masses of healthy new grass.

I walked back around the arm of the river to Youvarou, treading on semi-dry mud which was flaking and cracking like

The Inland Delta

crazy paving. The flakes that weren't on a dry base slipped aside under my feet, and twice I fell in shin-deep. The wind was bowling me along and I played at being an aeroplane and taking a course to give me no headwind until I reached Youvarou.

In the afternoon I was lent a Land-Rover and driver to visit some fishing camps. We rattled off across dry lake beds, the flatness changing colour as we passed former tide lines, from green to the red of dried ground weed, gold sand and black mud. Small fishing camps loomed like mirages floating above the flat horizon. In every direction the skyline was flat, a round flat world like a plate. Scattered herds of cattle and donkeys didn't begin to fill it. Some huge vultures were wheeling in the sky; they'd obviously sighted their next meal and soon we drove past it, a dead calf.

We came to Tielde with its picturesque barrage of fishing baskets and fish traps thrown across the river. Here hundreds of small fish were laid out on the ground to sun dry, others were being smoked on racks over clay fireplaces. Most of these would have been thrown back in the old days. Now they were so scarce the fishermen kept them, rather than let the folk in the next village catch them.

One man told me they used to catch fifty or more different kinds of fish in the past but now there was only a handful of species left: red carp, or tilapia, sardines, Nile perch, dogfish and catfish, the last now the most expensive fish on the market. That surprised me, I thought catfish usually had a muddy taste because they lived on the river bottom, but my driver said they smoked well.

Locally people considered manatees give a good tasting meat. The adult mammal, at six feet, is often believed to be one source of the mermaid myth. Their mating takes place on land and being rather noisy, can end in the hunter's triumph. But as the manatee is a protected species, no one admits catching them.

Tielde had been inhabited for a month, before which the land was submerged. This Bozo community would stay until July when the river dried up, then they would move on to another island until that, too, dried, and so on, down the delta. There were two types of fishermen: the Seminor, or Diaka, a boatman caste dating back to the Mali empire in the fourteenth century, and the Bozo fishermen who were also hunters and gatherers. The Seminor are the sharp businessmen of the delta. The Bozos

155

sell them their fish and the Seminor offer the Bozos credit to buy grain or fish nets. But once the Bozos take the credit bait they are hooked, and obliged to give the trader all the fish they catch. Loan sharks operate the same way the world over.

The next day, talking to Richard, I understood better how the people of the delta are now having to put their energy into everything: fishing, agriculture and livestock, learning each other's skills in order to spread the risks, and giving up their traditional specialisation. The delta is a complex territory of nomadic, transhumant and sedentary peoples, but no one stays completely still. The herders move out at the beginning of the rainy season, going into the drylands to barter milk for wild foods and grains such as 'hungry rice'. In October they barter milk for millet, and return on to the flood plains just in time for the rice harvest, exchanging milk for enough rice to last them through the dry season. If the rice is not sufficient they have to sell animals at the market, but they don't like to sell their stock.

Later that evening Richard pointed out that rainfall and flood are not the same thing, since flood is caused by rainfall in Guinea, and the river runs in clay beds not giving to the water table. It's the local rain which controls the grain and grazing. Rainfall here is marginal for several species of flora and fauna, and a very long dry spell knocks them out. But it is a changing environment rather than a dying one and the problem is persuading people to adapt. People don't expect something to grow where it's never been before, and they cannot understand how changes in water-levels mean a crop will no longer flourish where it always has in the past. But sometimes something like burgu grass comes along to give everyone fresh hope.

The delta was endlessly fascinating and next day I explored a bit more of it by canoe. The canoe was a *pirnas*, a long craft with a mid-section awning made of straw mats over arched bundles of poles. Ali, the boatman, smart in his red pompom balaclava with blue embroidered soldiers, moved from prow to stern by running along the top of the canopy, and soon we were chugging out of Youvarou's river arm into the main river. On the long shallow spit at the confluence we saw flocks of terns, ruffs, plovers, sacred ibis, grey herons, and one white egret flew inches above our bows, stretching and re-kinking his neck in flight. The neck motion seemed to pull his body forward and create enough speed for him to clear us.

The river widened and the *pirnas* rolled and pitched in the sideways waves. Greenish muddy brown water, the spray came over on to the deck and I was quickly soaked. I began to relax, enjoying being part of the delta traffic: the canoes had decorative panels at bow and stern, colourfully painted with arabesques and prayer symbols; we passed open *pirogues* being punted along, short-haul ferries, big *pirnas* laden with fish and fire-wood, and a houseboat canoe with washing lines and straw canopy to both ends.

Ali was going about twenty miles upriver to see a friend at Ambiri. We paused en route at Kabe village where a boat repairer was standing in the shallows organising a group of men to beach a fifty-foot canoe. Nearby a man was making a new canopy for an even bigger one flying the green, white and green Nigerian flag.

Along the waterfront each hut had a different pattern of mud brickwork, inset pyramid outlines and lacy geometry. A tomb-mosque nearby sprouted clay crowns from its corner poles, with more moulded crowns in its west niches. We walked half a mile to the main village, across a mud-flat to a raised circle of land, to greet the maribou.

As traditional spiritual leader, the maribou's influence can take in his people's political beliefs and their economic welfare. The military government has not succeeded in breaking their power, which is based on superstition mixed with the Koran. Maribous are often also sages, healers, or soothsayers. Ali already knew the maribou. We were ushered through a gateway into a walled area containing various houses and a beautiful old mosque edged with spiky crenellations. Near it was a day chamber where the maribou sat with his hands on the heads of two small boys, to whom he was giving a quick blessing. It was the custom for families to give their third son to a maribou; the first son's role was to keep his parents, the second to go into commerce; the third, as a disciple of the maribou, would carry a begging bowl and sing for his food like the urchins I'd already met at cafés in Sévaré and Mopti.

The maribou told us to sit on the straw mats in front of him, and after exchanging greetings we discussed how he uses astronomy for instructing people when to plant and sow their crops. The relevant stars for this are the Seven Sisters, which stand for agricultural events. Ali later added that most of the maribou's income derives from donations after good harvests. A sick man came along to ask the maribou to lay hands on him,

157

so we gave the sage a thank-you gift and let him get on with his work.

Upstream from Kabe the river branched. Both forks were shallow and I was glad Ali knew the way, snaking from bank to bank along barely navigable channels. The banks were sandy beaches that continued backwards to distant tree mirages.

Low cliffs rose on the left and two spits of sand almost closed the river. We swung left up a creek, islands and sand-banks appeared, and Ali wove our path through shallows and out into deeper water again. Around one bend a lot of wild ducks had a staging point, taking flight in pairs and small groups as we approached. Occasionally we passed fishing camps where men were shaking out nets, or inspecting them and hanging them to dry. Some nomads were setting up their domes of matting. The river widened with tributaries and lagoons.

On reaching Ambiri, Ali rammed the sandy shore so I could jump out and push a metal stake in as our mooring. The first part of the village was the Bozo quarter. Each homestead had a gate-room, usually an empty room between courtyard and alley, with doors made of thorn bush. Separating the Bozo and the Peul areas was a sand dune and the fallen remains of some once gigantic trees. That seemed to sum up why the village existed, inhabited by peoples who could no longer live as pure nomads because of the encroaching sands and the dying of the trees.

Ali took me to a two-roomed whitewashed house. His Peul friend, Yorok, was out; an infant was despatched to find him and his wife welcomed us into the front room dominated by a row of nine hanging basket frames made of coloured grasses, holding an assembly of calabashes, pots and pans, about seven pots on each hanger. Ali said they were marriage presents. It didn't look like the bowls ever got used, they were more of a status symbol.

Yorok's wife wore a gold nose ring and two rings at the top of her ears; her hair was scalp-braided, all braids meeting at the top of her head where they sprayed into a fountain. Before she made tea she offered us water, kept cool in pottery jars on ornate moulded clay pedestals. These flanked the sides of the double-arched access to the back room, a bedchamber with a rush mattress on a carved wood frame. On the wall between the arches hung a silver hammer with a yard-long handle, puzzling because the hammer end was narrow.

Yorok arrived and was delighted to see Ali; their greetings were performed with huge smiles, Yorok's eyes shone with happiness and there were many hand claspings for all of us. The two men had local news to exchange, and I relaxed watching small ruby breasted birds flitting into the room chasing insects. A chicken was squawking as Yorok's wife tried to corner it in the yard. I suspected the chicken was for lunch. In fact it wasn't, Yorok gave it to me as a present, tying its legs to make it sit at my feet.

Later, when I showed the family my postcards and photos of England, Yorok wanted to keep the one of my parents, preferring it over all the sights of London. Ali told him about Pegasus and tried to describe it, and I drew a picture of it which everyone in the yard came in to see. The children's heads were shaven both sides leaving a long cock's comb, all the same except for a girl with triangles of hair left on the top of her head and a circle around her skull. The boys taught me to count from one to ten in Fulbe, the Peul language, while an older boy played a one-string guitar.

Lunch arrived in a wooden bowl with conical straw hat to keep off the flies: dark millet and fish, and my tethered chicken pecked up any bits that fell in her reach.

When we left Ambiri, Yorok accompanied us down to the beach and made it his concern to collect our canoe from where it had drifted, a gesture of respect to Ali. Yorok had a gorgeous smile, and stood with both palms up in farewell as we chugged away downriver.

A mile later and without warning my chicken jumped out of the boat into the water. It flapped wildly, trying to get a grip on the water, beating the air, going nowhere as I rescued it and tied its string firmly to a crosspole in the *pirnas*. As we moved downstream the waves were rolling with us and a bit of spray came as welcome rain in the hot sun. The chicken spread its feathers to dry.

Back in Youvarou we had supper that night with Richard Moorehead. Over our groundnut stew, we talked about how a microlight could be used in this area where rivers and mud made land vehicles impractical. Detachable floats would enable one to land on the lakes.

This made me itch to fly again and the next day we went to take a bird's-eye view of the Lake Debo region. We could see canoes with big square sails. Once these were made of grass matting but now old food aid sacks were handier. We flew low over Tielde twice and everyone waved. It was nice how no one resented our little aircraft, they thought it was fun. And it was.

Twelve

Tombouctou

We didn't know how many days it would take us to fly to Tombouctou, and the strength of the north-easterly wind meant we might not get there at all, but I was keen to try. From Youvarou we flew up the route I'd taken in Ali's *pirnas*, passing Kabe village, seeing more boats under repair and the maribou's impressive mosque, and flying quite low over Ambiri so I could wave to Yorok.

Then the river went north and we followed it but our progress was poor; the wind had increased and we were hardly moving forward, so we landed at a fishing settlement with the mud village of Gamou behind it. What had looked like a flat cracked clay beach proved to be a dry wallow-hole with deep cattle hoofprints. It gave us a very rough landing.

Our first task was to detach the microlight's wing and lay it flat on the sand, then David opted to rest on guard while I went off to look around the Sonrai mud-walled warren of a village. I found a marriage in process. Wedding ceremonies usually last a week and this one was on its third day. I met the bridegroom first in his uncle's house, swathed in a blanket. '*Jon wiley*,' said I, which means hello in Fulde. Apart from returning greetings he wasn't allowed to speak, only to listen. His expression was hang-dog. His friends told me he was thirty-two, and had paid 70,000 CFA (£170) for his bride, being helped by his father and friends. The couple were allowed to meet at night but had to spend these seven days apart, indoors among their respective friends who were giving them last-minute advice.

After some tea I was taken over to meet the bride at her mother-in-law's house. She was on a bed hidden behind a screen and a mosquito net. She was wearing a sheet and keeping her face averted. Her two best girlfriends sat on the edge of the bed, and the room grew packed as people came to look at the

161

foreigner who had come to greet the bride. My entourage included a young fisherman who was my translator since none of the women spoke French. In theory no man was allowed in the room but an exception was made so we could all chatter and get translations. The bride was sixteen, and looked like she needed a spell of fattening up. Outside the door women were dancing, stomping and hissing through their teeth.

Inside the room some had big amber beads in their hair, and one flashed a set of gold capped teeth. After half an hour I went to the house of the bride's elder brother, a lovely hut hung with Malian rugs. My entourage tried to follow me in so I shooed them all out; I felt like an invasion wherever I went. My host was a boatman doing business hiring out his three canoes, and he had recently bought his third outboard motor to fit a canoe of one hundred tons. His other canoes were thirty-five tons. He said none of them could get through to Tombouctou in this season, the water-level was too low and wouldn't rise until next year. The three outboard engines were clamped to the end of his bed, making me think of high-speed bedsteads.

Someone brought me a baby and said it was dying. It lay listless and dehydrated, no fever, no breathing problems, just wasting away. Its father told me there were two types of illness, one you could cure with medicines and the other caused by *djinns* which could only be treated by a maribou. Not wanting to give false hope I said I knew nothing about medicine except that the baby would have a better chance of survival if it could be persuaded to drink some of its mother's milk. One man suggested it would recover if someone saw or found an owl. Owls worked in close conjunction with the spirit world. We didn't find an owl but a maribou turned up. He felt the babe's skin and pulse rate, and he made movements to pull out the bad spirit, spitting to each direction to expel the disease. Then he gave the parents some dry plant medicine for inhalation and told them their child would live.

When we took off we followed the river's course north over a landscape of red dunes on the right bank and white dunes and pans on the left. There were no running tributaries, just an occasional damp wadi. We climbed up to 3,000 feet, below the top of the inversion layer and it was cold. Sooner than expected we saw Niafounké, where David had left a fuel stash a few days before. A pity to waste all that height but we had to come down, spiralling slowly to avoid damaging our eardrums. We refuelled, hoping to reach the regional capital of Goundam before nightfall, but as dusk fell we came to a huge lake. The far side of it was invisible, though according to our map the lake was not too wide. David flew around the edge for a short way then decided to go direct. I hoped he could swim, and we discussed how we'd ditch in the water if we had to.

It was dark when we spotted Goundam airstrip and since it was about ten miles from the town and we needed water and more fuel, we carried on. In the darkness we could just make out two colours of land, pale sand, probably soft, and darker sand, hopefully hard.

Before landing David cut the throttle back to idle so the motor's noise wouldn't attract attention. We chose a clear space a mile from town, touched down and parked by a sandy mound. I set off to town on foot with the empty jerrycan and water-flasks. As I passed some Peul tents on the outskirts two dogs rushed at me and I had to stand, swinging the jerrycan at them and yelling for some time before gruff voices cursed the dogs and called them away. A volley of stones rattled past my ears. I hoped they were aimed at the dogs not at me.

In town a man on a donkey told me there was no fuel station, no public water pump, and no cafés selling food. But there was a large building with a light inside. So I walked up its impressive stone stairway and in through double doors. It was very grandiose, built, I guessed, as the old colonial governor's seat of power. Voices murmured in the inner sanctuary. I called hello, and a chorus bade me to come in.

I had interrupted a meeting of the regional administrators. I explained about needing fuel and water, and they summoned a gendarme to show me the house of someone who sold black-market petrol. He also filled my flasks with water and helped me buy some round cakes of bread. By now the officials had finished their meeting. I bumped into one of them and thanked him for their help, and he invited me into another great hall up a different stone stairway.

Inside, seated around a large table, his colleagues were about to tuck into supper. 'Join us,' they said and ordered a servant to lay an extra plate. Between mouthfuls they discussed arrangements for the forthcoming visit to the region by the president. I didn't stay for the whole meal, as I knew David would be waiting for me.

Pegasus's wing lying rigged on the sand gave us two flat spaces underneath where we slept sheltered from the cold desert wind. At first light we were woken by the Goundam Male Spitting Choir, four youths who stood clearing their throats and hawking repeatedly in appreciation of Pegasus. They stayed for ten minutes then left. Dawn was too windy for take-off, and though part of me wanted to fly off to Tombouctou, part was quite happy to be delayed in such an odd place.

I discovered the hospital where they refilled my water-bottle and the doctor showed me round. Only one of the ten beds was occupied, by a woman who'd had a Caesarean birth. She already had seven children, and the doctor feared that next time would be a Caesarean job again. There were taboos which prevented these Moslems using contraceptives, and a woman needed her husband's permission. In this hospital's region there were only two women using family planning.

The operating theatre was tidy with boldly labelled cupboards and a book recording details of every patient seen. Deaths were fairly frequent but that was usually because people came here as a last resort, after their traditional medicine had failed, and it was already too late to save them.

Consultations were free. Medicine used to be but it was not valued. The doctor said now people had to pay a small charge of 100 CFA (24p) for a vaccine, and they were beginning to believe in it. Before this change, he had 160 patients daily, now he averaged sixty.

He invited me for lunch so I explained about David and went to fetch him. On the way back a boy on a fiesty strong horse noticed me admiring it and offered me a ride, thinking I'd be afraid. He wore no saddle or bridle, just a halter rope, and his right legs were hobbled to each other. He tried to bite me as I vaulted on to his back, so I growled at him. The ride was enormous fun because, with his legs hobbled, he couldn't buck or gallop. He paced along with short fast steps, like an explosive charge on a short fuse.

In the afternoon a Tuareg called Mohammed Ali took me for a walk in the encroaching dunes. After three miles it occurred to me that I might have put myself in a dangerous position. In the past I've had many a male escort through remote places and have never been harmed. But this time my companion wasn't an ordinary man, even for a Tuareg. There was a strange intensity in his piercing eyes. But it wasn't worth panicking,

164

common sense would do, and keeping the conversation respectable.

We were walking where dunes of red, gold and white sands met, and beyond them was a black flat-topped mountain. Mohammed described the dunes we had to climb as being five steps high, or whatever number of paces it would take to reach the ridge, bearing in mind how the very first step would start creating a slide from the top. It's not your footsteps that slip, it's the whole slope that moves.

Nearer the black mountain there were some nomad domes, and the sands had occasional plants and bushes. As we walked Mohammed told me how his family had been forced to come here by the drying desert, and were too poor to do anything about their fate. His own skill was as a specialist in the medicinal use of desert plants. He said he tried never to infringe on the hospital's role and he usually only took cases after the doctor had pronounced the illness incurable.

I pointed at a ground creeper of bush apples, an acid fruit that not even goats would eat, and asked if it was used in traditional medicine. 'It's a difficult plant because it's so poisonous, but it can be used for certain liver diseases,' Mohammed replied. 'You stew it, then drink and vomit. It should burn the illness out of the patient's system, though if it's taken too strong it's often fatal.' A moment later he went on, 'I had to make that medicine for myself in 1984. I'd become ill in the bad years when we lost everything, and the doctor said there was no treatment nor possible cure for that disease.' He had combined his traditional remedy with a strict diet. 'For a week I was close to death, but within another week I was back to strength. Illnesses are either hot or cold, blood or water, day or night. There are all kinds of opposites that apply and help you know how to treat the illness. There's no disease you can't diagnose by seeing and talking to the patient.' He had a curious way of clicking a tsk noise to emphasise his points. 'Tuaregs do also use sorcerers, and maribous use incantations, but I only deal with the reality of plant medicine.'

We paused to sit in the shade of a thorn tree. 'The dry thorns of this one are useful for pulling out infection, though for heavy infection we use a black stone.' I asked if this would be a black stone like mine from central Africa, and he said they were still carried up here on the old trade routes. He lit a pipe of tobacco, fashioned from a piece of carved bone.

Slowly I realised that here was a gifted man deeply involved with his knowledge; no wonder his eyes were bright. He was now working to catalogue all the medicinal plants and what treatments he used them for, making a book which he hoped would one day be used for research by Western doctors.

The majestic old colonial buildings of Goundam faded into the distance as we flew north again. The river began to meander in multiple loops and seemed to shrink, and in one bend the water disappeared altogether, leaving a dry bed. It reappeared on the next bend, seeping back out of the sand. Half an hour into the flight we had to make an emergency landing when one of the engine's two cylinders cut out. David swapped the spark plugs over and we buzzed back into the sky. We spent the night at a Sonrai camp in a sandy cove, and I bought some potatoes and tomatoes from them to add to our supper. We had misplaced our salt bag, so David suggested opening the Pilot Survival Kit. What a lousy package it was; no salt! It did have some tea-bags but they tasted of mixed Oxo cubes and chocolate, which had been packed together and melted.

Early next morning we spotted Tombouctou.

The image of Tombouctou as a fabled city of gold miles from anywhere visited by Western man owes its origins to Mansa Musa who was emperor of much of West Africa in the fourteenth century. When he went on a pilgrimage to Mecca he took 60,000 men, and eighty camels each carrying 300 pounds of gold dust. On his return to Tombouctou he decided to emulate the glories of the holy cities. He strengthened his lines of trade, built a palace and a mosque, and set up 180 Koranic schools. Tombouctou became a centre of culture and learning. One celebrated savant, Ahmed Baba, had a personal library of several thousand books.

In 1494 the much travelled Spanish Moor, Leo Africanus, visited the city and recorded in his *History and Description of Africa* that Tombouctou had 'a great store of doctors, judges, priests and other learned men, that are bountifully maintained at the king's expense'. But by the time the first Europeans, Laing, Caillie, Barth, found their way there at the beginning of the nineteenth century much was changed. The mud-based architecture had suffered the ravages of both weather and repeated invasion, so Tombouctou and its faded glories received a less than ecstatic press, perhaps disappointment coloured by the difficulties of getting there in the first place.

David and I had lunch beside a fountain in a garden restaurant on the edge of town and then I went to explore.

The first thing I noticed in the alleys was the thick wooden house doors studded with decorative brass designs and large round knockers. Above one door I saw a plaque telling me this was the house of the British explorer Gordon Laing, the first recorded European to reach Tombouctou, which he visited in 1826 after crossing the desert from Tripoli. But Laing did not live to bring back traveller's tales of the fabled city, as he was murdered by his Arab escort while recrossing the Sahara. The house was small and falling into ruins. It had one lower room and front terrace, and an upper enclosed balcony leading to another room. I climbed up the rubble of fallen masonry to peer in, despite a warning that the floors were about to collapse. Also I saw the house of Heinrich Barth, a German explorer, which was large and in better repair. From there I walked to the oldest mosque in Tombouctou, in the Jung Gareva quarter, unspecial, except for its ornate doors, so I carried on to the central market to buy provisions.

On the way back to the airport I got a lift with a handsome young Dutchman called Tom who was working with a Unicef irrigation scheme for growing rice. As David had not arrived at the airport, Tom took me off to lunch at an Italian colleague's house. The party also included a French man, an Arab lady and an East African girl from Burundi. Our Italian host, Michele, had prepared a fabulous lunch of *spaghetti aglio olio e peperoncino*, and *parmigiana di melanzane*. The talk was about rice husking machines which Tom was introducing and Michele explained how this project was unique in that its three million dollars had been funded by Italian socialist workers donating some hours' pay. Solar pumps were also being fitted to wells. 'But we don't tell people the pump is a gift, we say it's on loan and that they must pay a fee for it each year. The pump will only last about eight years, and the fee is one eighth of the cost of a new pump, so we keep the money for them and will use it to buy a new pump when the old one breaks.' What a clever way of keeping the system going.

They also used the 'food for work' scheme, though next year Michele wanted to try 'cash for work' since imported food aid did not help the economy, while cash would re-energise the local market. In addition the 'food for work' was open to bribery demands. The distributor would take his cut first; the driver who had to be hired to carry the nomads' sacks back to their families would take twenty per cent and every petty official and roadblock along the way would demand their share. Money might stay more intact.

After coffee I reluctantly said I had to get back to the airport. Tom offered to drive, and Michele said if I came back later in the day he'd lend me his horse, a Tamashek stallion.

At the airport David was working to adjust the carburettor, and it wasn't going to be ready to test for half an hour. And since we hadn't begun filing a flight plan, which should be done an hour before departure, it seemed sensible to postpone our next leg until the morning, giving David time to finish his work and let me take a short flying lesson, before going back to have a ride on Michele's horse.

I piloted badly in the lesson, my landings were shocking and my circuits lop-sided. I was mesmerised by the view of white dunes being blown grain by grain from the core of the Sahara and moving inexorably towards Tombouctou. Michele's house sat at the edge of the dunes. I could ride east from there for miles, the sands went on for ever. My concentration wasn't on my flying. On the third turn of a circuit I had my hands full with the turn and checks for finals, I forgot to slacken the throttle, so Pegasus climbed instead of descending. We came in to land trying to dive at the runway from 1,000 feet, twice the correct height. I should have enlarged the loop and done several things differently, but didn't. The landing was about to be so bad I let David take it over from me.

But when the stallion pranced out of his stable I felt relieved, here was something I did understand. Michele pointed to his four white hooves and said the Tuareg considered this a sign of distinction, a horse fit for a chief. He added that, conversely, in Italy four white feet were thought unlucky. The bridle was red leather with tassels and the usual strict bit. His saddle was traditional Tamashek with high pommel and back, usually worn without any girth strap. The Tuaregs don't put a saddle on a horse before mounting, they vault aboard with the saddle in one hand, putting it in place, then landing on it, and holding it there by the feet in the stirrups.

I set out west into the white dunes. The horse was fresh and we made good speed along the dips and basins, leaving the town far behind. Apart from some well-worn goat paths the sands held no footprints. We slowed to a walk to climb the sides of dunes, going up diagonally, heading for some ultra white dunes another mile away.

Rounding them we went down into a dry wadi, its flat course ideal for the horse to lope along at whatever speed he liked. The evening sky cast its hue on to the sand. Ahead I could see riverside cliffs and as we passed them the twilight began fading. It wasn't worrying because I felt sure the horse knew his way home. I turned his head east and threaded a route between the dunes, the horse skilfully and speedily picking his way through patches of soft sand. Night fell but I could see the distant lights of Tombouctou.

Back at Michele's garden gate, his houseboy couldn't open the catch because he held a baby-bottle of milk in one hand and a day-old goat in his arms. I dismounted and held the goat while he took the horse to be rubbed down. The goat nuzzled my hands and drank greedily from the bottle as I carried it into the house and wandered around seeing how the traditional Tombouctou layout gave a central living room with a corridor around and rooms leading off it. The corridor encouraged a breeze and this cooled the walls of all rooms.

On the living-room walls Michele had hung his collection of masks, camel panniers, and artefacts. I sank down to rest on the Malian floor rugs, and two kittens bounded over to play. The baby goat had finished suckling so I put him on his feet beside them. They chased around him, he took a few wonky steps, then a bound into the air, and landed sprawled flat. The kittens sniffed him and tapped him with their paws until he shook his head, got up, and sprang back into my lap for security.

Michele, David and I had supper at Tom's house and spent a marvellous evening eating more Italian food and examining the model of a cog-wheel pulley system that Michele wanted to offer as an alternative to water pumps. There are 180,000 of these still in use in Morocco, and they existed here until about 1959 when Mali became independent and threw the pulleys out as being too old-fashioned.

'And since 1959 there's hardly been a water survey done. I'm working from a 1952 aerial picture and archive records about the levels of the water table. We need to build up an idea of the current trends, and I'd like to know if a microlight would be suitable for aerial surveys and locating potential sources of water.'

This sparked off a whole new conversation which lasted late into the evening.

Tom and Michele came to wave goodbye at the airport. We were making an early start to get across a 140-mile stretch of desert. We would need to land and refuel somewhere, and were carrying the extra petrol. It gave me a curious thrill when David switched on the radio and gave our call sign. 'Tombouctou, this is Gold Mike Tango Lima Golf, ready to take off.' Not just the excitement of a journey, more simply the reality of being there, and leaving with good memories. Tombouctou would no more be just a name on a map. It was February 16th, exactly three months since we had arrived in Africa.

Thirteen

Masked Dancers of Bandiagara

We flew south towards the Niger River, which lies six miles from the town. 'Isn't that one of Tom and Michele's irrigation schemes?' David said as we overflew some neatly laid out rice fields with straw windbreaks. Beyond them was the river, then only the desert, rows of parallel dunes remarkable for their red tops and white valleys. The colours blended on the slopes into shades of pink.

Our engine temperatures were not reading evenly, one cylinder was much too hot. We hoped the instrument was misreading. By pressing the glass David could make the needle drop to normal. I suggested we flew along with him making the gauge read a safe heat.

We thought we were on a straight line course, heading ultimately for Douentza again, but as usual it was impossible to tell how the wind at this height was affecting our line. There were few landmarks to judge by. After one and a half hours we expected to pass the west tip of Lake Garou and go over Lake Niangay. At one and three-quarter hours we still hadn't seen any lakes, only scrubby bush desert. Niangay should have been twenty-three miles wide, how could we miss it?

David thought he could pick out the shape of a dry lake-bed which he said must be Lake Niangay. People in Tombouctou had assured us the lakes still existed, and I felt certain that, even if they were seasonal, not permanent as the map showed, they could not have leafy bushes growing in them.

Then we spotted a derelict-looking village which tied in on the map with David's theory of dry lakes. Refusing to agree, I studied the map and suggested the village could be one of several we might see if we had drifted east with less of a crosswind than anticipated. It still frustrated me not being able to know either our ground speed or the sideways drift.

Below us was another vastness of parallel dunes in pink and white. Twenty minutes later we saw a lake. It shouldn't have been there. Its shape bore no relation to anything on the map.

David did some rapid calculations and said that if by chance this was Niangay, we were flying into headwinds and we'd never make it to Douentza. We climbed to 4,500 feet to give us a better view, then we cruised around in loops, casting for signs. In one bushy basin I thought I saw an elephant, but this was too far north for elephants, I told myself, it was more likely to be an anthill. I switched my attention back to looking for shapes which might be marked on a map. As before, none of the ground features fitted any part of our map. It was time to admit we were lost.

Our fuel gauge showed ten litres left; we needed to stop and refuel from the jerrycans, and our muscles were stiff from two and a half hours' flying. We landed on a spacious purple gravel sweep, with a few anthills and many dead trees, skeletal white in the glaring sun. While we sat in the shade of the wing and pored over the maps, some Peul tribesmen appeared in billowing robes and with swords slung from their shoulders. I asked if they knew where we were.

Unfortunately none of them could speak French, only Fulde. Twelve years ago I had learnt some words of Fulde, useful phrases like 'Where is . . .?' and now I racked my brains to remember. *Ipi* sprang to mind but I suspected that was 'where is' in Zulu. Slowly some words came: *ndiam*, meaning lake or water; *dar larde*, in the bush; and *me ander*, I don't know. With these and by watching the Peuls' reactions to area names and finding out which ones were local, then pointing in the direction of each name, we attempted to centre our position. The men were puzzled but helpful, though their idea of direction could be totally misleading, as we had found before.

The man beside me had pulled out a dainty silver tobacco pipe of tiny trumpet shape whose wider end was beautifully engraved with patterns, and, after filling it with dusty Tuareg tobacco he lit it by striking a knife against a stone flint over a scrap of fluffy tinder.

Despite our pact that we would never fly in the midday thermals, we decided it would be better than sitting in the heat of the desert. So we took off, and David lopped one of the wingtips into a dust-devil to help us gain lift.

172

Pegasus purred along comfortably; there were stretches of calm air and stretches where we bubbled along on soft thermals. Below us the pale sand had dark smooth outcrops of rock like stone dunes. Sometimes the whole view looked like a burned pie crust.

Moving south we came to some belts of scrub, which we guessed might be Benzema pan since our map marked water-holes there. Benzema was where there were still some herds of elephants, said to be the remnants of the herds that supplied Hannibal with his elephants for crossing the Alps.

An hour later we spotted a 3,000-foot mountain barrier dead ahead. This was reassuring, our map showed we should follow them west and they'd lead us to Douentza. These were the mountains we had already flown along the southern side of when we had camped the night in a wind trap.

The north side was no better. Turbulence broke out around us and with one fearful jolt we rocketed up faster than the gauge could show. We were still a few miles from the north-facing cliffs of the mountains but obviously we were encountering seething wind currents spinning back from the wall. A lurch sideways made me grab for handholds, a wump down, and another, I tightened my seat-belt.

It was like hitting holes in the air; we seemed suddenly to stop flying and drop straight down. David stayed silent and concentrated on flying us through it. Twice we 'went negative' as gravity forces shot fast towards the border of human limits, and I wondered how much more stress the microlight could take before breaking up.

We tried to climb out of the turbulence, and at 6,000 feet we reached the top of the inversion layer. The air was very cold but less rough. It was rather stunning to fly along level with the flat plateau on the mountain massif, seeing down the sheer drops of its cliffs, and being able to pick out impressive isolated cylindrical peaks towering 1,000 feet higher.

The visibility was deteriorating rapidly with thick dust in the air. And we were tiring fast, we had been flying for four and a half hours. I didn't know whether to feel thirsty and hungry, or sick from the continual pockets of turbulence. We gritted our teeth and went on.

It was with great relief that we finally landed at Douentza. In the evening I met someone who said there had not been water in Lakes Niangay and Do since 1973, and when I asked

173

about the lake we'd seen to the south he said, 'Oh yes, that's Benzema, it's a very flooded water-hole.'

We had both been right: Lake Niangay was where David had seen its shape, but it hadn't been a lake for so long that bushes had grown. Even the elephant had been in the right place. The incident boosted my faith in David's navigation. He had never actually been lost today, and as a pilot he had certainly come through an evil rough flight with flying colours.

At sundown I sat for coolness on the roof of Fiona's house and was busy writing when I heard music. It was the thumpings of many women pounding millet with wooden pestles, each thud echoing off several mud walls, combined with the hand-claps by some women on an upstroke, and others snapping two fingers together or calling a thrilling ululation to encourage their companions, all blending into a rhythmic harmony.

Dawn on the rooftop was punctuated with calls to prayer: '*Allah-ah-hab! Allahaaah-washbar!*' The last two syllables came out with terrific gusto and abrupt staccato endings.

I piloted the morning's flight, to make myself get over the horrors of the last one. At take-off Pegasus didn't do her usual hurtle forward and pop away from the ground; this time she seemed reluctant to let go. David explained he'd moved the trike's hang-pin into its front hole which changed its pitch and made the wing take longer to reach flying speed, less economical on fuel but it would give us greater speed in flight, and meant the aircraft would be more quickly responsive to my hands on the bar.

We were heading in a good tailwind south-west back to Sévaré and the delta. Visibility was great, showing all the cracks in the mountain range beside us; deep sheer ravines made black knife-sharp shadows. From the ravine's narrow mouths came tongues of white sand, dry stream-beds seasonally running a short way into the desert.

A bit of light turbulence sent me scurrying up to 3,000 feet where the air was smooth. It was lovely flying. Northwards I could see for about forty miles, infinite dune crescents which made flecked scrolling patterns. After an hour, despite our altitude, thermals started bursting off the ground and catching us quite forcefully.

It was hard work keeping the microlight on course. The air was jerking around and we were forced along with it. 'Don't fight it,' said David, so I relaxed and discovered that by using the bar lightly but firmly, I could feel how to fly.

We saw the River Niger and the glint of lakes in the delta after one and a half hours' flight; my muscles were aching from having to recorrect our course, and the turbulence was increasing as the sun's heat hit the land.

The wind-sock at Sévaré airport was horizontal, indicating a fifteen-knot crosswind, as we descended and made a pass over the runway because our radio wasn't working. The controller couldn't hear us, but we could hear him telling us, 'You are inedible. Say again. You are inedible.'

Then he saw us, recognised us and cleared us to land.

In the next two days David and I brought my flying hours under instruction up to twenty. I should have made more progress, but conditions had not always been favourable. In among the pretend emergency landings we had two real power failures. They taught me why I should get my glide assessment right.

It was time for David to take the engine apart and de-coke it. We wheeled the trike into the airport's passenger lounge, turning it into a temporary workshop. As David's work would take several days, it gave me the chance to go off for a jaunt along the Bandiagara escarpment.

By noon I was standing beside the Bandiagara road waiting for a lift. The morning wind had blown into a duststorm, which blasted along the unpaved road picking up heavy clouds of grit. I hunched my shoulders and pulled down the brim of my hat.

An old jalopy bulging with passengers trundled past, followed by a brand-new Toyota which stopped for me. The driver was an Italian Protestant missionary whose stereo cassette machine was playing choirs backed by organ pipes, like heavenly pops. Dust-devils fifty yards wide spun away to both sides of us.

Southwards the ground became rockier until the whole landscape was filled with rock, flat knobbled expanses, low cliffs, wind-sculpted boulders, and an occasional clump of fan palm trees or a Dogon village. The missionary explained that this escarpment area was an enclave of Dogons, culturally isolated from outside influences by living in a cliff 1,000 feet tall and so steep there were few ways up or down. In the middle of strongly Moslem country, they were still ancestor-worshippers, their beliefs expressed in amazing funerary celebrations famed for their masked stilt dancers.

'Do you convert many to Christianity?' I asked, and the missionary replied there were few. To be exact, his church had converted one family, and they were Tuareg not Dogon. But the record was better than for their mission in Tombouctou which had only one convert.

After forty miles we reached Bandiagara, which was still fifteen miles from the cliffs. The next day a young contact called Ibrahim took me out by Mobylette to the remotest southern section and a clifftop village called Jiggi-bombo. Something was happening there. A man was standing on a rooftop, pacing to and fro shouting and gesticulating. Ibrahim said this was the start of a dance to honour the dead and the man was standing on the roof of the deceased villager's hut calling out the good deeds he had done in his life. Men's spirits are believed to linger in the cliffs and can cause disharmony in local villages. The dance is to console them and reconcile them to being dead.

Masked figures dressed in black bush-fibre skirts clambered up a ladder on to the flat roof and, as each set foot on the top he began a vigorous solo dance with many high jumps in the air. The small rooftop became crowded, the costumed figures kept dancing, now joined by a second type of mask: long-mouthed black ones which encased men's heads and had eye-holes rimmed with cowrie shells, and a kind of cockerel's comb on top also embellished with cowries. Their arm bands sprouted grasses sticking up to head height and the dancers pumped their arms to and fro while stomping with knees raised high.

On the ground a crowd gathered around huts bordering an open sandy space. Masked men ducked out of sight and hastened into position, each waiting his turn to emerge into that space for solo and troupe dances. Six lizard masks appeared and began to gyrate.

Coming towards me were two men whose masks led up in to twelve-foot poles topped by red tufts; the men balanced the poles with caution and moved into a steady rhythmic dance, while behind them some cow masks were whirling and twisting, bending over to smack their wooden horns on the ground. Another twirled and slapped his horns into the dust like an angry bull.

Ibrahim told me that each dancer was free to choose his own mask, and make it or ask the village blacksmith to do so. Only

176

the best dancers could carry the tall masks. Their dance took on precise steps according to the symbolic meaning of each mask.

The importance of masks is their reputed power to transform the wearer, breaking through the human bonds into a different aspect of the natural world. Wearing a mask representing a cow, hare, snake, tree, another person, or even a building, the man takes on its character and temporarily loses his own. Some masks I could not identify Ibrahim named as Kananga and Soulinge, a fifteen-foot-tall mask, from Dogon religious mythology.

One of the masks slipped and the man retired to re-attach it, helped by a hyaena-masked friend who introduced himself with the customary hand-clack of Dogon initiates. Dancers in masks are forbidden to speak to each other in normal words, they must use a language called Sigi So. This may only be spoken by initiated men in mythological story-telling or while masked. Masked, the men find Sigi So comes fluently even for those who had never really learned to speak it.

Onlookers wore conical straw hats and carried ancient rifles. Some held drums which they beat while a chorus chanted and two tiny women trilled in their throats. Masked raffia devils circulated in the crowd to seek out and frighten rebellious women. One singled me out, leaping around me as a warning to behave and be unobtrusive about photography.

Two men on stilts five feet tall strode along above the crowd's heads; not the type of stilt with hand extensions, these ended splayed under the men's feet and were bound on with cloth cross-straps. Their legs were encased in red grasses, below long black bush-fibre skirts, and cowrie bedecked masks whose cloth chins hung down to their knees. The performance of the stilt men was prefaced by paying respects to the village elders, the men touching their elbows and putting their hands behind their backs, symbolically asking permission to dance. The deceased man being honoured at this party had died about three years before, but for Dogons it was usual for a family to save for up to three years in order to hold this event. At the 'dama' ceremony, which happened every few years, dead men's names would be given to their grandchildren, to ward off disaster and to establish the dead as ancestors.

A procession took off through the village and Ibrahim beckoned me to follow. The winding alleys threaded among tall square granaries with thatched tops. I found Ibrahim waiting for me beside a half-built granary, its clay base divided into four bins, and on the outside there was a series of dots in the mud to show how much grain it was expected to hold. Below the door were white dribbles which my friend said were an offering – juice of wild grapes mixed with millet flour, fermented, and splattered on to the granary's outer door to protect grain for the future. On the village's outskirts we noticed isolated women's menstruation huts, also daubed with protective magic against harmful influences.

The most spectacular house was home of the spiritual leader, the hogon, who told people what to sacrifice if he saw a bad omen and appeased the ancestors who could ask the gods for mercy. The hogon seldom went out, except to make offerings, his needs being tended by a young disciple. A hogon's house is called Ginna which means 'mother of houses'. The front of this one was tall with many square niches containing offering jars. According to the anthropologist Marcel Griaule, 'there should be eight rows of ten niches each, representing Lebe, the eight primordial ancestors with their descendants. These niches are the final abodes of those ancestor spirits and should never be walled up because the spirits need to breathe fresh air. Ten swallows' nests are put in the ten round niches at the top because the swallow is the bird of the ancestors.' This Ginna also had a line of cows' horns, poking out singly at eye level from a border of decorative stones.

From there Ibrahim took me to the edge of the village to see the fetish shrine, a small grey mound of cracked mud with stones and forked sticks around it. I was not allowed to approach the fetish since I wasn't initiated. Ibrahim said that inside the mound is a statuette occasionally sprinkled with the blood of black cows.

From the main square we could still hear drumming although most dancers had by now disbanded. The day was growing hot, it was time for us to continue a mile further and find the way down the 1,000-foot sandstone escarpment.

Ibrahim knew the way down, following a dry watercourse over smooth sloping rock bulges and scrambling vertically down beside a waterfall. It had gouged holes through the rock in its first drop. The holes went straight down and out of a cave below. At the base of that waterfall we turned along the edge of a greater gorge. Pressed to a sheer wall, we had to squeeze between boulders on a kind of natural staircase. Down over knobbled rocks and ironstone rims, finding hand- and foot-holds, I kept having to stop and dig thorns out of the soles of my sandals, only knowing they were there when I stepped hard on rock and the thorn tips jabbed into my feet.

Ibrahim slid out of sight over a ledge and called me to feel for a notched wood tree which served as a ladder. Gradually, in descending into the final canyon, the path became clearer, its steps better placed. Some huts came into sight, tucked in under the base of the cliff, and a derelict hogon's house. At one p.m. we reached the bottom. It was hot with a hot wind. A mile further we came to Kani Kombole village and went to see a friend of Ibrahim who helped me hire a horse. I wanted to make a jaunt of several days along the cliff base with its extraordinary Dogon life, and see something of the plains afterwards. There are 300 villages along 120 miles of cliff, an extraordinary concentration.

Our lunch of sweetened millet gruel, *la crème de mille*, was surprisingly filling. Then everyone lay back and went to sleep. The horse had been sent for. I fell asleep too, and didn't wake until the mid-afternoon call to prayer echoed off the cliffs.

Blackhorse III arrived, a little mare. Her red and yellow leather saddle was comfortable, with trowel-sized stirrups, but the bridle had no reins; just a halter rope and metal bit, though easy to steer with the single rope by holding it out or against her neck.

We loped through a woodland of baobab trees growing in rock falls. They were ring-barked in two parts, the fibre being used for the type of costumes I'd already seen; the branches now leafless and bare except for an odd round pod too high for people to knock down with stones. Monkeys and squirrels scampered away over the rocks. Birds flitted around the cliffs, tiny red birds, a big turquoise kingfisher, and hoopoes with curved beak and swooping flight.

Villages were more scarce, and so naturally camouflaged they were hard to pick out. I saw a boy shouting at the cliffs and assumed he was mad, until an answering voice came from the scree and I realised a village was sitting there almost invisibly. Further back, up where the scree met the cliffs, there were the ruins of Tellem villages.

These cliffs have been inhabited since about 500 BC. The

Dogons didn't arrive until the fifteenth or sixteenth century, probably coming from the Mali empire which had begun crumbling. They found a flourishing Tellem culture already here and simply took over its territory, customs, art, carvings and masks. Everything I had seen of Dogon culture had belonged originally to the Tellem.

Blackhorse III offered a very good jog and an eager walk, belying her low head carriage. She had a sweet nature and was well trained; when I dropped her rope she stopped, and waited patiently without moving off while I wandered around on foot. Re-mounting was made complicated because her girth strap couldn't be tightened and now that she'd stopped puffing out her belly the cinch hung very loose. The saddle slipped when I tried to hop on from the ground so I looked for a mounting block.

The closest candidate was an anthill. I led her beside it and climbed up but at the vital moment the anthill collapsed. My feet went into a hollow, red fire biting; I leaped up brushing off the ants and stamping fiendishly until all were gone. A fallen rock made a safer block and we continued south-west. The evening was breezy, though with no sign of the duststorm I'd encountered that morning.

In Kani Bonzon village, which was reputed to be where the first Dogons settled, I noticed some stunningly carved little wooden doors set in the sides of granaries, depicting masked men and mythical animals. One had a catch worked by entwining a man and woman.

Some children ran after me as we left the village and, wanting peace and quiet, I urged Blackhorse into a gallop. The saddle slid horrendously forward on to her neck. Rather than go through the whole re-saddling process I looked for uphill ground where I could wriggle it back underneath me. There was one hill, a vibrantly red clay tongue, that extended for miles, which was fortunate since I didn't dare ride downwards, and it led me around again to Kani Kombole where I spent the night. My host, Boureima, was a leather worker. Sheep's leather saddlebags decorated with tassels were slung over his knees, he sewed with an awl and leather thread, cutting strips for leather tassels and using an arc-shaped tool on a deeply grooved flat bit of wood. His wife Howah winnowed millet and the goats scampered around grabbing any grains that fell. I listened to the village; some talk in raised voices came booming off cliffs

180

while murmurs eddied around. For coolness I slept on the roof, reached by climbing an unsteady notched tree ladder.

Dawn crept over the village roofs, then women with clay pots silhouetted on their heads went in ones and twos to the well. My neighbour's wife carried her babe slung under her arm to suckle as she walked. All the women exchanged morning greetings with an old man who was leaning on a stick at the path corner. The greeting had a rhythm consisting of repetitive sounds at changing intervals. They started with two voices, then one and a new, then another new fresh voice, each joining in with the same pattern of response, starting with *'Na?'* *'Sewo'*, *'Gisewo'*, *'Sewo'*, *'Yapo'*, *'Sewo'*. Translated, *sewo* meant good, fine; *yapo*, you come here gather water/food; *gisewo*, without children; *nisevey*, with children. Perhaps the music was in the way the second voice took over from the first part and saluted a new voice, or voices answered in chorus, and when two groups passed each other I heard a double chant, carrying on distantly as they went their separate ways, greeting other different voices down the path.

Blackhorse and I made an early start. It was such glorious countryside, I revelled in the shape of the cliffs, the colossal shelves of overhangs, the occasional villages halfway up, and Tellem remains up even higher where paths had fallen away. Unreachable, their granaries were now roofless and derelict, just tall rectangular boxes raised off the ground on small stone platforms. Angular shadows of the wood prongs and hanging poles stuck out in lines from the granary walls.

Other poles were used to haul dead bodies up into the cliffs high above the villages, a funeral rite still practised here. The body, in a shroud, is pulleyed up on long ropes of baobab fibre tied on to a makeshift stretcher, to be walled into a rock niche or mud-walled tomb to stop birds getting in. Near the body are left the things it might need: oil, mask, gun, hat and farming hoe. In death, people simply move up the cliff. Ancestors are closer to God and can intercede on behalf of the living. Men, women and infants have separate nooks and there are reputed to be other caves for victims of infectious disease.

The cliffs towered ever higher. Blackhorse picked her way through the rock falls. The day was oven hot and windy but water abounded. We passed occasional villages. In the shade of a tree a man was shaving a boy's head, leaving only a tuft at the front, centred above the forehead. He explained that each family has a different design, so their children can be recognised and identified.

I was on my way to Ennde market where we stopped to rest at a delightful courtyard full of small clay ovens with tunnel entrances, and square dumpy granaries with doors of decorated wood. I bought a bale of hay for Blackhorse and went to the market. The noisiest women had tattooes on their stomachs in spreading tree patterns and arabesques.

Later I climbed up the cliff scree to some Tellem ruins and an old hogon Ginna. A dark cave beckoned and in it I found some ancient Tellem stilts, and raffia costumes which seemed to fall apart at the touch.

When the heat of the afternoon had passed I rode off once more along the cliffs until sunset threw red daggers across the sky. The sound of Blackhorse's hooves cantering on baked clay awakened a long moment of pure rare joy. It took me back to my very first black horse, Diablo, twelve years ago in Cameroun. I had realised then that horse travel was special but not all the wonderful places it was going to take me, up the Great Rift Valley of Kenya, across the New Guinea highlands, and from Lake Van to Mount Ararat.

Two stallions grazing free near a village looked up at our hoofbeats and began to follow my mare. Catching up with us, one got pesky, crowding Blackhorse from behind, and to protect her honour I had to get the whip out to threaten them to stay away.

I had planned to spend the night at Sadia which was reputed to have an interesting mosque. But when I arrived there I found I had ridden into a celebration to mark the circumcision of small girls. About twelve of them, only five years old, had been circumcised a week before, and were now being re-presented to their community. The maribou sat cross-legged in the fading sun outside the handsome multi-buttressed mosque. I asked someone if the maribou was also the hogon, but the people couldn't understand my French. With patience I managed to learn that the circumcision was done by an old woman in the village, the knowing one. Boys are also circumcised at about seven years old. As to the purpose of female excision, they said: 'She must or she'd be ashamed. No Dogon would marry an uncircumcised woman. It keeps her faithful, and if she were unfaithful her friends would sing songs about her badness. Infidelity is uncommon.'

Masked Dancers of Bandiagara

The infant girls stood nervously in a line before the assembled population perhaps wondering what was going to happen to them next. Women went forward and hung necklaces of polished stones around each girl's neck, adding layers to their already decorative appearance. We watched the benediction of the infants by the maribou. Following his lead, everyone raised their hands in prayer, then made circular emcompassing hand movements and prayer responses.

Facing the mosque, behind the infants, was the *case de palaver*, where men gathered daily to discuss village life. The roof, of deeply mounded millet stalks, was held up on stumpy forked posts carved with women's breasts. These erotic supports symbolised the eight ancestors of which Amma was the chief father and the creator.

I arranged to stay with the village trader, Amadou, who also had a horse. We tethered Blackhorse by a front hoof to a stake. Wanting to keep her strong I bought millet and hay but the moment I put it down beside her a flock of sheep rushed over to eat it. The only solution was to employ a small boy to chase them away. Innumerable children came to stare at me and I asked some larger ones to chase the others away. The little ones scarpered so fast and blindly that some ran straight through the millet-stalk fence, punching holes with their bodies.

A tea boy began swinging a fire basket to light the charcoal, waving it to and fro with a mixture of wood embers, then in full overarm circles. Amadou's stallion was also tethered by a front leg, near the fence where there was a hole and sheep went through. The horse was playing a game of trying to bite the sheep as they passed. When children were chased through, the horse tried to bite them too. He was an unbroken yearling, good-natured but bored with the tether.

While sitting drinking tea, a boy leapt up and smashed a scorpion, a pale sandy colour, two inches long. He said the sting hurts for three days but isn't fatal. If it stung a chicken the bird would die in a couple of minutes.

When I asked Amadou his age he answered, 'Wait, I have to look on my birth certificate,' then, showing it to me he boasted, 'it's a rare man who has one of these.' He had two wives, one of whom was at home and she showed me her room, going in through a door embellished with burnt circle designs and an elaborate Dogon catch. The second wife had an identical adjoining front door into an identical but mirror opposite room. Even

183

with such equality, Amadou admitted that having two wives was unrestful. It's fairly common for a husband and wife to live apart until several years after their marriage. She visits him and if she doesn't produce any children there can be divorce. When she moves in with her husband she may leave her first one or two babies with her parents to recompense them for her departure.

Many of Sadia's women wore brass nose rings. Among their children I noticed some very distended bellies, probably due to worms not malnutrition since their arms and legs looked healthy enough. To amuse them I lent out biros for a drawing competition. Paper had to be shared. One boy ventured to admire my skin colour, saying it was more useful than black skin since you can write on it in biro.

Supper was millet with fish sauce in a green slime of baobab leaves, and I was hungry enough to find it good.

In the morning I helped Amadou's wife with the daily chore of feeding termites to the chickens. To collect the termites she had put a cloth containing cowshit into an anthill hole in the ground. Overnight the cloth had attracted scores of termites. She said she did this every morning and evening, and that the chickens didn't mind what type of termites, large or small, though certain ones were tastier.

The circumcised infants were being washed and dressed early in their best clothes for the next stage of their celebration. Plastic beads and desert stones were being hung around their hips and necks. The jewellery was not being given to them which seemed a bit unfair after all they'd been through. It stayed the property of their mothers and would be used again for younger sisters when their turn came.

That day I rode north-east under the cliffs. At Guimini village it was market day and I saw some women whose teeth had been filed to points, six at the top and six below, which reminded me of the Dogon dentist who'd fixed my tooth after I fell off the cliff near Douentza. One woman wore a tall comb on her head, with the sides of her hair braided to the scalp but the top section was pure punk, standing on end and bound into a crest like a Roman soldier's helmet. Her baby howled at the sight of *me*.

Near Guimini was a route up the cliffs, one of the few, and I sadly knew that, once I had returned Blackhorse, this was the way I should have to go back to Bandiagara to rejoin Pegasus and David.

Masked Dancers of Bandiagara

Going up the cliff was more complicated than coming down. The Mobylette I hired to take me from Kani Kombole to Guimini gave up the ghost halfway and I had to continue on foot. I joined a group of women who were returning to their village, Yawa, at the top of the cliffs. They walked in a line, five women with pots and baskets balanced on their heads, all equal height and moving in step. I marched at the back, feeling incongruous. Halfway up the cliffs we began climbing steeply. At sunset we were still climbing, following a ledge up a ravine. Light faded but the moon and the stars were bright enough to see by. I was very tired by the time we reached the top.

Yawa was set on a great slab of rock worn into different levels on the end of a bluff. I was allowed to camp in the chief's yard which overlooked the vast plain. After breakfast one of the women from the previous day's climb took me to salute the chief's father, who was now retired at the age of ninety-eight. Finally I paid my respects to the current chief who gave me a bowl of creamy milk with gobs of delicious yoghourt-butter floating in it. He said he had thirty cows and employed Peuls to graze his herds in the bush. He also had three wives, and suggested I became the fourth. The region was so beautiful, I was almost tempted to accept.

FOURTEEN

Mauritanian Sands

Later that day I arrived back in Bandiagara to find that things had not gone smoothly for anyone else. I located the microlight and David at the Catholic mission station, but David had already been through the hands of Bandiagara's worst rogue, a conman known for his cheating and bullying of tourists. My friend Ibrahim had tried to extract David from his mercenary clutches but failed, so Ibrahim had tried to come and find me, fearing that I'd got stuck at the cliffs. He had spent a whole day searching for me, which made me feel very guilty. On top of that Ibrahim had been temporarily turned out of the hut he rented because its owner had come to stay. Part Malian, part Moroccan, he was considered to be a descendant of Mohammed, and he brought with him the servants and disciples his position warranted, leaving little room for Ibrahim. And Ibrahim was unhappy because although the man was wise and religious he kept finding fault with things, making my friend afraid to go home.

We were housed by the Catholic mission, though they didn't normally take guests. I particularly liked the Frenchman, Father Paul, who used to be a water diviner, or as the locals said '*un sorcier de l'eau*'. He used the pendulum method; it would turn right to indicate clean water, and left for undrinkable water.

Father Paul said he had not intended to be a diviner, indeed had scoffed at the idea. But dabbling once with a pendulum, he had received extremely accurate responses. So he was tested in Dakar, with cups of oil, water, petrol, diesel, sweet water and dirty water hidden under a sheet. The priest was handed labels and told to place them on the right cups and he went around with his pendulum until he discovered the nature of each.

186

As an officially certified diviner he worked in conjunction with some geologists. They would tell him about the strata below, and at what levels water might lie, coupling their knowledge with his talent. It was not always an easy relationship. Near Bandiagara the geologists had tried seven bore-holes and blamed him for their failure to find water. They hardly listened when he said there was plenty. But he had insisted they tried again and this time they hit an artesian gusher at twenty-five cubic feet per second.

But a diviner's life is tiring, Father Paul said. He hadn't ever slept well; receiving jumbled messages through his subconscious, it was unrestful. Now he had given it up, reverting to the tranquillity of simple priesthood.

After hopping back to Sévaré to load the rest of our gear, we set off on the first leg of a 300-mile flight to Mauritania, leaving them repainting the cleanest airport in Mali for the presidential visit.

At sunset we spotted a hamlet in a sandy open area among baobab trees on the western edge of the delta. We landed a bit heavily, our wheels scoring into the clay, then hit a bump which threw us into the air at an angle. That was a bad moment, especially when we could hear we had chipped our new propeller on its first day out. We re-landed safely, dodged to avoid an anthill, and came to a halt under a big spreading baobab.

The propeller had a small chunk torn out of one blade, and David set about mending it with Araldite. We camped there under the baobab, with plenty of firewood and a great starry sky. It was heaven. Some people from the hamlet brought us milk, dried meat, and tea. They were Bello, former slaves of the Tuareg. Most of them only spoke Tamashek but one called Ali spoke French and introduced me to his elder brother, who had a wooden leg, and was the tribe's wood carver. I asked if he could find us a couple of hardwood prongs to fix our damaged wingtip baton ends. They had been scraped on the ground so often they were at breaking point. He began hunting around for the right wood.

David's gluing of the propeller had been successfully filed to a smooth edge, and many people came to help us clear a runway. They didn't really understand why we were brooming the desert, and admittedly we looked ridiculous, but all helped willingly. Some men turned up on camels and I noticed their saddles were Moorish not Tuareg ones. This Moorish version had stubbier fronts and two large wings at the sides.

Before we left, Ali's brother hobbled over to present me with four beautifully carved wooden forks, a perfect fit into the wing batons.

By midday we were being buffeted by thermals over massive rice paddies. Fuel became critically short. I watched the level in the gauge fall until only an inch of fuel showed, meaning we would run out in approximately six minutes. We came down fast, on what looked like a flat smooth dry mud. But as we touched down I realised there was an irrigation ditch right across our path.

'Look out,' I yelled, and David whacked on full power to get off the ground again, but the ditch was close. At the last instant he pushed the bar out to flare the wing, and Pegasus hopped over the ditch. We landed, rolling at speed, and saw a second ditch coming at us. David jammed on the brake, a metal bar against the front wheel, though we weren't going to stop in time.

So he accelerated again, without the speed to jump it but the mound of earth along its side threw us up enough to get across. Down and again trying to brake, still no possibility of stopping before the third ditch. The microlight went straight over it; fortunately it was filled in with sand, only jolting us, and finally we did manage to stop just short of the fourth channel. I made rude comments about entering Pegasus for the Grand National next year.

Our display had been spotted by the rice-workers who came running over. When we asked where we were we learnt we were only five miles north of our heading. The next fuel stash, at Sokolo's gendarmerie, was only eight miles away.

I went looking for the irrigation project manager to apologise for landing in his field, and found, not surprisingly, it was being run by a Dutch team. They wondered cautiously about the use of microlights for crop spraying. But they told us how they had learnt you cannot plunge headlong into improving innovations. They explained they had bought some mechanical bird-scarers to frighten the birds off the crops, but had never used them when they discovered half the local children ex-pected to be employed for this job and it was an important contribution to the family income.

Between Sokolo and the frontier at Nara our map was featureless, a marvellous chance to get lost with no idea of our speed or drift, though our shadow moved fast over the sand. Buffeted by more thermals that sent us into negative gravity on the up force, I was very aware that I couldn't have flown this part. David was using all his strength. As Pegasus lunged left David's arms shot out to counterbalance. Another gust sent us into a hole of negative forces. I wished we were down on the ground, but at the same time I dreaded the idea of landing, it would be turbulent. David was equally worried about the prospect.

One and a half hours into flight, we had not seen any of our way-points and had no way to find our position on the map, so when we next saw a village we landed in the sand nearby. Blinded by the glare of heat we didn't see a tree stump in our path but David did a quick swerve and it missed our nose wheel, passing harmlessly under our back axle wires. We rolled to a halt; it was two p.m. and the land's heat hit us like a furnace. The villagers said this was Nowalena, one hundred miles south of Nara; we had missed our mark rather widely. After lunch with the villagers we re-oriented ourselves to the wind-striated land and set an angled course.

Eventually in the late afternoon we sighted Nara and our last fuel stash in Mali, and the following day I concluded the Customs formalities with some friendly policemen who insisted on sharing their goat's rib meal.

Our way-points over the Mauritanian border were a sickle-shaped dry seasonal mud-pan and a dry stream. But the shapes we saw on the open sandiness below could have been interpreted in many ways and we were soon disagreeing amicably in our guesswork. At one point we might have been reduced to guesswork for the rest of the trip as, glancing at the map case, I saw with horror it had come open facing downwards and the ruler and protractor were sliding out. Not only would they have been irreplaceable here, but they were likely to be whizzed into the propeller. We had already broken one propeller when a string came untied. Both David and I grabbed to close the case in the nick of time. Suitably chastened, when we saw a big village ahead, we landed to ask the way.

We were taken to the chief, a large old man and the most revered maribou of the region, claiming direct descendancy from the Prophet, who lived in a clay house with pillars at either side of a canework dais on which he sat cross-legged. There were red and blue Arab carpets on the floor, and tin trunks and chests containing his possessions, all rather Arabic.

Strictly an Islamic country, I was aware of a complete difference between Mali and Mauritania. Various men shook hands with David, but not with me. Instead they put their hand to their chest in salute, unable to touch a strange woman. I had to be extra polite, since it was considered an insult for a man such as this maribou to have to speak to a woman. Men came in and greeted the maribou, kneeling to kiss the palm of his hand then press it to their forehead, and he passed his other hand over their head while muttering a benediction.

We were given a wooden bowlful of *zrig*, sweetened cow's milk which looked as if it had sour gobs on it but was actually delicious. Even David drank his share; normally he was too worried about catching tuberculosis. Next came a tray of gooey dates, different from the dried ones we were accustomed to crunching, and these we dipped in rancid butter which made a tasty combination.

People were talking in Hassani, a dialect of Arabic; their faces weren't narrow like Peul or broad-eyed like Tuareg, and they said they were Moors. Mauritania has several ethnic groups and about seven castes, the dominant and most noble being the Hassanes, descendants of Arab warriors who came here in the 1500s. They ensured the protection of the maribous who formed their spiritual aristocracy. The maribous were Zouaya or Tolba people from Berber stock, masters here long before the Arabs arrived. Nowadays they advised the Hassanes over disputes, instructed their children, and made talismans.

The Zenaga, a less noble caste of Berber blood, served as agriculturalists and herders. These top four groups were considered as Beidanes (white races). The Harratin were blacks, conquered here when the Berbers invaded. They were cultivators who kept slaves. Abid meant slave class, and the final categories were Igaouene, who were wandering minstrels, Maallemine, who curiously combined being artists and blacksmiths, and Nemadi, who were the hunters.

One of the men I talked with said, 'Presumably you know about the recent attempt by the blacks to overthrow our president? They failed, they had to fail. Would you let England be ruled by slaves?'

For the heat of the day the maribou gave us an empty hut and sent over some carpets for us to rest on. We learnt we were only fifteen miles from our next fuelling point at Néma. The ground outside was still sizzling like a frying pan when we went out for runway clearing duties, and to rig Pegasus's wing we had to put on our leather flying gloves because the metal was too hot to handle.

It was a long take-off run then we sailed up over a sea of crescent dunes. After four miles we met the tar road, 'La Route d'Espoir', symbolising the hope that trade would reach this back end of Mauritania. Stretches of it were already obliterated by sand. The road ended abruptly at Néma in two large signs saying *Déviation* and pointing to the sands.

The airport didn't look very international; there were some dilapidated buildings with dunes advancing into them, and a fire engine with no tyres. The runway markings had worn off and the wind-sock was in tatters, its shreds indicating a strong crosswind. There was no reply to our radio calls so we circled and landed on the apron.

The airport commandant turned up; his control room was full of equipment which either didn't work or no one knew how to operate it. Predictably, there were no passport facilities at the airport. We would have to go into town.

The immigration police were rather intimidating, looked at us with hard mistrust and asked for my flight authorisation papers, which I didn't have because the Civil Aviation had assured me I didn't need such things. They finally backed off but held our passports overnight pending an official signature. Tourism is not common in Mauritania; apparently last year's figures showed that only a hundred tourists had visited the country. We found our jerrycans with the préfet, who also offered us mint tea and hospitality. Everyone slept on the verandah for coolness, though it was very windy and my covers kept being blown off. Innumerable goats, dogs and children curled up in the lee of the adults, and at dawn I was woken by two baby goats jumping on me.

From Néma I wanted to visit Oualata, lured by stories of its former glory and strangely painted buildings, all becoming lost beneath the desert sands. Historically, Oualata had been equal to the empires of Mali, Ghana and Songhai (Gao), and for a long time was the rival of Tombouctou. Now it was an insignificant village, sixty miles north in the desert, almost unreachable by land vehicle. David was not willing to fly there since the cliffs which ran from Néma to Oualata would certainly produce much turbulence and there was virtually no ground traffic because the track had been swamped by impassably soft sand dunes. Eventually I found a truck from the Mauritanian Institute of Scientific Research which was due to take supplies to Oualata and I rode on the back, seated high on sacks marked 'Wheat, Gift of Canada'. After much praying we set off across a flat desert of gravel sweeps, stony and barren. Two hours later we stopped at a tented camp to unload some dark-skinned long-haired Cherva people and some grain. Someone passed me a bowl of *zrig*, more refreshing than water.

We continued across the desert following old tyre tracks for six miles to a hamlet. The children were terrified of me, and when I took a step towards them their faces crumpled with fear and they fled. I was tempted to sprint and catch one, but it was too hot for such strenuous games.

The tracks ended and we went by the driver's instinct. Just before dark someone spotted a pair of ostriches, the male running at an astonishing speed. The men debated our direction, the back of the truck discussing it in one group, the front in a separate huddle, then the two sides conversed. Arabic always reminds me of turkeys gobbling.

The moon was up and nearly full. I lay back on the sacks, holding on as the driver engaged four-wheel shift and we clambered along up and down dunes, often sinking and stalling. At one point someone got out to deflate the tyres a bit. Perhaps it did help; after a seven-hour drive we reached Oualata.

The village was dark and asleep, I went to the préfet's house and asked if I could sleep on his verandah for protection. It must have been something of a shock to his constitution as he hadn't been near a woman for two years; the Oualata ones were hidden and anyway local people didn't fraternise with the administration. The préfet's wife was living in south-west Mauritania with his mother, and he said he couldn't ask her to come to such an end-of-the-world place. Apparently none of the officials or the gendarmes stationed here brought their wives, preferring to leave them with their mothers, who kept a sharp eye on their behaviour.

The préfet showed me inside his house, the main salon ornately painted by an Oualata craftswoman in red ochre patterns on a white background, with red borders to decorate doorways and windows, and geometrical friezes on all the walls. He slept inside, I slept out. It was another windy night.

Mauritanian Sands

It was February 29th. I was up at dawn and wandered through the town's alleys, so narrow that if you met a donkey one of you had to give way. There were many two-storey houses built of mud and stone. Some beside the alleys sprouted grey slate benches built on to their red-plastered walls. The old wooden doors were studded with metal discs, and framed by elaborately painted designs.

Spotting a man at work replastering a wall, I asked him about the paintings and he said that they were always done by women, or the village blacksmith, and they did it because God gave them a hill of coloured clay.

As I reached the middle of the town I became aware that many doorways were below alley level, with steep paths dug down to them. They hadn't been built like that, the town was being engulfed in sand. Dunes lay heaped against houses, pouring steadily in through their windows, slowly swallowing the buildings whole.

I struggled to climb the dunes in the town centre, passing the eleventh-century mosque which had already half vanished beneath sand. Up behind the village, the old ruined town stretched back up the hillside. I climbed through the ruins, which was like being in a maze, since if sand filled a room you couldn't pass under the doorway and had to backtrack.

Down in the living village a girl in flowing pale blue beckoned me through an arch into a courtyard and in an adjoining salon I met a very fat lady lounging on the carpet, so fat her flesh seemed caught in at elbows and wrists, and the rolls around her waist that I glimpsed as she suckled her baby were impressive. She showed me her incense burner and said that Oualatans used a type not found elsewhere in Mauritania. It was small, made of clay with four handles, and the incense was mixed by the fat lady to her own recipe from sap crystals and perfume. A girl brought in a bowl of milk and the lady lethargically pulled out some money and threw it on the floor for the milkmaid to gather. Outside in the yard a man servant was frying small pancakes, three frying pans going at once. Around him played children and livestock, and the four inner courtyard walls were each painted with bold white emblems.

When I left Oualata, returning with the scientific truck, a fellow passenger was a man leaving home. His mother stood beside him, holding his hand between both of hers as she muttered a prayer for him. Then they each planted an index

193

finger on the other's forehead, said another prayer, removed the finger, kissed it and put it back, still mumbling prayers. Maybe he'd be lucky to return, people said the road would be completely cut in a few years. Oualata would be marooned, unable to exist, with neither access nor resources.

There was one other woman passenger. Invisible beneath a thick indigo-black shawl, she lay cringing on the floor of the truck. Her husband had a marvellously strong handsome face and billowing blue robes caught in by a wide leather belt above baggy knee-length pantaloons. He put his hand on his wife's head and made sure she stayed hidden, passing her a tin can when she started to be sick. Poor girl, she retched for the next six hours. I thought she might have been less ill if allowed to sit up with her head in the fresh air.

The truck dropped me at the airport but David wasn't there and I found another lift into town, going along the tail end of the dune-covered Route d'Espoir. The driver came to a large dune and put his foot hard on the accelerator to motor up it, and not until we reached the ridge at full speed did we see that the far side was a sheer four-foot drop. That kind of experience made me happy to get back to travelling with Pegasus. We should have had to carry extra fuel on the next leg to Ayoun, but decided instead to break the journey at Timbédra and trust to chance.

At dawn we flew away above a desert of dunes and flatness. Chatting over the intercom, David said that the founder of the Paris–Dakar rally had been killed in a mysterious air crash in Mauritania some years ago. It had been suspicious because the man was a very good pilot and there were rumours he'd been shot down. I asked if machine-gun holes could rip open our wing, and David said not with luck.

I thought about great women aviators who had taken this same line across Africa, like Amelia Earhart who set out to fly solo around the world. It was in the 1930s and she had been exactly my age when she started that flight. Her route went east via Gao then on to Khartoum. She was three-quarters of the way around the world when she went missing while flying over Papua New Guinea and no trace of her or her plane have ever been found.

After one and a half hours we reached Timbédra and landed since we needed more fuel. We used the airstrip beside the town which was a mistake, we should have learned that lesson by now. We got mobbed by the enthusiastic population and I left David to them while I sought out the fuel station, a chunk of the crowd following me when I set off. The fuel was at the far end of town, too far to carry twenty-five litres in that heat, so I hailed a donkey-cart which here served as a taxi.

Hoping to lose my crowd of followers, I was dismayed to see their number growing and getting more excited. The cart was a flat board I sat on with the driver, and his donkey set off at a trot. My mob began yelling and running behind, making such pandemonium the donkey started galloping down the main road. The crowd loved it and ran faster to keep up, and finally the donkey laid back its ears and bolted.

After collecting the fuel I was called for an interview with the police. It wasn't that they were very threatening, they just all looked like terrorists. The donkey-boy refused to take me any further. Finally I got back to David who'd had an equally difficult time. It was now one p.m. and we decided to escape immediately; the thermals couldn't be worse than the pressure on the ground.

We flew, sighing with relief, into one and a half hours of violent thermals bouncing from the grilling desert. One thermal pillar alone bumped us up 1,500 feet in a single lift.

We landed in the desert to eat our lunch and made a fire for coffee. Then the calm was broken by a duststorm which went on in squalls and surges for nearly three hours, until, in a lull at five p.m., we decided it was now or never to fly out. The wisdom of staying on the ground doesn't always hold. In some cases special circumstances allow one to fly against the rules. Although these conditions were definitely outside my piloting ability, David could probably handle them. Blowing thick clouds of dust, Pegasus needed both of us to pull the bar and keep control of the wing when we taxied across the gale. Sand swirled up in our faces, but not for long; our take-off run was only ten yards long.

As we rose I wondered if we were crazy to be flying into a duststorm. But David was always conscientious. To both sides the visibility wasn't bad. It was the ground that was worst affected, though ahead looked pretty dark. We gained height and, fortunately for us, the storm was indeed only at ground level. Beyond it the sky cleared. Miles passed and, after checking the fuel gauge, I warned David we only had enough for fifteen more minutes' flight. Ayoun was not far away.

Five minutes later we sighted the town in the gloaming on a rocky plateau. The map showed an airport a few miles north but we couldn't find it, daylight was fading fast, and we had only four minutes of fuel left. We circled the northern plateau, with its tall thin rock cores. Beyond it in the desert were other dramatic outcrops of rock. Finally the fuel gauge showed empty. The engine spluttered at the same moment as we spotted the airstrip markers.

There was an old watchman at the airstrip, who spoke only Hassani, and another man who was very self-important and kept getting in our way as we dismantled the wing. I smothered a laugh when he adopted a casual pose, leaning against Pegasus's exhaust pipe which was still scorching hot, and jumping away with a yell. When he left we made ourselves at home on the sand near a shed. The watchman brought us some milk and I cooked a stew for supper on thorn firewood which produced a lovely smell: its living bushes had fragrant yellow pompom flowers. Lightning was flashing over the western desert, and the full moon was rising. I wriggled into a mound of sand and slept, exhausted.

The following morning we went to claim our fuel from the préfecture, and I revised my mistrustful opinions of Mauritanians because everyone we met in Ayoun was helpful, and totally likeable. When I asked if we could hire a trailbike to scout out the rock formations, the reply was, 'You can't possibly hire our motorbike, but we would be pleased to lend it to you.'

So we borrowed the bike. Our excursion led north for twelve miles along tracks in drifting dunes of soft sand. Trying to ride over sand spills was unnerving because both wheels slid in opposite directions. David reckoned going faster was better than going slowly. He hadn't ridden a motorbike for years and never in soft sand, but he seemed to be coping well. The next instant we both went sprawling with the bike on top of us as we skidded out of control. By the third time this happened we both reacted quickly enough to leap clear at the vital moment, and congratulated each other on mastering the art of falling off a bike.

As we bounced north we could see outcrops of rock like breakaway arms of the plateau, flat-topped islands 200 feet above the sand. Some were waisted with mushroom tops. The first we stopped at had been hollowed by erosion into deep chambers at high level, with shelving floors of many-banded sandstone which created natural tables and seating. The banded walls were covered with ancient writing, an Arabic-like script interlaced with many designs. This was Grebi Nimish, inhabited many centuries ago. A man in Ayoun told us the writing noted the grandeur, riches, deeds and valour of this vanished race. Pearls and pieces of gold had been found here, but I saw only fragments of pottery.

One chamber was like a council room, high overlooking the plains, with natural smoke holes in its ceiling. We clambered up a chimney and out on to the mushroom top where David found a flat polished table-sized rock with four holes scooped in it. Perhaps it had been used for pounding special ingredients, or as an altar, or a game board for guards on duty.

Half a mile away we visited an enormous natural arch, the size of Marble Arch, with a sand dune banked against its front, and through it I could see a semi-hidden valley of sand and trees enclosed by cliffs. Nearby single pillars were waisted like an apple core. It was a magic region. To the south nestled a small oasis of palm trees and an encampment of nomads with camels and goats. We were reluctant to leave but time was moving towards night and the bike didn't have lights. On the way we paused on a rock to watch the sun set magnificently through clouds which lit up in full glory. So enchanted were we both with this amazing sandstone landscape that we stayed on another day exploring its incredible beauties. I couldn't understand how my guide book could say there was nothing worth seeing.

FIFTEEN

To the Atlantic

From Ayoun our next destination was Kiffa, about 150 miles away, which would need a refuelling stop en route. The moon was still shining when we got up, long before dawn, to finish rigging the microlight, load it, make coffee and, as the sun rose above the plateau, we puttered out on to the runway. There was already quite a stiff crossbreeze and we had an extra heavy load, carrying an additional twenty-five litres of fuel in the black bag. Pegasus let go of the earth and purred effortlessly into the sky; it seemed that we had come through all the problems of making the motor run well, and its performance now with overweight proved that the trouble had lain with our lack of experience with Avgas, no fault of the motor.

We circled once more to gain height and gaze for the last time at Grebi Nimish, black and gold in the dawn, then set off along the rim of the plateau, fabulous cliffs tumbling to rosy dunes, and out into the desertscape. Our visibility was over a hundred miles.

The flying seemed calm so I took a turn with the bar. The aircraft was nose-heavy with fuel and tended to sink. I tried to feel for level flight, counterbalancing the excess weight by pushing out the bar, but that slowed us down. Suddenly it was nearly jerked out of my hands, a violent wind current whapping us hard, followed a split second later by another. As the jolting continued spasmodically I gave control back to David who said we were in a wind sheer where two layers were in conflict; the sharpness of the turbulence was worrying, and very uncomfortable. We climbed to 4,000 feet to try and leap clear of it. Visibility was still magnificent, well over a hundred miles of canyons to the furthest mountains; it was a joy to be airborne, and I felt privileged to be seeing the distant islands and pillars which are invisible to those who travel by road. To me, nature's creations are more impressive than anything man can build.

At 4,000 feet it was extremely cold. I pulled my flying suit legs down over my ankles and the cuffs over my gloves, and didn't stop shivering. Some of this was probably fright, since the air was still turbulent with sharp wallops. 'This is evil stuff here,' David remarked, 'and it'll be worse when we cross Kiffa's mountain range tomorrow.' In fact, it was likely to be horrific. He suggested sending women and baggage on ahead, and I countered with appropriate bravado that it would be an opportunity for me to pilot Pegasus through as my first solo flight.

It was still very cold and David gave me control for a while so he could warm his hands. Neither of us could concentrate because the cold had also hit our bladders making us long to land for a minute, but landing in the canyons would have been madness. We reached a large dry lake-bed and followed its shore, a headwind slowing our progress to about 20 mph, painfully slow. Having used twenty-five litres of fuel in two hours, Pegasus was now lighter at the back and even more nose-heavy. We approached a river, not quite dry, then a lake full of green trees, making a wonderful combination of vibrant blue and green, with a few nomadic white tents in the sandy wilderness. Suddenly beside the lake we spotted a derelict airstrip.

We landed and both dashed off behind bushes, then came back to refuel and decided to fly on. The ground wind was now north-east while the upper wind was definitely south-west so we opted to fly low. It was a short take-off run with nomads scattering out of the way, then we flew low along the river. There were a few plots of cultivation around water-holes, groves of palm trees, and a large troupe of nomad families moving camp with camels nearly hidden by huge loads of baggage. Then we branched away across a vastness of flat sands interrupted only by distant conical hills. At low altitude we made good speed and I took over flying for the last half hour.

Kiffa town came into sight, and a high mountain range beyond it. The airfield was a couple of miles south of town, enough for us to land unnoticed and relax in peace, make fire, coffee, lunch and take a siesta. Then it was David's turn to find fuel.

He came back with a United Nations team of dam builders

and nutritionists, who arranged our fuel and invited us for supper. Also staying there was a Catholic priest whose parish of 2,000 square miles had sixty Christians. One thing I learned about foreign aid was that only a third of it was supposed to be distributed free. The rest, according to international agreements, was intended to be sold off by the administrators, who agreed to put the money into further projects. This made sense when you consider how local markets must suffer when you flood a country with free food.

During supper we discussed our next problem, how to jump Kiffa's mountain range. David thought we could avoid the turbulence if we went to 8,000 feet, but I wasn't keen. I felt wiped out with tiredness and next morning woke with a pounding headache and temperature. So that resolved the problem; David could hop the mountains and I'd meet him a little way down the road, at Mokta el Hajar where our next fuel stash was located.

Nursing my fever, I caught a bus and dozed as it trundled down the road into a wide gorge. We passed four sugar-loaf mountains in a row, the last two with 1,000-foot sand dunes stacked against their lee sides. Orange dunes rose like an angry sea from a foreground of pure white dunes. Visibility was good but on the ground dust was starting to blow. Gradually the gorge closed in on both sides and we went through a 'gate'. It led us across a mountain ridge and down to a string of palmy oases.

When the bus stopped to pick up a passenger a voice I knew requested 'to Mokta el Hajar.' It was David, who had landed short of fuel, five miles from our destination.

From Mokta el Hajar we flew through duststorms. Whenever I lifted my visor I could feel the grit hit my face. At our next overnight fuel stop, Boutilimit, we sat out the worst of it. Sand scrunched between my teeth. I took shelter, as David had already done, by sliding under the wing. In the morning the storm intensified; sand pelting against the sailcloth, wind howling and whistling around the batons.

Then we heard a new sound, of camels grumbling. I peeped out from under the wing and was confronted with the extraordinary sight of a hundred camels in a wide group coming straight at us through the foggy blowing sand. At twenty paces the ranks split to pass both sides of our camp, engulfing us with blurred, almost opaque images, even at close range. At twenty paces beyond us the two groups came together again, plodding slowly, grumbling and grunting, becoming invisible from the feet up until only their heads and humps showed. Then they were gone.

Gradually the wind slackened but the dust stayed thick in the air. We emerged from our respective crannies. Our baggage was partially buried under new dunes. We ate a rather gritty lunch pestered by scores of flies, and, since we had to wait for the visibility to improve before we could get airborne I went off for a walk up a wide valley between great sand dunes. The valley floor was carpeted with white sea shells, whelks and cockles, which made me realise that the Atlantic Ocean was now only a hundred miles away.

Mid-afternoon we began preparing to leave: Pegasus looked filthy, the baggage looked as bad, I felt begrimed, and David's face was thickly coated in orange dust. Surely when we reached Nouakchott on the coast we would leave no one in doubt that we'd come across the desert.

The valley of shells made a good runway and we took off easily. Pegasus rose slowly to 7,000 feet and continued going up. We passed through all the layers of claggy dust, leaving the murk behind and emerging gradually into brilliant sunshine – 8,000 feet, then 9,000 feet, now higher than we had ever been before. The sky was intensely blue. It was glorious. I took over the flight bar for a while; the air was silky smooth but extremely cold. We were longing to see the ocean. It meant something to us in terms of having succeeded in getting there, although we were still about 500 miles from the end of our journey. We looked forward to ambling down the Mauritanian coast to Sénégal, and camping on the beaches; there was no need to hurry, we still had about two weeks of the journey left and one major thing to achieve: I had to start doing some solo flying. We hoped I was ready.

Below us the dust clouds caught the sun like a pearly cloth. Then at last we saw the ocean and Nouakchott where we were entertained magnificently by Mobil's local director and his Peul wife, who turned out to be the niece of the large maribou we had dropped in on near Néma.

On March 9th we left Nouakchott and flew down the beach on a flight plan that gave us several days in hand. The coast was a straight unbroken line of silver sand backed by the desert. Within the first twenty miles we saw four shipwrecks, one washed up against the shore, others half-submerged and being pounded by surf. Beyond the waves the ocean was deep jade green, holding an occasional jellyfish and a few fishermen in canoes, whose camps were set nearby on the sand.

I took the control bar for half an hour, making good speed and keeping a low altitude of 500 feet. The coast stayed straight though a string of salt lakes now appeared between beach and desert, and a scrubby line of bushes. Flocks of oyster-catchers were out feeding, and a solitary dog-like animal at the tide line was trying to catch a crab. Hearing our motor it fled, a strange zigzagging dash at great speed into the bushes. It certainly wasn't a dog. Five minutes later we saw another, again alone and far from any fishing camp, chasing crabs, and shortly after there was a third. Each fled but by this time I'd recognised them as hyaenas.

Desolate and windswept, there was nowhere ideal for camping but after one and a half hours we reached a blind lagoon with big dunes on its northern edge, offering some sheltered dells. The tide was out so we landed on the firm damp sand. When we tried to taxi up the beach our wheels sank in soft sand. We would only be able to take off from the harder stuff exposed at low tide. We made ourselves at home in the prettiest dunes overlooking both the ocean and the lagoon with flamingoes and pelicans wading in the shallows.

The day was hot and cloudless but the wind strong and cold. I relaxed and went wandering. On the high tide line I found a dead sting-ray and some useful firewood. Sudden yells came from David. 'Help, quick, the tide's coming in!' Pegasus was still sitting in soft sand, now only a few feet from the incoming waves. The firm sand was awash.

I could see David desperately pushing at Pegasus whose nose wheel had dug itself in, and I ran over via the side of the lagoon to check if the ground was hard enough for a second landing, which it was, and we pushed and pulled at the stuck microlight. Waves swept in ever closer, and as they pulled back we saw that David's best chance of taking off was to use the wet sand between waves. 'That'll have to do, I'll give it a try,' he called, and swung Pegasus to face into wind. His take-off run on full power was only six yards, well clear of trouble.

We did an afternoon flight east for twenty miles to the nearest village where Mobil had deposited our last fuel stash in Mauritania. The ticket on the fuel drum said eighty-five litres so we mixed it with our two-stroke oil for that quantity, then discovered the drum was actually only fifty litres. The engine could probably run oil-rich quite easily, but we were worried it might not like our all-up load.

In the evening we did a more proper flying lesson, though I couldn't help reminding myself that the wind was still very strong, the fuel was over-rich, and the runway was soggy enough to sink into. As I took off, a skein of pelicans came in to land at the lagoon with a bunch of them in the fore and then a tight line of followers. The lesson was revision in medium turns, climbing and gliding turns, height awareness, and landings by glide assessment. My first landing attempt failed because, although I was right on target, I hit a funny rotoring wind behind the dunes, so I put the power on and went round again. The second one was complicated by David giving me a mock engine cutout, and also as I landed he hopped us forward nearer the camp but one wheel caught against a ridge of shells. A close shave – I was glad to stand on the ground. The ocean birds were wheeling and noisy, out for supper at low tide.

The flamingoes were feeding again at the lagoon, their pink standing out against its pale metallic blue. The evening air felt very damp after the desert, our clothes were moist, and there was a heavy dew after sunset. But it was an idyllic night.

The next leg of our flight would take us to St Louis, the old colonial capital of Sénégal at the mouth of the Sénégal River. From there it was only a day's flight to Dakar and the end of our journey.

We took off with me piloting, and immediately both heard a different note in the whirring of the propeller. A blade must have been chipped by a stone or shell during take-off. But it wasn't serious enough to force a landing. I kept just out to sea to avoid being bumped by thermals off the beach. We passed a man on a camel trotting along the tide line. The Sénégal River appeared, looping along beside the beach for many miles before reaching its estuary and St Louis, set on an island in the mouth as well as on the mainland, its palm trees and wide boulevards leading to shabby genteel mansions.

At the airport I joined the circuit; there was a small plane taxiing out on to the runway and when the control tower mentioned another plane I assumed that was it. He took off and I couldn't understand why the tower asked if I could see him. In my landing approach I checked the sky along finals, all clear, and descended steeply to land. Suddenly the controller started shouting, 'You are second to land, there's a plane coming in under you!'

I swung violently left in standard evasive action and a small plane scooted past just underneath. It wasn't a near miss because I felt sure the other pilot had seen me and had been ready to divert right. But it was a valuable lesson; I hadn't properly looked for other air traffic. It was a mistake I could not afford to make again.

Checking in with the airport officials was surprisingly easy, bearing in mind that microlights are banned in Sénégal. Fortunately we had special permission. While I was in the control tower David met some people from the aero club who gave us space for Pegasus in their hangar and room for us to camp in their clubhouse.

Intensive flying lessons were the order of the next day, despite harsh turbulence below 500 feet, and twenty-knot winds above it. The run-ins to landing were horrible since we sank vertically against the wind then hit 'tsugs' (gusts backwards!) being the pressure holes following gusts. Caught in a tsug we dropped like a stone.

'You've got to put on speed through the gust to avoid falling in the tsug,' David yelled as another gust caught under my wing at twenty-five feet. I nearly missed the runway, was knocked sideways and landed on the gravel edge. But David was delighted with my progress. We did twelve landings in the first hour.

The next session lasted an hour and a half, again turbulent and gusty, and David admitted that conditions were worse than he'd ever asked a student of my level to cope with, and were probably trickier than most new pilots would have encountered. We were practising engine failures at 150 feet, fifty feet, and at take-off. The hairiest were from fifty feet, since you must pull on speed immediately, while the ground comes rushing up. A radical flare is essential just before you hit the ground then you need pitch authority and to float along, with a last flaring round out of the curve on the instant of touch-down.

The following morning I piloted our flight upriver for sixty miles to the plantations at Richard-Toll. David had now handed the responsibility of flying over to me; he said it was my job from here onwards. At first I blew it, assuming that he had done the calculations, so there we were with no worked out way-points and little idea how to find the airstrip at the other end.

I guessed and muddled my way through; luckily the air was smooth though the visibility was dreadful. David ticked me off because according to flying rules I should not have taken off at all. But I flew well enough for him to relax and fall asleep.

Sugar plantations stretched to the horizons at Richard-Toll, headquarters of CSS, Sénégal's sugar company who had invited us to visit and demonstrate Pegasus.

After an excellent four-course lunch we made an air tour of the plantations because David wanted me to grow familiar with the surroundings before he sent me off solo. Each sugar cane field was separated from its neighbours by a dirt road or an irrigation canal, making a geometrical kaleidoscope of greens, the colour changing according to the cane's age. Harvesting was in process and some plots were being prepared for harvest by burning off the cane leaves, a quick very hot fire that didn't harm the stalks. Seeing the air fill with pale smoke and ash I headed away from the flames, remembering way back to Cameroun where the bush fires had produced dreadful thermals.

As one lot of workers cut the cane, another group came along planting for the new season. They used segments of sugar cane, each knot producing new roots, like the burgu grass in the Mali delta. The newly planted furrows were then irrigated and made patterns of organ pipes, multiple watery lines of differing lengths glinting in the sun. David kept checking I'd got my eye on potential emergency landing places.

We celebrated his thousandth hour of flight that evening; he deserved congratulations, a lesser pilot might not have come through unscathed. My feelings about going solo were mixed: I was a little afraid but was looking forward to it. I wished conditions could be easier, the wind was strong, gusty, and always across the runway; I'd yet to make a normal classic landing.

The next morning found me again practising landings in crosswinds, trying to avoid hitting the corrugations on the right side of the runway and fly through turbulence. The propeller got gashed on the last landing, so David stayed to mend it and I went off to have a look around the sugar factory.

It had been bought second-hand in India, and shipped in

parts, then reassembled on the new site. It was a noisy place where one's feet sometimes stuck to the floor, but working well, and with friendly efficient staff. Its vast furnaces were fuelled by the crushed fibre of previously squeezed cane; juice frothed down inside pipes, vats of it bubbled, and turbines spun centrifugal tanks to separate the crystals into granulated sugar.

In the afternoon David attached a jerrycan of water to the back seat of Pegasus, as ballast. It was time for my first solo. The wind had wrapped the wind-sock around the top of its pole. Six helpers with long sticks unwrapped it for me. I taxied along to the end of the runway, then waited. People might think I was afraid to take off, not entirely untrue but in reality the engine temperatures needed to warm up before going for full power.

When I put my foot flat on the accelerator, Pegasus surged forward; I pushed the bar out and she left the ground, soaring upwards. Her nose was so high I couldn't see ahead, but I understood the danger of stalling if I took my foot off full power before I'd reached 300 feet. I pulled the bar in a touch, trying to get the nose down, so that I'd be able to cope with an engine failure if necessary. My main problem was that the accelerator was sticking, not answering the pedal, so my first landing came in much too fast. I put in an extra flaring check, mistimed something, hit the ground and bounced ten foot back into the air. Then, remembering my pitch control, I brought her down more neatly.

For my second solo landing I missed the runway, and landed at an angle on the verge. On the third landing the propeller got damaged again, and I was happy to adjourn for repairs. The continuation was an hour's solo flight in the morning; the throttle was still sticking but at least I knew about it. I did standard exercises above the airstrip, then cruised over to circle the CSS club. A sudden whap of turbulence like a sharp ripple made me catch my breath. But there was no problem, except for the dicky throttle.

Later that day David gave flights to the CSS managing director and the field director who were delighted with the possibility of using a microlight for crop inspection, and were seriously thinking of ordering one or two. It didn't matter to them that microlights are banned in Sénégal; CSS, employing more people than any other private company and indirectly contributing to the welfare of one in four Sénégalese, hoped to obtain permission.

I completed my map calculations and triangles of velocity for the morrow, which would be our last flight, via St Louis, to Dakar. My time sums indicated the flight could take me as long as four hours. The morning visibility was poor but not enough to ground us. I did the pre-start checks and soon we were away. My navigation suffered because I didn't think of looking back at the airstrip to judge the compass heading in relation to the wind force and direction. Lost in cross country, I opted to follow the river and cut the bends, which meant I wasted fuel and missed all my way-points. What was special was a chance sight as we passed a cloud and I saw a circular rainbow reflected on the cloud and in the centre of the rainbow was the shadow of my Pegasus.

St Louis came into sight. I landed to refuel at the airport, and noticed how differently Pegasus handled fully laden in low level turbulence, more stable but dropping faster. While David topped up the fuel I filed the flight plan for Dakar, and was told I'd be allocated runway four which was normal for light aircraft.

We flew on down the coast, and in the next two hours we saw only a couple of fishing villages, their canoes out at sea setting circles of nets on floats. Behind the beach dunes were some lakes, and one of them was bright pink, Lake Rose. Its colour was natural but lying in creamy sand by green ocean it looked weird. This lake was my final way-point, telling me we were entering Dakar's airspace. Our radio battery was again almost dead but we managed to raise the control tower and made contact.

Dakar is set on a peninsula, the furthest point west in Africa. The airport came into view; one of the runways was vast and there were several smaller ones to the side. The control tower gave us permission to land, saying, 'Take runway number one.' I looked at the size of it, built for Jumbo jets and Concorde, and wondered if perhaps the controller couldn't see how small we were, but as David said, 'You don't argue with the tower, just do what he told you.'

I turned along finals and began our descent. The great runway was clear of traffic, I'd have to get down and out of the way before the descent of the Boeing now circling above us. I pulled our nose down and zoomed in pretending to be Concorde; we were exactly on path, the white dashes on the runway sped beneath us. 'Check at fifty feet, check again,' I muttered, keeping my concentration pinpointed ahead, and with a final flare of the wing we touched down perfectly.

It was after midday. The tarmac taxiway led between two rows of monstrously large aeroplanes that made me feel as small as one of their wheels. 'Put your plane in parking bay number ten,' the controller instructed, but this time we didn't obey because the effects of large jets taxying past would have been disastrous. So I parked nose in against the control tower and went to offer my papers.

Mobil were delighted with our arrival and we all celebrated enormously. They had done a marvellous job for us right through our journey, from the directors down to the petrol pump attendants. Every fuel stash had been in place and not a mistake had been made anywhere along the line. Over such challenging and varied terrain it was no mean feat and a tribute to the efficiency of their operation in West Africa.

Our last task was to dismantle Pegasus and fold it into two crates for airfreight back to England. When this was done David flew back and a day later I followed him. It felt odd to sit in a normal passenger plane. As we taxied out on to the big runway one my mind rolled through the checks of CHIFWAP and when I got to 'w', wind strength, I laughed aloud remembering the times controllers had assured us 'The wind is calm' as it howled across the strip. Now there was no fuel gauge to check, no likelihood of power failure, no feeling of adventure: I sat encapsulated beside a window, cruising at five hundred miles an hour; it was all too easy.

Even when we hit turbulence there was only the flight stewardess saying, 'Please fasten your seat belts', and the big plane cut through it, not swinging and dancing like Pegasus. It made me think that in the last four months and 7,000 miles, I had perhaps earned the title of pilot.